Supporting People
through Loss and Grief

of related interest

Talking With Bereaved People
An Approach for Structured and Sensitive Communication
Dodie Graves
ISBN 978 1 84310 988 4
eISBN 978 0 85700 162 7

Setting Up and Facilitating Bereavement Support Groups
A Practical Guide
Dodie Graves
ISBN 978 1 84905 271 9
eISBN 978 0 85700 573 1

After the Suicide
Helping the Bereaved to Find a Path from Grief to Recovery
Kari Dyregrov, Einar Plyhn and Gudrun Dieserud
Foreword by John R. Jordan
ISBN 978 1 84905 211 5
eISBN 978 0 85700 445 1

Writing in Bereavement
A Creative Handbook
Jane Moss
ISBN 978 1 84905 212 2
eISBN 978 0 85700 450 5
Writing for Therapy or Personal Development series

Effective Grief and Bereavement Support
The Role of Family, Friends, Colleagues, Schools and Support Professionals
Kari Dyregrov and Atle Dyregrov
Foreword by Magne Raundalen
ISBN 978 1 84310 667 8
eISBN 978 1 84642 833 3

Pathways through Care at the End of Life
Anita Hayes, Claire Henry, Margaret Holloway, Katie Lindsey, Eleanor Sherwen and Tes Smith
Foreword by Professor Sir Mike Richards
ISBN 978 1 84905 364 8
eISBN 978 0 85700 716 2

The Essential Guide to Life After Bereavement
Beyond Tomorrow
Judy Carole Kauffmann and Mary Jordan
Foreword by Ciaran Devane
ISBN 978 1 84905 335 8
eISBN 978 0 85700 669 1

Silent Grief
Living in the Wake of Suicide
Revised Edition
Christopher Lukas and Henry M. Seiden
ISBN 978 1 84310 847 4
eISBN 978 1 84642 610 0

Supporting People through Loss and Grief

An Introduction for Counsellors
and Other Caring Practitioners

John Wilson

Foreword by Dodie Graves

Jessica Kingsley *Publishers*
London and Philadelphia

Figure 5.1, Lois Tonkin 2007 on p.118 is reproduced with permission of Port Hills Press, Christchurch, New Zealand.
Figure 5.2 from Stroebe and Schut 1999 on p.121 is reproduced with permission from the authors.

First published in 2014
by Jessica Kingsley Publishers
73 Collier Street
London N1 9BE, UK
and
400 Market Street, Suite 400
Philadelphia, PA 19106, USA

www.jkp.com

Library of Congress Cataloging in Publication Data
Wilson, John Frederick.
  Supporting people through loss and grief : an introduction for counsellors and other caring practitioners / John Wilson ; foreword by Dodie Graves.
    pages cm
Includes bibliographical references and index.
ISBN 978-1-84905-376-1 (alk. paper)
 1. Loss (Psychology) 2. Grief. 3. Counseling--Guidebooks. I. Title.
BF575.D35W55 2014
158.3--dc23
                                        2013040579

British Library Cataloguing in Publication Data
A CIP catalogue record for this book is available from the British Library

ISBN 978 1 84905 376 1
eISBN 978 0 85700 739 1

Printed and bound in Great Britain

This book is dedicated to Paul Wilson,
born September 1981, died December 1982.

His short but happy life is the reason I do this work.

Contents

Foreword

Whether you are an experienced counsellor or someone beginning to support people who have been bereaved, there can be, and perhaps should be, some trepidation about entering into dialogue with someone whose world has been shattered by death. For those of us who speak to bereaved people on a regular basis, there can be a sense of mystery as to how we can support and help anyone through the darkest times of his life. There is mystery and there can be a sense of awe in witnessing how courageous people are, and how much they have to face in dealing with the reality of their loss and grief.

While we know the therapeutic relationship is always important for the client's progress and we must not underestimate its power, at the same time we can feel that we need something more. When we meet with someone who is struggling we can feel helpless and out of our depth. What is needed at such times is an 'old hand' – someone who has lots of experience and has walked this way before, many times. We want some reassurance that what we are doing is at least not going to damage anyone. More than that, however, we need some ideas as to what may be helpful and significant for someone in the middle of gut-wrenching pain and loneliness. John Wilson is one of those 'old hands' – someone who has studied his subject and thought about the supporting role he and others have in this process and someone who has sat with people in difficult situations and has seen them come through the process. He shares his wisdom and experience with us sometimes in a learned way, and sometimes in a very practical way. In this way, he provides a good mix of the two, so that those who are looking for a theoretical underpinning will be satisfied, as well as being able to find solid advice and helpful approaches to assist them in their practice.

What you will also find in these pages is the content of a training course that John and others at his hospice deliver for trainee bereavement support workers. When he first mentioned the idea of this work to me I was instantly delighted that a book of this kind would be available to those who train volunteer workers, as well as providing a knowledgeable framework for counsellors and other caring practitioners. As a professional who is involved in training, I would most value a book that provided the content of a course that covered what I wanted to train. Here is such a book, and what is really beneficial for us is that the work has already been done: the theories have been researched in some considerable depth and the results of that labour are succinctly presented so that we can weigh up the theories and the approaches and use them as we wish. The theory and the practice are vital for us as practitioners, and it is good to learn afresh through the perspective of another professional. I particularly think the 'notes for trainers' are an excellent addition and certainly not an afterthought at the end of each chapter.

Making a book on this subject interesting is quite a challenge, and the best way forward is to inlude real-life stories that explain and illustrate the way we can do or say things. You will find many helpful insights from the anecdotes and stories shared here. Sometimes we only need to have someone else's way of phrasing or handling of a situation in order to set us on a different path with our clients. Because John works with the wider bereaved public than those who are bereaved in a hospice setting, there are many examples of different kinds of deaths and illustrations of the ways the bereaved people they have left behind have been supported. The chapter on families and grief is of particular interest, incorporating as it does a good deal of theory alongside practical hands-on approaches that have been tried and tested. The chapter on working with difference is not only informative but also challenging; in it we are reminded of the value of both understanding and working with differences of culture, beliefs and life experiences.

The scope of this book is ambitious in the range of subjects it covers, but it also reflects the depth and breadth of the knowledge, understanding and skills needed to be involved in working with bereaved people. If you are looking for help in training volunteers for a bereavement service, you will be greatly supported by the content of this book that could help you formulate your sessions and provide guidance along the way. If you are a counsellor, or professional care practitioner, wishing to enhance your understanding of loss and grief as you work with bereaved people, you will find much to help you in these pages. There is wisdom and a wealth of good practice here, and I have learnt much along the way from someone who is a good, safe pair of hands.

Dodie Graves
Counsellor and author of: Talking with Bereaved People: An Approach to Structured and Sensitive Communication *and* Setting Up and Facilitating Bereavement Support Groups: A Practical Guide

Acknowledgements

A book like this is never written by one person. The perspiration is mine but most of the inspiration belongs to others. I would like to acknowledge these people.

Most importantly I would like to thank my clients who have taught me so much about loss and grief. I would like to thank my colleagues at Saint Catherine's Hospice, in particular the Bereavement Supporters who have taken the time to ask about the project's progress. Thanks are due to my PhD supervisors, Lynne Gabriel and Hazel James, for helping me manage my research alongside this project, and to my counselling supervisor, Lucy Birtwistle, whose knowledge, skill and compassion continue to play a role in my professional development. Warm appreciation goes to my immediate colleagues Jan Pocknall, Flynne Readman, Martyn Tinker and Ann Wells, for both the loving support and the professional conversations that have contributed to this book. A very special thanks go to my Manager Kath Atherton and our Service Coordinator Mollie Woollard, similarly for their love and professional reflections, but also for tolerating my distracted lapses in departmental paperwork. I apologize for the extra pressure this has placed on you both.

I wish to express my gratitude to Katherine McGilly, Hilary Minter and Greg O'Sullivan for reading and commenting on chapters, to Stacey Sutton for proofreading the final draft and to the researchers and clinicians in this field that have taken time to read and comment on those sections of the manuscript that draw on their particular expertise: Sharon Cornford, Dodie Graves, Linda Machin, Robert Neimeyer, Colin Murray Parkes, Margaret Stroebe and Lois Tonkin. Chapter 7 owes its existence to Golnar Bayat; in essence, the text of this chapter is hers.

Thanks to those who have generously granted permission to use diagrams I have taken from their own work and to Curtis Brown Ltd, agents for the estate of Laurie Lee, for permission to use the quote at the head of Chapter 1.

Final thanks go to my wonderful wife, Sandra, in part for putting up with the back of my head for the past six months, but especially for her ability with English grammar. Her contribution to punctuating the text has considerably improved its readability.

Introduction

It is now more than 30 years since pioneers like Colin Murray Parkes at St Christopher's Hospice in London and Marilyn Relf at Sobell House Hospice in Oxford took the courageous step of recruiting volunteers to work with bereaved people. At the time, many professionals regarded these new services with some suspicion, until in 1981 Colin Murray Parkes published a paper that demonstrated the efficacy of this kind of bereavement support. As more hospices opened, more bereavement services came into being. Most were based on the pioneers' arrangement of one or two paid staff coordinating a team of volunteers. The professional staff tended to come from nursing, social work or counselling backgrounds. Everybody concerned was learning as they did the work. St Christopher's Hospice and Sobell House took the lead in providing national training, positions that they retain today. In 1987 the widows' charity Cruse, also organized on a volunteering model, became Cruse Bereavement Care.

Recognizing the need to disseminate the knowledge and skills required to support bereaved people, a team of experts in this fast-growing field came together to produce a teaching pack. This large volume was edited by Ann Faulkner and Susan Wallbank and the contributors included Marilyn Relf. The writers adopted a bereavement counselling approach to helping, and their ambitious project, entitled *Bereavement Counselling: A 60 Hour Introductory Training Course*, was published by Cruse Bereavement Care and Help the Hospices in 1998. It was the pack that was used to train me when in 1999 I joined the bereavement support team as a volunteer at Saint Catherine's Hospice in Scarborough. Eighteen months later I accepted a professional post in the service as a bereavement counsellor. Within a few years, perhaps due to my background as a teacher and lecturer, I was helping to teach my colleagues, also using Faulkner and Wallbank's teaching pack. Of course, the knowledge base of bereavement theory does not stand still; on the contrary, knowledge in this area is always expanding and developing. Due to the outstanding contribution of Margaret Stroebe's team at Utrecht University in the Netherlands, worldwide research into bereavement has been brought together in a series of research handbooks (Stroebe, Stroebe and Hansson 1993; Stroebe *et al.* 2001; Stroebe *et al.* 2008). In my role as trainer, and with these weighty volumes by my side, I found that I was constantly updating the content of our volunteer training, to the point that little remained of the 1998 teaching pack apart from its philosophy of experiential learning, which I have embraced throughout my teaching career. Over the past six years, my colleagues and I have developed a completely new module, moving from the 60-hour training of the original pack to a full module of 150 study hours, including two written assignments that we assess to a university standard. The ideas of Faulkner and Wallbank that do remain in our teaching materials are duly credited and correctly referenced, just as they are in this book. Our successful students have included counsellors and psychotherapists, social workers, palliative care nurses, health visitors, care home staff, teachers and chaplains. Many of our students go on to work with bereaved people.

I am privileged to be part of an amazing team. Our Bereavement Support Service began operating in 1993 and two of the original Supporters deserve a mention. Sheila and Sue have clocked up many hundreds of hours of client work, training and supervision. Although we are part of a hospice, we are a community-based service and our clients may be bereaved from any cause. Most referrals to our service come from general practitioners (GPs, known in some countries as 'family doctors'), and because we work with such vulnerable people, we expect a high standard of professionalism, with mandatory supervision for everyone and a requirement for all team members to keep up to date with new developments in the field. Our service has a substantial library of classic and recent publications. We provide monthly training in-house and team members are also encouraged to attend external training for continuing professional development (CPD). Many of our volunteer team are qualified counsellors or psychotherapists, either accredited by the British Association for Counselling and Psychotherapy (BACP) or working towards BACP accreditation. All recruits are required to complete the training module that forms the basis of this book before they work with clients.

Since many of our volunteers come from caring backgrounds other than counselling, we all call ourselves 'Bereavement Supporters'. The title is always written with a capital 'S' in recognition and respect of the status it deserves and the hard work needed to acquire and retain the title. We operate no hierarchy, either between paid staff and others or between one paper qualification and another. Everyone in the service is valued equally for the contribution she or he makes, an ethos that permeates Saint Catherine's Hospice. Resting quietly 250 miles from London, Scarborough, where we are based, ought to be a sleepy place. In fact this is a vibrant and successful seaside town with a hospice that any community would be proud of. When I read Sheila Payne's hospice research (Payne 2001, 2002), in particular about the tensions between paid staff and volunteers, I was thankful for what has been achieved in our service. This is no accident; it is due to the management styles of my first manager, Hilary Minter (now doing great work a little further up the coast), and my current manager, Kath Atherton, both of whom I acknowledge for their skill in helping staff and volunteers feel so valued.

I'd like to explain the aims of this book and, as I do so, I hope that the choice of title will make sense. Although some of the chapters are devoted to a counselling model of support, there are other, equally valid, ways of working with loss and grief. These include social work and befriending models as well as the spiritual models used by hospital and hospice chaplains, and within religious communities under the umbrella of temples, synagogues, churches and mosques. Many hospice bereavement services also include support structures that are not based on a counselling model.

Most of the chapters are written with any helping practitioner in mind and the skill of active listening has a value in any caring situation. We also have to remember that many people who seek help in their loss and grief have experienced losses not necessarily through bereavement. In my private practice I have supported clients with other losses, including loss through radical surgery, loss of relationships and lost assumptive worlds through retirement, redundancy and ill health. In fact many people who seek bereavement support are experiencing multiple losses, some of which they may not have been fully aware of until they begin counselling. This book can also serve as a useful guide to counsellors in general practice, since most issues that clients bring to us involve one or more kind of loss.

There may be those who would say that the style, content and density of academic referencing I have used puts this book outside of being an introduction to the topic. I would profoundly disagree with any such criticism, on pragmatic grounds alone. This book is no more than an expansion of the teaching materials my colleagues and I have successfully used in teaching those who come from a range of educational backgrounds, many of whom go on to become our talented volunteers. I have worked in adult education for more than 25 years, in which time I have learnt that highly motivated adults with a breadth of life experiences are capable of amazing achievements. We select our students carefully and support them well. Raise the bar high and students will strive to reach it if they feel you believe in them. That said, I would not expect students to read anything other than a fraction of the journal articles I have referred to, nor some of the more specialist books. This book is also written for lecturers and trainers presented with the task of introducing bereavement support to others, however, and it would be plagiarism on my part not to refer to all my sources.

I would also say that expectations of bereavement services have changed as theory on the grieving process has developed. In Stroebe and colleagues, 2001 research handbook, the Utrecht University team published *The Efficacy of Bereavement Interventions: Determining Who Benefits* (Schut *et al.* 2001). This review of several efficacy studies concluded that routine referral to counselling for normal grief had no significant effect but that there were benefits in counselling for complex grief, with the finding that the more severe the grief reaction, the more likely it was that counselling was likely to be of benefit. In the light of this, Colin Murray Parkes has asked the question, 'Is the day of the volunteer counsellor past?' Parkes questioned if it remains reasonable, in the wake of Schut and colleagues' (2001) conclusions on counselling efficacy, to expect volunteers to work with clients at risk of complex grief. He concluded that from his experience, well-selected, trained and supported volunteers are particularly good at working with clients with attachment-related grief complexity, possibly being better in some instances than 'clever professionals whose paper qualifications may outweigh their ability to handle human relationships with sensitivity and tact' (Parkes 2006, p.267). I completely concur with that sentiment. When, towards the end of their counselling, our clients are asked what they have found most helpful, the most common response is that our support has given them the opportunity to share with a stranger the thoughts and feelings it would have been too difficult to share with family members.

There are two related ideas underpinning this book. The first is that each of us sees the world through the lens of our life experience, and the second is that a significant loss or catastrophic event changes the view through this lens. We see the world differently for a time; it may look so distorted that nothing makes much sense. Both ideas go under the heading of 'construct theory', based on an explicit recognition that each of us maintains a life narrative, that is, a soundtrack of our place in the world that informs who we believe we are (and can become), what we believe we are worth and how emotionally secure we feel. This soundtrack informs our values, our beliefs and our actions. If it is disrupted, our world for a time becomes chaotic and we have to accommodate the changes before health and wellbeing are restored.

Throughout the book I have tried to teach and reinforce this theory in two ways. In the early chapters I have drawn attention to the life histories of the researchers and practitioners who have contributed so much to the field of bereavement theory. I have tried to show how our narrative soundtrack directs the course of our lives. I am grateful in this respect for the example of Robert Neimeyer, who in explaining construct theory better than I can, movingly describes his father's suicide and its consequences:

> Many of the subsequent emotional, relational and occupational choices made by my mother, my brother, my little sister and me can be read as responses to my father's fateful decision, though their meaning continues to be clarified, ambiguated and reformulated across the years. (Neimeyer 2009b, p.294)

In the last chapter I have attempted to teach and reinforce these ideas by inviting each reader to consider his life narrative and reflect on how it plays a part in choosing ways to be in the world. With our own students, my colleagues and I model the thinking, experiencing, behaving (TEB) cycle (see Chapter 9) with our own openness and transparency, something I can only do in print with the personal stories it has seemed appropriate to share. The TEB cycle is based on Kolb's learning cycle (1984), which in turn draws on the theory of constructivism adumbrated by Jean Piaget (1952, 1954). Our experience of successfully facilitating students' learning and personal reflection in this way (evaluated by the quality of their written assignments), would suggest that trainers who adopt this book as a source of knowledge, ideas and techniques would do well to consider a similar open and honest approach in delivering its content. If we model openness, we encourage others around us to take the same risk.

For the individual who intends to use this book as part of his own practice, I suggest trying some of the personal development activities in the final chapter, including, perhaps, keeping a journal of your process.

A note about third-person singular pronouns in this book

In English we so often struggle with this. In other languages, for example Persian, there is one pronoun for both genders, but in English, if we say 'he' when we mean 'he or she', our language discriminates. Writing 'he or she' every time soon gets tiresome to read, as does '(s)he'. To avoid this I have used 'she' in the first chapter and 'he' in the next, and so on, alternating between the two.

A note for practitioners not working to a counselling model

You will see that throughout I have referred to 'clients' rather than 'patients', meaning to encorporate 'patients' but to avoid writing 'client or patient' because it interrupted the flow of the text. I hope that readers will adapt, by using their own mental substitution, if the word 'client' feels inappropriate to their profession.

The case studies

At the end of Chapter 5, I draw trainers' attention to the pitfalls of using case studies. I have used a variety of approaches in this book. Some examples are taken directly from my experience, but disguised by changing gender, occupation or cause of death. Others are created by combining the stories of two or more clients. Where stories are entirely fictitious I have said so. In all cases I have used pseudonyms.

An introduction for trainers

In my work setting we believe that it is ethical to select our volunteers very carefully, because of the vulnerability of our client group. We make it clear when we advertise the module that it is not suitable for those experiencing a recent bereavement. Those who express an interest are invited to make a formal written application and are interviewed. We look for volunteers who are self aware, prepared to work alongside others in a spirit of cooperation and who show evidence of valuing diversity. During the training we monitor and foster those qualities. Before the start, students are made fully aware of what they can expect from the module and what we expect from them. Personal development is central to the course. We ask students to keep a journal and invite them to explore their learning processes with a journal sheet for each activity (Appendix 9.1). In general, didactic sessions and learning activities take place in our morning sessions. We find it helpful to have two tutors/facilitators present. One takes the lead in teaching and the other monitors the teaching and learning process. This also means that one tutor is available to support any student who may become distressed during a class activity.

In the afternoon sessions we divide the group into triads and practise counselling skills. We encourage students to use real events and situations to bring to the triad, but emphasize that this is not a therapeutic space to bring serious or complex issues. We have found that trust within the triad builds if students stay in the same group throughout the course. As tutors we monitor the triads and assess each student's developing skills. Students are issued with a skills checklist (see Figure 4.1) for each session. Appendix 9.3 suggests a programme for the delivery of this book in module form.

Each chapter in this book ends with additional notes for trainers. It is my belief that the lead trainer should have read widely so as to be able to answer students' questions, as well as having a breadth of experience in the field.

Chapter 1

The Nature of Grief

For the first time in my life I was out of the sight of humans. For the first time in my life I was alone in a world whose behaviour I could neither predict nor fathom: a world of birds that squealed, of plants that stank, of insects that sprang about without warning. I was lost and I did not expect to be found again. I put back my head and howled, and the sun hit me smartly on the face like a bully.

Laurie Lee (1959, 2002), *Cider With Rosie*

Loss is part of life. Our first experience of loss is leaving the physical, physiological and psychological security of the womb. From this moment our life is punctuated by losses. Not all of them are unpleasant, since there are many that are deliberately planned – if not by us, then by our parents. A childhood loss familiar to most of us comes with leaving the house of our birth. The old house was familiar and helped us to feel secure, but the new house offers new opportunities. At first the unfamiliarity may be frightening, as the three-year-old Laurie Lee found when in 1918 he arrived on a carrier's cart in the Cotswolds village of Slad. In every life there will be other losses. Most of us will have memories of losing a pet or losing the safe family atmosphere of our first school in exchange for the larger, comparatively impersonal school of our teens. We may have experienced one parent moving out of the family home. In our teens, the chances are that we will eventually experience the heartbreak of losing our first love. If we are really unlucky we will experience loss due to illness or disability, be it our own or that of a close relative.

Losses can be grouped into two broad categories. One is termed *circumstantial loss*. Illness, miscarriage, radical surgery, bereavement, divorce, burglary and sexual abuse are all examples of circumstantial loss. The other kind is grouped together as *developmental loss*. These losses are associated with growth and maturation, and will include loss of mother's breast and, at onset of puberty, the loss of childhood. Adulthood may mean the loss of home with our parents. As we age, we find that there are some things we cannot do as well as when we were younger, including loss of fitness, hearing loss or deterioration in our eyesight, even loss of our sharper mental faculties. As we grow and mature, we experience a succession of transitions from one period of our life to another. Although we may be gaining new experiences and delights we may also be leaving things behind. Becoming parents can bring joy but also loss of freedom, of being unable to be spontaneous in our plans, something we take for granted in our youth. When the children become adults and leave home, many parents find their new freedom is tempered with a loss of parental purpose. Becoming a grandparent is usually joyful. It has little of the responsibility of parenthood: as all grandparents will tell you, it is good when you can hand the grandchildren back before bedtime. At the same time there is a loss to be acknowledged in becoming a grandparent: we can no longer pretend that we have our own youth. Retirement may bring freedom, but with it a loss of status and income.

Loss disrupts the ordered narrative of our life

The way that losses affect us is determined by the meanings we attach to them, by the support and feedback from those around us and by our ability to accommodate and accept the changed circumstances. This is because loss disrupts the ordered narrative of our life. If we are emotionally secure, we adapt and accommodate all but the most severe and traumatic of our losses. Even difficult adaptation is for most of us possible, given sufficient time and emotional support. Little losses in our formative years help us learn to cope with bigger losses. Recovery from significant and painful losses will often prepare us for the next significant loss, providing that two do not come too close together. When faced with the next loss, some of the territory has become familiar. We have learned how to negotiate it. Our ability to deal with change, in particular with the loss of somebody we are emotionally bonded to, will be determined by our level of attachment security. This is something that John Bowlby spent a lifetime investigating, which is why Chapter 3 is devoted to exploring his work. In recent years, Bowlby's colleague Colin Murray Parkes has re-examined the link between grief and attachment style in his book, *Love and Loss:*

The Roots of Grief and its Complications (2009). Our ability to adapt to change and to accommodate new aspects of our life after a loss will also depend on the lessons we learn from how our family and the culture we are born into deal with change. When I talk about learning in this context I am not suggesting that our family or others within our culture deliberately and actively teach us how to deal with loss. In fact, quite the opposite is true. We learn by example even if it was not our family's intention to set a pattern in our behaviour. Let me give you an example from my own upbringing.

When I was about five years old I found a wild mouse in a field near my house. Obviously it was sick, otherwise it would not have let me pick it up and take it home. My father made it a cage and I fed it grass seeds. The next day, when I returned from school clutching a handful of grasses for my new 'friend', the mouse was dead. I remember to this day how distraught I was. This was my first loss. My father, who could not bear my unhappiness, scooped me up. We went to a pet shop and got a new mouse. Without anybody consciously teaching me, I learned that grieving could be avoided by replacing. When, some 14 years later, a much-loved cat died, I was at the cat rescue centre choosing a kitten, also a ginger male, before my pet's body was cold. It has taken me many years of adult life to learn how to grieve.

Working definitions

It is easy to become confused by the terminology used to describe aspects of grief, so here is a quick guide.

Bereavement is what happens to you. *Grief* is what you feel: the affective and cognitive state you are likely to experience following a significant loss. Whereas grief is a state, *grieving* is a process: what you do as a response to your grief. Some writers use the term *mourning* interchangeably with that of *grieving*. I would argue that *mourning* describes a more public face of your grief that is often linked to culture, religion and tradition. Grieving is often more private. Some authors, it seems to me, confuse the state of grief with the process of grieving. My firm belief is that we can understand both more easily if we are clear about the difference. I follow these definitions throughout this book.

Chambers's 20th Century Dictionary tells us that 'bereavement' is derived from the Old English word *bereafian*, meaning 'to plunder'.

The word 'grief' is from the Latin *gravis*, meaning 'heavy'. This gives us some insight into our cultural heritage in which we see loss as something precious to us being violently taken away, leaving us with a feeling of heaviness and depression.

Grief in a historical account

On May Day 1633, Venetia Stanley, an heiress of the Estates of the Percy family of the Earldom of Northumberland, died suddenly. Her husband, Sir Kenelm Digby, found her dead in bed. We have to thank for the quality of the public record, letters that Sir Kenelm wrote to his friends and family during his mourning. These were faithfully copied into print by Professor Vittorio Gabrieli from 1955 to 1957 and published in *The National Library of Wales Journal* as 'A new Digby letter-book: in praise of Venetia' (Gabrieli 1955, 1956, 1957). These letters provide an intriguing glimpse into one man's grief. They are now digitized and available to all on the National Library of Wales' web pages.

Three weeks after his wife died, Sir Kenelm wrote a long and moving letter to his sons extolling her virtues, rather as a father might do now for children too young to understand, so that in time they will have an impression of their mother. He wrote many letters to his brother during the first few months of his loss, including one in which he recorded: 'For four dayes together I did nothing but weepe (as you can well wittnesse)' (Gabrieli 1956, p.450). He wrote of his difficulty in concentrating: 'Never since my wife dyed, I haue bin able to looke upon a booke to any purpose; and if I force my selfe to read a few lines, I understand them not, although the matter be never so plaine' (Gabrieli 1956, p.460).

In letters that followed, he wrote of his struggle to enjoy anything, his loss of appetite and his tendency to suddenly burst into tears. He also wrote of his guilt at his marital infidelity, believing that her death was God's punishment to him (Gabrieli 1956, p.448). He noted near hallucinatory experiences: 'I can sometimes fansie to my selfe particular passages betweene my wife and me so strongly y[t] me thinkes they are even then present wth me; I see her and I talke wth her' (Gabrieli 1955, p.138). After six months it appears to have become easier. He reported, 'I lye quietly upon the ground and am contented with my fall, it lyeth gently upon me' (Gabrieli 1957, p.93). He did, however, continue to grieve for the rest of his life, including making sure that when he died he was buried with his wife (Jupp and Gittings 1999, p.166).

Evidence of the universality of grief

This account of one man's grief and grieving, almost four centuries ago, suggests that grief and the process of grieving is to a great extent universal and part of what it is to be human. Of course there are significant cultural factors to take into account; few modern autobiographical accounts would concentrate so fully on the interpretation of religious meanings, nor would there generally be such explicit eulogy. However, all the features of Sir Kenelm Digby's grief are found in current-day studies of adult grief, and this account is similar to that which C.S. Lewis wrote in *A Grief Observed* (1961) following the death of his wife, Joy. Wolfgang and Margaret Stroebe concluded that crying as part of grief is a universal response (Stroebe and Stroebe 1987, p.39). In no culture is bereavement treated with complete indifference, although the duration of overt grief reactions can vary across cultures: from days, to months or even years (p.54). James Averill (1968) drew an analogy between grief and sexual feelings, since both are human universals channelled by culture into elaborate sets of social rules. When we are working with a grieving person we need to be aware of cultural differences and cultural sensitivity. For this reason, Chapter 7, 'Working with Difference', forms an important part of this book.

What is grief for?

Grief is, to a greater or lesser extent, almost always a painful and unpleasant state so it may seem strange to reason that it must perform some useful function for our species. If it served no purpose, so the biologist's argument goes, then it would have been selected out of the human gene pool long ago. After all, a grieving person is less likely to perform at full potential and so will be nowhere near as competitive as her peers in finding food, keeping offspring safe or seeking a mate. In a book chapter entitled 'An Evolutionary Framework for Understanding Grief' (2006), Randolph Nesse has compared pain and grief. He has pointed out that physical pain is a biological adaptation that warns us when we are sick or injured and motivates us to attend to the situation. A creature that did not feel pain would soon die of blood loss or infection before passing on genes. He suggests that grief may be a similar painful phenomenon that has the effect of keeping us safe. The sad behaviour that follows a loss, says Nesse, may confer an evolutionary advantage, including successfully undoing the loss, preventing further losses and warning kin of the danger (p.206).

Against this view, prominent evolutionary biologist John Archer (1999, 2001, 2008) reaches a different conclusion. Grief, he argues, has no evolutionary purpose: it is the unfortunate but worthwhile price humankind pays for the evolutionary benefits endowed by attachment behaviour.

My own view is that grief is not *for* anything. Although it may present humans with some of the fringe benefits suggested by Nesse, the significant evolutionary advantage it confers is due to it being inextricably bound to attachment behaviour, which, as we will see in Chapter 3, performs a vital biological function for many species. The distress we experience when we are separated from those we love and on whom we depend for our safety and security, motivates us to stay close to them. It keeps us bonded into family units in which children are born and are able to thrive in safety, and it has probably been that way for at least 100,000 years. Family members separated from one another will search for an extended period of time until either the lost one is found, or all hope is lost and despair sets in. The despair, sadness and depressive mood that follow the initial, animated grieving, may prevent any more energy being wasted on a fruitless striving for the unattainable, allowing old bonds to be broken in order that new bonds can be created. The extended family group, as in apes and chimpanzees, would in early human communities have been instrumental in survival and procreation. In evolutionary terms, those bereaved individuals of breeding age who relinquished old attachments and forged new ones would have increased the likelihood of passing on their genes to the next generation. In such groups, even grandparents past breeding age would have been less successful subsidiary caregivers at the times when they were impaired by grief, so here too there may have been selective pressure for a rapid recovery to health and usefulness. Hence, although grief is not *for* anything, both the ability to strongly bond *and* the willingness to form new bonds when bereaved are selected by evolutionary pressure. When we describe grieving as a normal and healthy process this is what we mean.

Factors affecting normal grief

We have already looked at some of the ways in which culture determines how we grieve. In Chapters 2 and 3 we will explore the part played by our attachment style and in Chapter 6 consider the role played by families in grief. We will be looking at the risk factors for complicated grief later in this chapter. The most helpful aide memoir I have found for remembering the factors affecting grief comes from the training pack I mentioned in the introduction (Faulkner and Wallbank 1998). The authors used the heading 'who, how, history and help'.

Who *has died?*

As one would expect, this will have a huge effect. To lose a close family member will generally be harder than losing a more distant relation. To lose a person on whom one depended, practically or emotionally, will cause difficulties. Most people would agree it is harder to lose a child than a parent, and harder to lose a parent than a grandparent.

How *did they die?*

Most cultures will entertain the notion of a good death. Sometimes a death at the end of a long illness is seen as a relief and a mercy. By comparison, violent deaths will be problematic, particularly if it becomes apparent that the deceased suffered. Suicides are generally perceived as being the hardest of all.

What *is the grieving person's history*

This will include the bereaved person's family and cultural history, the attachment style of the person concerned, any previous losses, concurrent grief and mental health history such as previous depressive episodes or personality disorders.

What help *does the grieving person have in place?*

Some people have supportive family, friends and religious communities to support them, but others are isolated. Some with a mental health history may already have a network of professional support.

The controversial nature of complicated grief

You do not have to study bereavement theory for very long before you meet lively discussions around complicated grief (CG). While most researchers in the field have no doubt about the existence of CG there is by no means a consensus of agreement over how to define it. Many practitioners are far less certain than researchers about either the existence of CG or its nature. All those who work in the field have been exercised by this for the best part of a century. Sigmund Freud, whose work on grief we will meet in the next chapter, attempted to distinguish between normal grief and what he called 'pathological' grief (Freud 1957, p.250). Freud's followers in the first half of the twentieth century continued to describe as pathological what we would now describe as features of normal grief. Part of the difficulty in defining what is normal grief and what is CG, stems from the fact that each share so many common features. In deciding whether the grief we are observing is normal or otherwise we may be determining the intensity and the duration of the grief reaction rather than looking for the peculiar features of one type or the other.

At this point let us assume that grief *can* enter a pathological phase. Pathological in this sense means unhealthy and likely to cause dysfunction in the individual, like a disease or an infected wound. Pathological grief would be unhelpful to the person suffering it and, like a pus-filled wound or fever, would impair the affected person going about their daily life. Any compassionate friend or relative would worry and would want her to be healed. In Chapter 1 of *Attachment and Loss, volume 3, Sadness and Depression* (1980) John Bowlby distinguished between healthy and pathological grief. Since Bowlby (whose work we explore in detail in Chapters 2 and 3) was medically qualified, it is of no surprise that he would describe some grief as 'pathological'. To understand this better, it may help to contrast it with healthy or 'normal' grief. Any disease is much easier to understand when it is viewed in relation to normal, healthy physiology.

Common features of normal, healthy grief

Below I have listed most, but not all of the feelings, behaviour and thoughts clients experience and want to discuss when they come for bereavement support. Perhaps the most obvious feature is sadness. Grieving people are sad, both for their own loss, and for the loss of a future their loved-one will no longer experience. Sadness is often expressed in tears: from tear-filled eyes, to quiet gentle sobs, through to heart-rending wails of pain and anguish. All of these expressions of sadness are considered normal and healthy, at least in the first few weeks and months.

Clients will often express their shock at and disbelief in the reality of what has happened. Shock is understandable if the death was sudden and violent, but you may think that an expected death at the end of a long illness would be easier to accommodate. In fact in many cases, the actual end of life can still come as a huge shock. Clients tell me that the illness has become part of life's routine, and a little bit of hope continues so long as the loved one is alive. Apart from the fantasized hope of a last minute miracle cure, family members can come to expect that there will always be one more day to share. The medical staff may know that death is imminent but the family may be partially blinded by the hope they need to cling to. With cancers, my medical colleagues tell me that the final weeks' trajectory of the disease can be unpredictable. This means that deterioration can appear to be very sudden to the family.

Following on from the shock is the disbelief at what has happened. I suspect that disbelief is a psychological mechanism to protect our emotions from the enormity of what has happened. 'Pretending' that the person is still alive seems to give us time to get used to the idea. The cognitive side of acceptance is much easier to resolve than the emotional side. Clients will say, 'I *know* he is dead, I just don't *feel* he is dead.' Clients also say that they sometimes forget: 'I thought to myself, "I'll tell Joan that story when I get home." Then I remembered that I can't.'

Perhaps associated with this phase of disbelief is a powerful sense of yearning for the deceased, which comes in waves or 'pangs of grief'. This can be compounded when the bereaved person searches for the deceased. Clients often say that that they saw the object of their grief in a shopping mall. They chased after her only to find that of course it was not the deceased, and as they tell the story they berate themself for their 'silliness'. In fact it may be that the yearning and pangs of intense grief are responsible for this apparently irrational searching behaviour.

With the pangs of grief and the yearning to be reunited with a lost love comes the risk that the bereaved person will begin to dwell on the memories of the deceased to the point where all else may be excluded. They may become preoccupied so that the loss becomes all consuming. For a time this may be helpful. It gives time to make sense of the death and find new meanings. However, it may lead to rumination. Rumination, which is discussed in Chapter 5, is a cycle of unhelpful negative thoughts that can leave a person confused and exhausted as she finds herself lying awake at night with thoughts going round and round, leading nowhere helpful. Disturbed sleep is another aspect of normal grief. None of this helps with the confusion, absent-mindedness and difficulty in concentrating that are also common features. Clients often worry about this, especially older people who are relieved to hear that this is unlikely to be an early sign of dementia. Bereaved people often temporarily lose the ability to read a book. They say that by the time they get to the bottom of a page they have forgotten the first paragraph, something we have seen Sir Kenelm Digby experienced.

Grieving people are often angry. Actually I would suggest that in my experience they are *usually* angry, although they may be unaware of their anger at first, and as it becomes slowly apparent, they may be reluctant to admit it; some even express guilt at feeling angry with a much loved person who didn't want to die. However, just as the mother and child separated from each other in a department store are often angry with each other when they are reunited, and just as father is angry with the teenage son who comes in late without communicating his revised plans by phoning ahead, this healthy anger is born of a need to stay bonded and attached to those we love.

A grieving person often expresses anxiety about whether they did enough for the deceased, and anxiety about how they will cope on their own. As William Worden points out in his book *Grief Counselling and Grief Therapy* (2009) some anxiety comes from the new awareness of mortality that bereavement brings. Grieving people may become anxious about their own death. Anxiety may be accompanied by a sense of helplessness.

With bereavement there frequently comes guilt. I recall a client whose sick partner, perhaps sensing that death was close, desperately wanted to stay at home. She begged my client not to call an ambulance. Eventually my client could stand the anxiety no longer and called the ambulance. As a result her partner died in hospital. There was, understandably, guilt at the hospital death and guilt at the delay in seeking medical help. Realistically, my client acknowledged, after talking to the doctors, the delay had made no medical difference.

The guilt that accompanies grief is often wholly irrational, although clients will hook onto some feature of the bereavement story to give credibility to the emotion. Other guilt-inducing scenarios include not noticing how ill the loved-one was, agreeing with the health professionals to turn off life support and consenting to 'do not resuscitate' (DNR) protocols. Deaths from suicide invariably leave a trail of guilt in their wake.

When I first meet a bereaved person professionally I find it important to check on changes in appetite, weight gain or weight loss. As may be expected, grieving people often eat very little in the first few days or weeks, so some weight loss is generally seen as normal (unless the client has a history of an eating disorder). In my experience, people grieving normally who lose weight just after the loss regain it within a few months. Not everyone loses weight in this way. Some people who lose a partner may feel disinclined to 'cook for one', especially in the early stages of grieving. They may resort to snacks and ready-meals or what they will describe as 'comfort food'. They may consume more alcohol. These changes in behaviour can cause weight gain. This is covered in more detail in Chapter 8.

With bereavement, especially following the loss of a partner, comes a change in social status. Any bereaved person will tell you how some people have avoided them, apparently for fear of saying the wrong thing and causing upset. Often new and unexpected people become helpful and supportive friends while other friends disappoint. Invitations that previously came to a couple seem to dry up when only one of the couple remains. Conversely, invitations to the bereaved survivor may come out of the blue. As one client put it, following an unexpected and uncharacteristic social invitation from an acquaintance, 'I think I'm being seen as a charity case at the moment.'

The bereaved, now single, person can feel strange surrounded by couples, and this may heighten the sense of loss. Add to this the exhaustion of grief and a lack of appetite, and it is not surprising that newly bereaved people lose interest in mixing with others. Another common experience of the bereaved is that they sense people's discomfort in their presence. Clients will often report that they pretend to be doing better than they are in social situations in order to protect others. This is hard work and another reason to avoid public appearances.

Grieving people often report very vivid dreams. Sometimes these are about the deceased. In the dream the deceased may be ill, as at the end of life, or may be restored to health. If the dream feels real, it is distressing to reach out a hand to the other pillow, only to find that your partner is not back, that she is still dead. Dreams that involve searching or problem-solving are also routinely reported. Clients commonly report sensing the presence of the deceased – 'feeling' that they are nearby even if not seeing them. One client, whose husband's work often involved him returning home at 2.00 am, was, for months after his death, woken by the doorbell every night at 2.00 am. Eventually she had the old bell disconnected and a new chime installed. However, each night at 2.00 am she still heard the old bell. Very common is a sense of smelling perfume or aftershave, even though none is actually in the room. In one case a client reported coming home to the smell of her deceased son's favourite takeaway food on the night of the week he usually brought it home. In some cases, the grieving person may even see the deceased in the room. Most often this occurs early in the morning and at night, when the grieving person is visited at her bedside. The deceased will often bring a message of comfort and reassurance that they are OK. I make a point of asking clients if they have seen the deceased in this way, because some clients would otherwise keep quiet about it, for fear that others would think they were 'losing the plot'. I do not want to get into explanations of what is 'really happening' here; I am just reporting the common phenomenological experience of many clients, an experience that is common enough to be regarded as normal by researchers and practitioners.

You may have noticed that I have avoided the word 'symptoms' to refer to the myriad of features displayed in normal grief. This is quite deliberate. As we shall see in Chapter 2, throughout the first half of the 20th century grief was often described in terms of its 'symptomatology' even when 'acute', as opposed to 'chronic', grief was being described (see, for example, the work of Lindemann 1944, described in the next chapter). In general, there is now a 21st-century consensus, even within the medical profession, to consciously avoid describing grief as a collection of symptoms. Nothing I have described so far is anything more than common manifestations of normal grief. To the person existing on this rollercoaster of thoughts and emotions, especially if this is the first significant bereavement in her life, it can feel very frightening. To the inexperienced practitioner faced with this client, it may appear to be an overwhelming constellation of difficulties. However, what your client needs from you is to be told that what is happening to them is normal and is to be expected. The relief that clients display when told this is often palpable, and just hearing this can alleviate the intensity.

To be told that these intense and frightening experiences of grief are normal should not be to dismiss them. Professor Robert Neimeyer presents a humorous scenario in his workshops. He invites his audiences to imagine walking down the street when just in front somebody falls from a window. He has broken bones and is writhing about in agony. Would you look up at the window, judge the height of the fall, conclude that the injuries are 'normal' in the circumstances and walk on? Of course not: you would offer compassionate help. Normal grief does not mean that the client can always manage without support.

Researchers' arguments for and against diagnosing complicated grief

Much of the work on complicated grief is based on two research teams in the USA. One is led by Professor Holly Prigerson at Harvard Medical School Department of Psychiatry and the other by M. Katherine Shear MD at the Columbia University Department of Psychiatry. Prigerson and her colleagues have argued that CG is distinguishable from bereavement-related depression (Prigerson *et al.* 1996). Prigerson (1995) has produced an inventory of complicated grief symptoms, known as the ICG. The IGC assesses whether the client is experiencing a range of grief symptoms, including invasive thoughts and memories, difficulty in accepting the death, longing and yearning, anger and a sense of pointlessness, avoidance of some situations and unexplained pains similar to those the deceased felt during the final illness. Prigerson and her colleagues (1995) claim that this inventory can be used to predict long-term functional impairment in response to loss.

Most bereavement practitioners would say that most or all of the IGC symptoms are observed in normal grief. Some would argue that the duration and intensity of the grief experience are bound to vary widely due to differing circumstances and individual personality variation. However, Prigerson and Shear continue to argue that CG should be classified as a distinct disorder (Prigerson, Vanderwerker and Maciejewski 2008; M.K. Shear *et al.* 2011). Shear and her many co-authors[1] argue that the potential benefits of diagnosing and treating CG outweigh any stigma that a mental health diagnosis may carry (Shear *et al.* 2011, p.107), and that without a diagnosis, individuals go untreated (p.106), resulting in mental and physical risk to health (Prigerson *et al.* 1997). Shear and colleagues also claim to have a treatment model for CG (Shear *et al.* 2005; Shear, Gorscak and Simon 2006).

If normal and complicated grief share so many features, just what has to be different in order for grief to be identified as 'complicated'? Could it have extra, qualitatively different features not found in normal grief? Maybe it could be the same features, but the intensity fails to diminish with time, such that grief is prolonged. Perhaps we are looking at CG when all signs of grief are initially absent and only appear either after a protracted length of time (delayed grief), or do not appear at all (absent grief). It seems reasonable to suggest that, for a whole host of reasons, bereavement will elicit a range of responses, and that some losses are easier to come to terms with than others. One may also expect that a level of grief complexity understandably described as CG will vary due to many factors, including the cause of death, the circumstances of the death and the relationship to the deceased.

An obvious question that all of this raises is how do we define the word 'normal'? In some situations our definition may be a statistical one, since most living things can be measured and fit into normally distributed ranges. I have difficulty buying shoes, since my feet are at the lower end of a normal distribution curve of the population of British shoe customers. This does not make my feet 'abnormal' because they are small. Diseased feet that are difficult to walk with could more validly be described as 'abnormal'. If statistical norms are inadequate to describe foot size as abnormal, then imagine the difficulties in describing sexuality using statistics. The majority of people in a population describe themselves as heterosexual, but most people would regard it as unhelpful, misleading and even offensive, to describe heterosexuality as 'normal'. The logic of applying statistics to the complexity of human behaviour falters at the first hurdle.

If statistical normalization is an over-simplified, unproductive way to determine the nature of CG, then perhaps, like diseased feet, biological dysfunction is a better starting point. If normal grief serves

---

1   There are 25 authors of the 2011 paper cited here.

a healthy biological function, then just as feet have evolved for us to walk upright, leaving our hands free to wield tools and weapons, so grief has evolved to perform some useful function. On the other hand, if this theory is wrong and *all* grief is seen to be dysfunctional, like a disease, then no grief is normal. Such a theoretical possibility was explored by George Engel in a paper he called 'Is grief a disease?' (1961), and we consider Engel's arguments in the next chapter. For now, however, I ask the reader to assume prevailing 21st-century thinking: that most grief does serve a biological function and therefore is not dysfunctional. Grieving is the way that humans healthily express feelings of loss. Only in atypical circumstances is grief so intense and so prolonged that it becomes dysfunctional and can reasonably be described as complicated. While few would claim that grief is *never* pathological, the debate for and against accepting the reality of CG is no more and no less than arriving at a judgement of when a grief reaction is atypical, given the circumstances of the loss. Academics and clinicians have devoted many thousands of words to this deliberation, and recently the debate has been encapsulated in a seminal collection of articles published as a book.

Edited by Margaret Stroebe, Henk Schut and Jan van den Bout, this collection is entitled *Complicated Grief: Scientific Foundations for Health Care Professionals* (2013). Some of the greatest experts in this field lined up to debate just the philosophical issues I have raised in this chapter, and I am indebted to their expertise in attempting to formulate a balanced discussion of the current state of knowledge. (The chapter numbers provided in the rest of this section refer to Stroebe, Schut and van den Bout's book.)

In Chapter 2, philosopher Rachel Cooper explores the concepts of dysfunction and disorder. She balances the argument between those who judge disorder to be merely a biological fact (for example, Boorse 1976, 1977) and those such as Wakefield (1992, 2007) who say that a biological dysfunction only becomes a disorder if it is considered 'a bad thing' (Cooper 2013, pp.13–14). Intuitively, we may feel that we would know when a biological dysfunction was harmful. However, what may be harmful in one culture or society may not be so in another. For example, in Western society, certain attributes of personality may be seen as mental health disorders. In Shaman societies similar attributes may be seen as a special gift (Noll 1983).

Jerome Wakefield contributed Chapter 8. He systematically questioned all of the arguments used by both the Prigerson and the Shear teams to link CG to the DSM-5 (the fifth edition of the Diagnostic and Statistical Manual of Mental Disorders published by the American Psychiatric Association (APA)) definitions of disorder. First, he questioned the concept of 'impairment', pointing out that even normal grief frequently stops us doing things we would easily do were we not grieving; second, he addressed the arguments against citing statistical deviance, and, third, he highlighted the fact that the DSM criteria states that for a harmful condition to be seen as a disorder, it must arise from a behavioural, psychological or biological dysfunction. In his view, neither Prigerson nor Shear's proposals meet this criterion. He pointed out that most if not all that is observed as CG is also found in what, by wide consensus, is viewed as normal grief. The distinction, if it exists, is about duration and intensity rather than quality.

Shear and Mulhare (2008) have claimed that neither rumination nor avoidance is observed in normal grief. My professional experience leads me to disagree. I have noticed that normal grievers *do* ruminate on their loss until such time as they have the opportunity to explore their confused thoughts with a counsellor. Once counselling begins, change is frequently rapid. My response to Shear and Mulhare's second claim is that my clients frequently avoid the total reality of what has happened, especially in the early days or weeks of grief. This seems to me a helpful adaptation to allow for the slow and gradual acceptance of the enormity of the loss. I would say that few of my clients who initially demonstrate avoidance are exhibiting CG.

Another DSM-5 criterion that both the Prigerson and Shear teams tried to meet is encapsulated in the claim, 'CG entails harmful dysfunction in that the normal healing process has been derailed' (M.K. Shear *et al.* 2011, p.105). Similarly, Prigerson *et al.* (1995) make the claim, 'Complicated grief, unlike normal or uncomplicated grief, is not a self-limited process' (p.23). In other words, the claim is that if grief reactions continue for more than six to twelve months without diminishing, the process becomes derailed and interminable. Hence at this point it becomes justifiable to classify it as a disorder.

Wakefield (2013, pp.104–105) cited the classical work of Bowlby (1980) and that of Parkes and Weiss (1983) to refute this 'interminability' claim. Both researchers cited examples of grief reactions that did not begin to diminish during the initial six to twelve months but that eventually had normal and successful outcomes.

There are other published case studies (see, for example, Horowitz *et al.* 1997) where grief that remains intense after six months satisfactorily and healthily resolves itself.

Wakefield also explored Prigerson's claim that CG is predictive of symptoms such as depression, suicidal thoughts, high blood pressure, substance abuse and distubed sleep and hence these symptoms can be used to validate CG as a disorder. Wakefield pointed out that so too may a bad marriage predict similar symptoms, yet this does not mean that such a marriage is a disorder.

Perhaps the most important symptom that could reasonably establish a difference between normal and complicated grief would be the incidence of suicide ideation. In fact, Prigerson and colleagues (2009) found that at six to twelve months after bereavement 10.1 per cent of the those assigned to a normal grief category were positive for suicide ideation, compared to 57.1 per cent of those in the CG category. Subjects were tested using the Yale Evaluation of Suicidality (YES) screening questions (that can be found in an article by Latham and Prigerson 2004). In particular, Wakefield questioned the validity of question 3, which reads: 'In light of X, have you ever had thoughts of killing yourself?' and is scored: no = 0, possibly = 0.5, and yes = 1.0. Preceding with 'yes', that questionnaire begins: 'Identify the most upsetting event (X): In the past year, what has been the most upsetting event or condition that you have had to confront? Sometimes people with X feel that this experience has affected their feelings about living.' He quite rightly pointed out that conclusions are dependent on the framing of the question. Many clients grieving quite normally will, if only for a brief time, have fleeting thoughts of suicide, so a question that asks '...have you *ever* had thoughts...' (my italics) and then goes on to offer 'possibly' as a response, will record and score the most tentative and transient suicide ideation. Even if a client has ceased to feel suicidal when answering this question, an honest answer will still attract a score.

Jerome Wakefield concluded that the arguments presented for inclusion of a grief disorder in DSM-5 were flawed, although he acknowledged the immeasurable value of the work done by the Prigerson and Shear teams in adding to our knowledge of grief.

In Chapter 4, Therise Rando shared Stroebe and colleagues' (2008b) view that complicated grief is not a single syndrome, and identified four forms of complicated grief:

- symptoms

- syndromes

- diagnosable mental or physical disorders

- death.

(Rando 2013, pp.46–49)

Symptoms, she said, may be 'psychological, behavioural, social, or physical', involving 'distress, disability, dysfunction, pathology, or loss of freedom' (Rando 2013, p.46). For these symptoms to be seen as CG, Rando stressed that they must have developed as a result of bereavement and must compromise, distort or disrupt the normal process of grief.

Rando listed seven syndromes described in clinical literature: absent grief, delayed grief, inhibited grief, distorted grief (for example, extreme grief and anger beyond that reasonably warranted by the situation), conflicted grief, unanticipated grief (for example, for an ex-partner for whom all emotional ties were presumed to have been severed) and chronic grief. To this list Rando added an eighth syndrome: prolonged grief disorder (PGD). She noted that PGD has been empirically investigated but that the other seven syndromes have been minimally or inadequately researched.

It is known that bereavement can cause a range of diagnosable mental and physical disorders (see, for example, Stroebe, Schut and Stroebe 2007), including somatic symptoms similar to those experienced by the deceased. The whole spectrum of mental illness associated with anxiety and depression may be experienced as a form of complicated grief.

In Margaret Stroebe and colleagues' 2007 article, the authors concluded that bereaved individuals face an increased likelihood of death, particularly in the first few weeks and months of the loss. This includes both an increased risk of fatal illness and a heightened risk of suicide. Rando noted a third form of grief-related death through self-neglect (failing to eat properly or take medication), self-destruction (substance abuse, including alcohol) and dangerous actions (drunk driving, excessive speed).

In Chapter 5, Kathrin Boerner and colleagues concluded that the complexity of some grief reactions may be an idiosyncratic, helpful adaptation to difficult circumstances. They reminded readers that once we understand the variety of possible grief patterns we are 'less likely to impose an expectation of how one should grieve' (p.64). Clients are not there to fit into neat theories; they are individuals. We can and should learn about grief by listening closely to their human experience.

If it is so difficult to separate complicated and normal grief using behavioural indicators, may some way forward be found in measuring physiological difference? In Chapter 15, Mary Frances O'Connor reviewed the current state of understanding in this field (O'Connor 2013). It is known that CG brings about physiological changes. However, so does normal grief, for example during tearful episodes, when heart rate and blood pressure have been observed to increase. Levels of hormones and neurotransmitters associated with stress[2] have also been shown to change after a loss, although this may be a stress reaction not specifically related to bereavement. An additional complexity is that where significant physiological differences between complicated and non-complicated grievers are observed, there is no easy way of knowing if these differences are caused by the grief reaction or are the result of some pre-existing tendency to physiological disorder that is triggered or exacerbated by bereavement (O'Connor 2013, p.207).

If physiological studies raise as many questions as they answer, what of the fast-expanding province of neurobiology? Recent developments have refined a technique known as functional magnetic resonance imaging (fMRI). This allows a brain scan to be made while the subject is performing a task. In the field of grief studies, many would consider O'Connor to be the leading player (Gündel *et al.* 2003; O'Connor *et al.* 2008). In the 2008 study, participants were shown images designed to elicit a grief response. There were significant differences in the brain scans of participants with CG when compared to subjects grieving normally. The CG group showed a significant activity in part of the brain called the nucleus accumbens, activated when something is strongly 'wanted' (in this instance, the deceased loved-one). Of course it may be that in earlier phases of grief, the non-complicated grievers would also have displayed increased nucleus accumbens' activity. Indeed, O'Connor acknowledged that the point may come that the intensity of grief is viewed on a continuum rather than there being a point at which grief becomes diagnosed as a distinct disorder we label 'complicated grief' (O'Connor 2013, p.214).

---

2   Some of this work has been carried out using animals including non-human primates.

The pros and cons of a CG diagnosis

With so much difficulty in deciding the nature of CG, does it matter, so long as grieving individuals receive the professional help that they need? If an individual experiences intense and unrelenting grief so severe that it is having an effect on day-to-day living, but is unable to get access to psychological care because they have no mental health diagnosis, then a CG label may help. On the downside, there is a risk that intense, prolonged but explainable grief is categorized routinely as CG, and that the pharmaceutical industry's attendant advertising will convince millions of individuals that they have a disorder that needs to be treated (Wakefield 2013, pp.111–112).

Risk factors for CG

As one would expect, those researchers who support the existence of CG have considered the risk factors for developing the disorder. Perhaps not surprisingly, there are similarities with the Faulkner and Wallbank (1998) list – 'who, how, history and help' – discussed earlier. Laurie Burke and Robert Neimeyer (2013) have examined the relevant peer-reviewed literature from 1980 to 2010. They grouped the factors into two groups: potential risk and confirmed risk. I would urge everybody who works with chronic and intense grief, including those who refer people to specialist bereavement services, to read this chapter. This list is a summary of the principal findings.

Confirmed risk factors:

- being either the spouse or the parent of the deceased
- low social support
- anxious/avoidant/insecure attachment style
- found, saw or identified the body in cases of violent death
- issues related to being notified of the death
- high pre-death marital dependency
- high neuroticism.

Potential risk factors:

- being young

- being female

- violent death

- age of deceased

- sudden, unexpected death

- low level of education

- loss is recent

- low income

- experience of prior losses

- problematic relationship with the deceased

- being non-Caucasian

- lack of family cohesion.

I would argue that these factors may well be indicators of the likelihood of CG. Equally, and this is important, they can also predict grief that is normal but intense and lasting over a longer than average period of time, such that the bereaved person's life is significantly affected. When this happens the individual may find it difficult to focus on tasks. Relationships may suffer, particularly in families where conflict and poor cohesion is already an issue. Going to work may be difficult. This may not be immediately problematic with a sympathetic employer. However, some employers will only be willing to accept a diagnosed medical condition as a qualification for sick leave and sick pay. This may present a case for the practical value of CG as a diagnosis.

Complicated grief and DSM-5

In May 2013, the American Psychiatric Association published the fifth edition of the Diagnostic and Statistical Manual of Mental Disorders (DSM-5). Neither CG nor PGD appear as specific DSM-5 disorders, and the picture is little changed from the previous version, DSM-IV,[3] in which it was recognized that bereavement sometimes triggers a major depressive episode, just as other losses and catastrophic

---

3   Note that the APA have now dropped Roman numerals, so that the latest edition is correctly called 'DSM-5', not DSM-V

life events can do. However, in DSM-IV there was a bereavement exclusion clause suggesting that, because of the perfectly natural grief reactions that could be confused with depression, a diagnosis of a major depressive episode could not be made in the first two months following bereavement. This clause has now been removed. The authors of DSM-5 say that this change removes the implication that grief typically lasts only two months, and recognizes that grief may in some circumstances last much longer. It also recognizes bereavement as a psycho-social stressor that can and does lead to a major depressive episode *in some circumstances and in some people*. Third, it recognizes that family history and past depressive episodes will also be factors. Removal of the bereavement exclusion clause means that a professional diagnostician can now diagnose a major depressive episode almost immediately following a stressing life event, including bereavement. There is still the expectation that symptoms should be observable for two weeks before a major depressive episode can be diagnosed.

Already there are critics of this content of DSM-5. For example, writing for the international news agency Reuters, journalist Sharon Begley (2013) stated, 'Now, if a father grieves for a murdered child for more than a couple of weeks, he is mentally ill.' In my view this is a flagrant misrepresentation of the actual content. I see DSM-5 as an enabling guide rather than as a prescriptive edict, but would urge readers to make up their own mind. A summary version can be found on the APA web page.[4]

A professional reflection

My own experience suggests that very few clients experience intense, prolonged and unremitting grief that perpetuates for more than two or three years with little or no observable change. I have worked with many instances, both where the onset of grief reaction was delayed and where grieving was prolonged. However, all of these clients did, with help, eventually reach a resolution to their own satisfaction. Only three clients' grief has been what I would describe as pathological. In none of these cases did grief diminish. After two years all were grieving in much the same way as they had been at six months, and weekly sessions of grief counselling remained ineffective. It may be helpful to look at what these clients had in common. All were white

4   www.dsm5.org

Caucasian, all were widows and all were bereaved under the age that one would generally expect to lose a spouse. Two of the spousal deaths were sudden and unexpected; one of these involved a violent death. The third case involved a spouse nearing the end of a life-limiting condition, but the way that death occurred was atypically sudden and dramatic and in a domestic situation where only the wife was present. All three deaths were reported to be traumatizing. All three widows had been in merged relationships with their husbands, and post-loss, expressed the view that they were no longer a complete person following the loss, nor could they ever be again. (A merged relationship is one where the boundary of individual self-identity becomes merged with another person, usually a parent, sibling or romantic partner. Merged individuals lose a sense of where they end and the other person begins, that is, individual identity gets lost.) All three had some ambivalence in their relationships with their mothers. All three women were childless. All three were in full-time professional employment.

A note for health professionals
referring to a bereavement service

Grief in the early weeks is often very intense. This can make it difficult to make a judgement based solely on the way that the patient is expressing her grief as to whether to refer her to specialist counselling. Many patients are helped by a simple reassurance that their grief is normal, and this is all the profession intervention needed. A far better guide for assessing the need for specialist support is a checklist of the risk factors that can be used to predict which patients are likely to have a severe and prolonged grief reaction and hence are likely to need specialist help. Reliable indicators are:

- sudden, violent and traumatizing deaths (especially suicide), and especially if the patient witnessed the death or its aftermath

- deaths unexpected because of the age of the deceased, especially the death of the patient's child

- deaths of people on which the patient was very dependent/ co-dependent

- emotionally and geographically isolated patients with low levels of social support

- patients with a history of depression and/or neuroticism

- patients unemployed or underemployed, perhaps with attendant financial worries, concurrent or closely consecutive losses and/or stressful life events

- patients for whom the relationship with the deceased had been difficult; this may include instances where the progress of the deceased's illness had resulted in personality changes (for example, as a result of brain injury or tumours).

As a rule of thumb, the more of these that pertain to the patient, the greater the risk of some form of protracted intense grief. Research suggests that women are more likely to be vulnerable than men (Burke and Neimeyer 2013).

Summary and conclusions

Life is punctuated by losses, some of which involve significant bereavements. A host of factors influences how we deal with loss, but it seems that personality and attachment style are particularly important factors. Grief is a human universal but with important cultural variation, and grief practitioners need to be culturally sensitive. Most theorists consider grief to be a normal and natural process most of the time. While it is generally accepted that grief can become pathological, there is an ongoing discussion within the bereavement research community as to the nature, prevalence and diagnosis of CG. The authors of DSM-5 have changed little from the view taken in DSM-IV that grief can trigger a major depressive episode in some people. They have not, however, recognized a separate disorder in the form of PGD or CG.

Notes for trainers

For the training module on which this chapter is based, the content is taught over three 75-minutes' sessions of class contact spread over two days. Sessions are broken down into activities, with time built in for discussion. I suggest beginning the first session with an activity on personal losses. Recognizing that this may stir up some difficult personal material, I first remind students of our confidentiality agreement, and of a personal responsibility to keep safe by taking time out if an activity engenders difficult memories. Students are given a random list of developmental and circumstantial losses and asked to circle those that apply to them. They are invariably amazed at how many losses they have experienced in their life and may need time to discuss these. After this, I offer a short PowerPoint presentation on the difference between developmental and circumstantial losses. This is followed with a personal time-line activity, inviting students to chart the chronology of their losses in graphic form (see Chapter 9). Again I allow time for discussion. Students come to realize that even pleasant key moments in their lives invariably have an aspect of loss associated with them. If tutors feel able to be open about their own personal experiences, this models openness for students. For example, I use the earlier story of finding a wild mouse that died.

The second session begins with definitions of 'bereavement', 'grief', 'grieving' and 'mourning'. I then read key extracts from Sir Kenelm Digby's letters, with the language modernized, and invite the students to date the account, which is of course not possible. Students are surprised at the age of this autobiography. I then present and lead a discussion on the universality of grief.

The final session is devoted to CG. I would suggest that all tutors are familiar with the appropriate material in William Worden's fourth edition (2009) and with Margaret Stroebe and colleagues' *Complicated Grief: Scientific Foundations for Health Care Professionals* (2013) so as to be able to present the material confidently, answer questions and lead a discussion. Familiarity with some of the original papers by Shear and Prigerson would also be helpful and with the original letters of Sir Kenelm Digby.[5]

---

5   These can be found at http://welshjournals.llgc.org.uk/browse/listissues/llgc-id: 127 7425

Chapter 2

Theories of Grief
Historical Perspectives

In this chapter I want to introduce the concept that will permeate this book: that ideas spring from human experience. The life narrative of the most objective of scientists will inevitably influence how he interprets the world. I have had the privilege of listening to some of the best current researchers in the field of grief studies. Often there is a story of personal tragedy and loss behind grief theory as a chosen discipline. This is in no way to question the integrity of the researchers but it is important for the reader to recognize that the possibility of total objectivity is a myth. In the straightforward science of chemistry and physics an experimental result can be reasonably unquestionable, although even in this field, what led the scientist to his investigations in the first place will be influenced by personal narrative. Take, for example, this account written by Sir William Stukely, an early biographer of Isaac Newton, who recorded this conversation with the great scientist in 1752. As they sat together in the garden drinking tea, Newton recalled a similar day 'when formerly the notion of gravitation came into his mind. It was occasion'd by the fall of an apple, as he sat in contemplative mood. Why should the apple always descend perpendicularly to the ground thought he to himself' (Stukely 1752, 1936). A chance event and a scientist in a relaxed but thoughtful mood led to Newton's laws of motion.

Another important factor in the development of scientific knowledge was explored by Thomas Kuhn in *The Structure of Scientific Revolutions* (1962). Kuhn concluded that once a researcher takes a theoretical stance this becomes resistant to change, particularly once the researcher has collected a community of colleagues and students as adherents and believers. Such a conclusion is hardly surprising. If you or I had spent many years perfecting what we genuinely believed was a sound theoretical model about loss and grief, had published several academic papers and had spoken at conferences where people nodded appreciatively and actively validated our ideas, it would probably take some very convincing discussion and evidence to get us to abandon so much work. It is hoped, however, we would be open to modifying and developing our theory in the light of new evidence we encountered. Yet even here we cannot be truly objective, because even what we choose to read will be coloured by our past. I, for example, am drawn to a branch of psychology called constructivism. I first became interested in this when as a teacher of young children it was my role to help them acquire scientific understanding. In a simplistic nutshell, a constructivist approach requires the teacher to expose children to observable phenomena, for example, a toy car rolling down different gradient slopes. The teacher listens carefully to the child's explanation of what is happening. With gentle and well-timed prompts, the teacher then helps the child to understand and interpret what he sees. When I became a bereavement counsellor I continued to use my skill of listening carefully to individual interpretation of personal events and I continued to help my clients develop an understanding of their experience. In time I discovered that I was not alone in this approach to counselling. My past experience, rightly or wrongly, means that it is towards constructivist psychotherapists, theorists and researchers that I am most drawn. It is their books and journal articles I am most likely to read and their ideas that continue to reinforce my own.

I have gone into this detail because I want you to consider the inevitable bias in how all of us – pioneer, researcher, reader and practitioner – approach the subject of counselling for grief and loss. In the bereavement support service I work in we have a very skilled and dedicated team. Part of my role is to train new volunteers and to support continued professional development in the service. In teaching I endeavour to put ideas in front of my colleagues rather than offer a prescription of how to approach this fascinating field. My hope here is that as I review the history of ideas in understanding grief, you will learn to discriminate and arrive at considered judgements, always aware that whoever we are, we view the world through the lens of our past experience. As I write about a century of grief theory, I will attempt to set the key players in meaningful context and weave together the threads of their history.

The promise of science

Towards the end of the 19th century and the beginning of the 20th, science was making such extraordinary progress that some commentators began to suggest that humankind would soon know all there is to know, particularly in physics and astronomy. On the back of this optimism rode those who believed that human nature could be explained by recourse to natural laws. Most influential in the field of psychology were the psychoanalysts, whose effect on bereavement counselling remains. First, however, I would like to introduce you to an intriguing character far less well known, and arguably a man born ahead of his time.

Alexander Faulkner Shand

Shand, Eton and Cambridge educated, was greatly influenced by the natural philosopher Herbert Spencer and by Charles Darwin's work, not only *On The Origin of Species by Means of National Selection* (1859), but also *The Descent of Man, and Selection in Relation to Sex* (1881) and *The Expression of the Emotions in Man and Animals* (1872). He was also inspired by the works of John Stuart Mill (1856) concerning a new science of human nature that Mill termed 'ethology'. Like many of his time, Shand believed that everything, including human behaviour, could be explained by laws that existed and that were waiting to be discovered. Rather than make field observations himself, Shand explored both natural philosophy and the classics of English and French literature to derive a science of character in which he proposed a system of emotions. He identified six primary emotions: fear, anger, disgust, curiosity, joy and sorrow. Shand did not develop a theory of grief but he did see grief as a particular aspect of sorrow. From sorrow as a primary emotion he derived four types: 1. expressive and tearful, 2. tearless and mute, 3. depressive and paralyzing and 4. frenzied and energetic. If sorrow becomes disconnected from the other emotions, he believed we are limited to becoming either depressed or excited. Shand saw sadness as 'a chronic state of subdued sorrow or grief' (Shand 1914, p.305). What makes Shand's work different from the psychoanalysts is his tentative suggestion that emotions derive from environment rather than from internally driven psychical forces. This idea was picked up by John Bowlby in the second two books of his trilogy: *Separation* (1975) and *Loss: Sadness and Depression* (1980).

Bowlby wrote of his appreciation of Shand's ideas. Within 30 years the concept of ethology had taken on a more scientific meaning, included field observations and, as we will see, changed the direction of John Bowlby's work.

Sigmund Freud

In 1876 Freud entered medical school in Vienna where he was tutored by Professor Ernst Brücke. In keeping with the scientific certainties of the age, Brücke believed that all phenomena could be reduced to their physical and chemical properties, an idea that greatly influenced Freud. Of course we understand now that this was naïve: that our infinitely complex behaviour is not easily likened to the laws of either physics or chemistry. Nevertheless, such ideas became popular, even in attempting to explain grief, its causes and its treatment. The seminal work on grief was Sigmund Freud's *Mourning and Melancholia*, written in 1917 and later translated into English (Freud 1957). In a view that paralleled contemporary physics, Freud saw instinct as a motive force driven by psychical energy: energy of the mind as distinct from the physical energy described and quantified by the physicists. Freud believed that psychical energy originated within the organism and that its purpose was to drive the body into action. Freud did not believe that melancholia (what we now call depression) was inevitable following bereavement. Indeed on pages 243 and 244 of the English translation of *Mourning and Melancholia* he is clear that he sees grief as a normal process but that melancholia becomes the reaction of those of a 'pathological disposition'. Freud explained the process as he saw it. Although the bereaved person knows the reality of the lost loved one, the libido becomes bound to the love object, which in turn becomes 'psychically prolonged' (p.245). Only by breaking this bond can a person be freed from his grief, a process Freud called 'the work of mourning' (Freud 1957, p.245).

What may have been the events in Freud's life that influenced his views on grief? In a paper by Esther Shapiro entitled 'Grief in Freud's life: reconceptualizing bereavement in psychoanalytic theory' (Shapiro 1996), she suggests that there are many personal losses that contributed to his fascination with grief. Freudian psychoanalytical thought has always emphasized the role of inbuilt psychic drive over environmental influence. Consequently, followers of Freud have out of loyalty, always played down the contribution his life events made to his theories. Freud's infant brother Julius died in 1858 just before Freud turned two years old. His father died in 1896 when Freud was 40 and more than 20 years before he wrote his essay *Mourning and Melancholia*. It is speculative to suggest how these bereavements affected his thinking but anybody who believes in the effect of life narrative on our social, emotional and cognitive development will fail to see how it could not. Anybody who takes a systems approach to family bereavements (see Chapter 6) will be familiar with the turmoil a child's death imposes on everyone in the household, even the youngest child (and some would convincingly argue, even on later family members still to be born). As Esther Shapiro (1996, p.554) points out, in his 1972 book *Freud: Living and Dying*, Max Schur, Freud's colleague and doctor in his last years, draws a link between the death of Julius and Freud's lifelong fascination with death. Perhaps as a result of his acquired personal understanding of grief, Freud dealt successfully with the loss of his father by breaking the emotional bond, as Freud would have phrased it, 'through decathexis with the lost love object'. His successful resolution of his grief would then, theoretically at least, inform his ideas.

Later in his life and after he had written *Mourning and Melancholia*, Freud's adult daughter Sophie died in the flu epidemic of 1920 and his grandson Heinnele died in 1923. Neither death was expected and both were potentially shattering to any parent and grandparent. Esther Shapiro (1996) records that three years after Heinnele's death Freud's colleague Ludwig Binswanger lost his own son and Freud wrote a letter of condolence in which he said that he remained inconsolable. In other letters Freud intimated that even the presence of his other grandchildren around him did not help. Three years later he wrote to Ludwig again, reiterating that he remained inconsolable but adding, 'And actually, this is how it should be; it is the only way of perpetuating that love which we do not want to relinquish.'

The poet Hilda Doolittle recalled in her 1956 book *Tribute to Freud* that when she was in analysis with Freud in 1933 they began to talk about the flu epidemic, and Freud intimated that he carried Sophie's locket attached to his watch chain. 'She is here,' he told Hilda (Shapiro 1996, p.128).

When Freud's 95-year-old mother died Freud was 74 and terminally ill with cancer. In writing to colleagues Freud spoke not of his grief but of his relief that she would not have to witness his death.

As Esther Shapiro points out, in spite of changing his views at a personal level and sharing them with colleagues and friends, Freud never modified the ideas in his academic writing. This firm belief that in order to escape chronic grief one had no choice but to break free of the bond that binds the bereaved to the deceased survived in academic writing for many decades and even entered popular Western culture. Equally important, Freud's academic intransigence and commitment to a theory of psychic drive had the effect of pathologizing anything but the most normal of grief. As we will see, this had the effect of putting treatment for grief firmly in the hands of the medical and psychiatric profession for many years.

Karl Abraham

Karl Abraham, a contemporary of Freud and fellow psychoanalyst, was originally reluctant to accept Freud's ideas about grief. It was not until he was faced with his own grief reaction following the death of his father, that Abraham recognized his own melancholia. In papers first published in 1924 Abraham (English translation 1949) reported that his hair turned grey for a time. This he interpreted as an introjection of his late father's hair colour, something that now would be seen as a somatic reaction to stress. The grey hair did, however, bring him to agreement with Freud that relinquishing the bond with the deceased is essential to successful grief work. Like Freud, Abraham distinguished normal from melancholic grief, although he concluded that introjection was a feature of both forms.

Melanie Klein and the schism with Anna Freud

An account of psychoanalysis and grief would not be complete without considering the life work of Melanie Klein. There seems to me little doubt that her ideas were greatly influenced by her life events, which you can read in detail in Phyllis Grosskurth's book, *Melanie Klein: Her World and Her Work* (1986). According to the Melaine Klein Trust website,[1] Klein's life was beset with difficulties and she suffered from bouts of chronic depression often associated with her apparently unhappy pregnancies. Depression became a subject she went on to write about extensively. When Melanie, the youngest of four children,

---

1   www.melanie-klein-trust.org.uk

was four years old her eight-year-old sister died. Her father died when she was 18 and two years later a much loved older brother Emmanuel died at only 25. Her plans to train as a physician were effectively ended by her marriage to Arthur Klein, a chemical engineer. She had three children from 1904 to 1914. Following the birth of her third child Erich, Klein entered psychoanalysis with Sándor Ferenczi, a professional colleague of Sigmund Freud. In 1918 Klein attended a conference where for the first time she heard Freud reading a paper on psychoanalytic theory. She became fascinated with his ideas and used his work on mourning and melancholia as the basis for her own ideas on manic-depressive states. In 1920 she met Joan Riviere, a psychoanalyst who became an important link between Klein and John Bowlby. In 1924 Klein managed to persuade Karl Abraham to analyse her, something he was apparently reluctant to do since by that time he regarded himself as a colleague and had written to Freud in praise of her work. A year and a half later Abraham died before Klein considered the analysis was complete, something which, according to the Melanie Klein Trust website, she found 'very painful'. Shortly afterwards she moved from Berlin to London where she was elected to membership of the British Psychoanalytic Society in 1927. In 1934 Klein's son Hans was killed in a landslide while walking in Hungary. The web pages of the Melanie Klein Trust report that she was too devastated to attend his funeral in Budapest. Meanwhile, having entered psychoanalysis with Edward Glover, a psychoanalyst with ideas opposed to Klein's, her daughter Melitta began to actively work against her mother's analytic technique and in 1937 formalized this attack with a paper called 'After the analysis – some phantasies of patients' (Schmideberg 1937). This was the beginning of a lifelong schism between Melanie and Melitta. The following year Sigmund Freud and his daughter Anna joined the psychoanalytic community in London having fled Nazi persecution. By 1942 the British Psychoanalytic Society was embroiled in a bitter struggle, with the Anna Freudians locked in conflict with the Kleinians.

Klein's position on grief was outlined in her paper 'Mourning and its relation to manic-depressive states' as published as part of *Contributions to Psycho-analysis 1921–1945* (Klein 1948). She recognized the significance of losing a parent. She accepted that children do mourn, that the effect of loss can be prolonged and that it will affect how, in adult life, that individual responds to fresh losses. The difference between her position and Bowlby's, which he outlines on page 36 of *Loss: Sadness and Depression* (1980), is that Klein saw the child's reaction as pathogenic, arising in the first year of a child's life in connection with feeding and being weaned. As Klein put it:

> The object which is being mourned is the mother's breast and all that the breast and milk have come to stand for in the infant's mind: namely, love, goodness and security. All these are felt by the baby to be lost, and lost as a result of his uncontrollable greedy and destructive phantasies and impulses against his mother's breasts. (Klein 1975, p.345)

Klein saw a child's aggression in relation to loss as an expression of the death instinct and believed that anxiety arose from the projection of this instinct.

Her critic, John Bowlby, found Klein's explanation unsatisfactory and said it 'cannot be reconciled with any biological thinking' (Bowlby 1980, p.36). Nevertheless he attempted to be constructive in his criticism. He stated her position 'to contain the seeds of a productive way of ordering the data' (p.36). He stated that he believed it was the whole person, the mother, or even the father that the child was mourning, not simply the breast, and that the child's vulnerability to loss extends way beyond the first year of life into adolescence.

Erich Lindemann

At just after 10.15 pm on 28 November 1942, a decorative model palm tree caught fire in the basement bar of the Cocoanut Grove supper club in downtown Boston, Massachusetts. Of the estimated 1000 people inside, 492 died and at least 160 were injured. The fire was soon out, but bodies were stacked shoulder-high at the blocked and jammed exits.

Boston psychiatrist and psychoanalyst Erich Lindemann went on to work with many of the families of the victims, who were understandably traumatized by the scale of the event and the horror of the situation. In 1944 he published a highly influential paper entitled 'Symptomatology and management of acute grief', the result of a study of 101 bereaved people. From a modern perspective, Lindemann's work needs careful examination. First of all, his sample of patients was hardly typical of a group of bereaved people at the acute stage of grief. He does not record how many of his sample were bereaved by the Cocoanut Grove fire but we can assume it was a large part of the work. Apart from this group he records that his sample also included 'psychoneurotic patients who lost a relative during treatment', as well as relatives of members of the armed forces and relatives whom it seems reasonable to assume also died violently since the research was carried out in wartime. It is also possible that many of his patients were also traumatized as well as grieving. Some were survivors of the fire who had been luckier than their relatives. We also need to recognize that Lindemann was pursuing a medical agenda as befits a psychiatrist, and that much of the language in the paper follows such a script: 'symptomatology', 'syndrome', 'somatic distress', 'prognostic evaluation'. All of these phrases suggest a medicalization of grief that some bereavement counsellors would be uncomfortable with today.

Lindemann concluded that acute grief is 'a definite syndrome with psychological and somatic symptomatology'. Outcomes depended on the success of grief work, which he saw as 'emancipation from the bondage to the deceased' (p.156) a task that Lindemann saw as requiring 'proper psychiatric management' (p.159). Both the essential breaking of a bond to the deceased and the necessity for 'grief work' owe much to Freudian ideas.

In a 2002 paper Colin Murray Parkes pointed to some of the limitations of Lindemann's theory of acute grief. In 1949, psychoanalyst Charles Anderson had observed 100 patients grieving as the result of war loss. Anderson noted that for many patients the eight sessions of 'grief work' that Lindemann had suggested were ineffective; these people were grieving chronically rather than acutely (Anderson 1949). Their grief did not diminish quickly over time but remained intense and emotionally painful.

George Engel

In 1961 George Engel MD wrote an article that he entitled 'Is grief a disease? A challenge for medical research.' In what he described as a 'Socratic dialogue', Engel began by listing the commonly observed symptoms of grief. If these were seen as a disabling syndrome then 'yes', he concluded, grief is a disease. Dialogic arguments that grief can be a normal process requiring no medical intervention were answered by Engel's assertion that this is true of many common ailments that no one disputes as forms of disease. Engel's justification for his medical view of grief was that it legitimized medical research and that it validated clinical intervention (pp.21–22). Engel cited stage theories of grief and some of the commonly observed effects particularly in the middle stages. Of the eight citations in Engel's references, three were articles he had written himself, one was co-authored, one was Erich Lindemann's article described above and a sixth was Sigmund Freud's *Mourning and Melancholia* (1957).

Engel's argument is well constructed and logical. It does, however, perpetuate the medical and psychiatric position that had become so established with Freudian theory. It took two great minds, independently at first and then collaboratively, to move away from the medical and towards the biological models of John Bowlby and Colin Murray Parkes, a model first hinted at back in 1914 by Alexander Faulkner Shand.

John Bowlby

There are a limited number of reliable sources from which to piece together John Bowlby's early life, and the influences that led him towards attachment, separation and loss. One source is a talk given by his son, Sir Richard Bowlby, in 2004 and published in book form as *Fifty Years of Attachment Theory* (Bowlby and King 2004). His son suggests that John Bowlby's motivation stems from the sudden loss of a favourite nursemaid, Minnie. John was the fourth of six children to become a successful London surgeon and in 1911 they were living in a large house with servants, as was usual for wealthy families at that time. The four-year-old John only saw his father on most Sundays and the occasional holiday, and his mother appeared for just an hour each day. The house had a senior nanny and at least one nursemaid who served as a surrogate mother, or main caregiver. From infancy, John had been raised by Minnie and he loved her as a child loves his mother. By all accounts Minnie felt a close bond to John as well. Then when John was four she left for a better job. In adult life, when he told the story to his son, Richard recalls him saying that he felt the pain of separation, although he was not traumatized to the point of not continuing with his daily life.

At the age of seven he was sent to boarding school along with his eight-year-old brother, Tony. According to Joseph Schwartz, Bowlby is reported to have said, 'I wouldn't send a dog away to boarding school at age seven' (Schwartz 1999, p.225).

Bowlby graduated with a first class honours in psychology from Cambridge in 1928, where at the behest of his father he had originally gone to read medicine. He worked for a short time at a school for what were then called 'maladjusted children'. It would seem very likely that based on his personal experience of separation and loss, he could identify with the boys and girls in his care. Bowlby returned to medicine at the University College Hospital (UCH) in London where he completed three years of clinical training. He quickly gained a post as a clinical assistant in psychiatry at the Maudsley Hospital in London. Bowlby joined the British Psychoanalytic Society in 1929. He was analysed by Joan Rivere, a psychoanalyst allied to Klein's ideas. Bowlby qualified as a psychoanalyst in 1937. In the previous year, his ambition to specialize in child psychiatry was realized at the London Child Guidance Clinic, although he continued to work part of the week as an analyst, for a time being supervised by Melanie Klein. After service as an army psychiatrist in the Second World War Bowlby joined The Tavistock Clinic in London in 1946 where he headed the children's unit. As he said when interviewed in 1977 (by Milton Senn MD, a pediatrician with psychoanalytic training, formerly Director of the Yale Child Study Center at Yale University School of Medicine) 'There was nothing I wanted more.' With the coming of the National Health Service (NHS), the Tavistock saw children from all economic backgrounds and sometimes from far outside London. It seems that Bowlby attempted to assert his position by changing the name from 'The Children's Department' to 'The Department for Children and Parents'. He reported a strong conservative influence from the Kleinian followers on the staff whom he felt did not appreciate the importance of the child's environment. As he said in the Senn interview, 'There were always members of the staff in the department who were keenly interested in my research work and keenly supportive and appreciative, although there have been an awful lot of others who have been none of these things.'

Even during the early stages of his professional development Bowlby was attracted to the idea that the child's environment was important. He was also keen that psychoanalysis should become more scientific in that it should offer itself up to testable hypotheses. Although he wished to remain a psychoanalyst and to be a member of the British Psychoanalytical Society, he was moving away from its dominant, arguably entrenched, ideas.

The origins and development of Attachment Theory

Bowlby's Attachment Theory is considered in detail in the next chapter, but for this historical account I will briefly mention the milestones, constructed here from the Senn interview and from Richard Bowlby's memories of his father when he spoke at the Donald Winnicott Memorial lecture in 2004 (see Bowlby and King 2004).

When, in 1928 Bowlby worked with troubled and delinquent children (see Chapter 3), he soon noticed that many of them had damaged or broken maternal relationships. It seems likely, even at this early stage of his career, that he was making an intuitive link between broken attachment and troubled behaviour. In 1948 he employed James Robertson, and the influential work they did together is described in the next chapter. The problem for Bowlby and Robinson was that it was difficult to convince academics of the importance of the child's environment when so many of them followed Freudian psychoanalytic traditions. Bowlby's work for the World Health Organization on children orphaned by the Second World War reinforced the link between attachment and emotional disturbance, but Bowlby, very much the scientist, was still looking for an explanation for the findings.

Two years later, Mary Ainsworth had moved to London with her new husband, and was successful in applying for a job in Bowlby's team. Her careful naturalistic observations on children in relation to their main caregiver (see Chapter 3) added to the impressive accumulation of data, but still did not give Bowlby an understanding of the biological mechanism he was seeking.

In July 1951 Bowlby read a translation of Konrad Lorenz's 1933 paper on imprinting (for example, that delightful phenomenon whereby newly hatched chicks and ducklings latch onto the first living thing they see and regard it as their parent). At the time the biologist Julian Huxley was staying with Bowlby's in-laws. Huxley knew Lorenz well. He arranged a meeting and also introduced Bowlby to Niko Tinbergen's work. Bowlby got to know Lorenz and the young ethologist Robert Hinde. This newly established science of ethology (a term that you will remember was coined by John Stuart Mill and that influenced Alexander Faulkner Shand) was the explanation that Bowlby had been looking for. His first paper using ethology was written in 1953.

Using this new interpretation of maternal attachment and separation, Bowlby published 'The nature of the child's tie to his mother' (1958). According to Klein's biographer Phyllis Grosskurth, this caused huge consternation at a meeting of the British Psychoanalytical Society. Even Joan Riviere protested. Anna Freud was not present, but wrote, 'Dr Bowlby is too valuable a person to get lost to Psychoanalysis' (Grosskurth 1986, p.404).

In 1960 Bowlby read his most controversial paper to the British Psychoanalytical Society. It was entitled 'Grief and mourning in infancy and early childhood'. In this paper he challenged Anna Freud's claim that a child cannot grieve due to insufficient ego development; this attracted huge criticism. When the printed version was published by the society, prominent members Anna Freud, Max Schur and René Spitz had, behind Bowlby's back, been invited to respond in writing to what they saw as Bowlby's challenge to Freudian theory. Although Bowlby remained a member of the Society he never again tested his ideas with the members. This was without a doubt a classic example of what Thomas Kuhn observed about scientists' resistance to change.

According to his son Richard, John Bowlby believed that that adult experience and reaction of bereavement could be compared to the childhood experience and reaction of being separated from one's main caregiver. As we shall see in the next chapter, it took him many years to piece together a coherent theory of loss.

Colin Murray Parkes

For reliable biographical details, a synopsis of an interview with Parkes conducted in 1996 by David Clarke for the Hospice-History Programme UK can be found online.[2] Another useful source of information is in Parkes's very readable 2002 paper 'Grief: lessons from the past, visions for the future'.

In 1956 Colin Murray Parkes became a trainee psychiatrist at the Maudsley Hospital in London. In 1960 he joined the research staff in the Social Psychiatry Unit at the hospital where he remained for two years.

In his 1972 book, *Bereavement: Studies of Grief in Adult Life*, Colin Murray Parkes recollects that when in 1959 he was reviewing the literature on grief in preparation for writing his dissertation for the

2 http://www.hospice-history.org.uk/byoralsurname?id=0086&search=p&page=0

Diploma in Psychological Medicine, he noted how little reference there was to grief in non-human animals in academic literature. With his dissertation complete and submitted to the examiners, he was shown a copy of a paper by John Bowlby containing conclusions very similar to his own. Parkes sent a copy of his dissertation to Bowlby and subsequently joined Bowlby's research team at the Tavistock Institute for Human Relations in 1962. This fruitful collaboration lasted for 13 years. In the mid-1960s Parkes was Project Director of the Harvard Study. In 1966 Dame Cicely Saunders, founder of the modern hospice movement, whom he had met previously in London, stayed for five days with him in the USA. She invited him to become honorary consultant at the hospice she was setting up in London: St Christopher's Hospice. He still holds this post almost half a century later. In 1970 Bowlby and Parkes jointly authored a paper entitled 'Separation and loss within the family'. From this emerged a four stage model of grief (see Chapter 3).

Parkes was able to use the findings of the Harvard Study in setting up a service, at St Christopher's Hospice, to support any bereaved relatives thought to be at risk of psychological difficulties. Parkes carefully selected, trained and supervised a team of volunteer counsellors who visited them in their homes to offer support. As he recollects in his 2002 article, not everyone, even at the hospice, believed that this would be helpful. After the suicide of a relative who had not been supported, Parkes (1981) carried out a randomized evaluation of the effectiveness of the service that showed significant benefits, particularly to bereaved men. Since that time, bereavement services run by combinations of paid professionals and highly trained volunteers have become widespread in the UK. A great deal of the work is carried out by Cruse Bereavement Care, which, with Routledge, now publishes an international journal called *Bereavement Care.*

Research by Colin Murray Parkes

The Bethlem Study

The purpose was to investigate atypical reactions to bereavement. Interviews were conducted from 1958 to 1960 on 21 bereaved patients of the Bethlem Royal and Maudsley hospitals. The results were published in 1965 (Parkes 1965).

The London Study

Twenty-two London widows were asked to rate their health at each of five interviews in the first year of their bereavement. Of those who reported a general feeling of ill health a significant number also reported feeling angry and irritable (Parkes 1970).

From these two studies, Parkes noted typical and atypical grief reactions. The questions this raised led to the Harvard Study.

The Harvard Study

Parkes headed a team of researchers at Harvard University. Conducted in 1965 and 1966, this study sought to explore why some people's grief proceeds normally while in others it becomes complicated. It focused on 49 young widows and 19 young widowers living in Boston, who were interviewed in their homes 3, 6 and 14 weeks after bereavement. Results from this study have allowed bereavement support practitioners to predict the course of grief and recognize likely complicating factors. Results were published in the journal *Psychosomatic Medicine* in 1972 in a paper entitled 'Health after bereavement: a controlled study of young Boston widows and widowers' (Parkes and Brown 1972). An important book followed. Published with Robert Weiss in 1983 it is called *Recovery from Bereavement*.

Other projects

From 1975 to 1993 Colin Murray Parkes was Senior Lecturer in Psychiatry in the London Hospital Medical College. Parkes researched the effect of loss following amputation and in the 1970s was one of the first to explore a psychosocial view of loss as a result of radical changes in an individual's personal world (see Chapter 5). In the 21st century he returned to an exploration of the effect of attachment style on grief reaction. The results were published in his 2006 book, *Love and Loss: The Roots of Grief and its Complications*.

Summary and conclusions

I have for several years pointed out to audiences the unbroken link, akin to a genealogical tree, from Sigmund Freud to Colin Murray Parkes, via Klein, Riviere and Bowlby. That particular PowerPoint slide always meets a ripple of surprise and interest and many people have told me that they had not before noticed these connections. I can admit now to an unfounded assumption on my part that this connection inevitably meant unconscious influence. Perhaps at times I even implied the influence to my audience. That was because I had not read widely enough. Only when I disciplined myself to read, from first cover to last, Bowlby's attachment trilogy, written from 1969 to 1980, did I begin to appreciate the genius of his original thought and the systematic way he challenged the dominant psychoanalytical thinking of the mid-20th century, while at the same time respectfully recording his points of agreement with Freud and Klein. Of course Bowlby was influenced by his academic forebears. That is, how a given discipline builds a knowledge base. In (Thomas) Kuhnian terms, Bowlby moved away from the Freudian paradigm to establish a paradigm of his own. The new paradigm – attachment theory – quickly gained researchers, writers, followers and even evangelists since this is an emotive subject. The theory survives and flourishes six decades on. The bereavement research and practitioner community owes a great debt to the continued and enthusiastic way in which Colin Murray Parkes built on Bowlby's legacy in continuing to evaluate the relevance of attachment theory to theories and models of grief. A key change Parkes brought about was to recognize what he has referred to as 'a grey area between mental health and mental illness in which both professionals and trained volunteers have valuable roles to play' (Parkes 2013b). This is not to say that a psychiatric diagnosis is never relevant, particularly in instances of PGD, where there may be advantages to the client in having such a diagnosis (see discussion of this in Chapter 1). In Parkes' view, even support for such complex grief could be provided by appropriately trained counsellors. His courage and determination to set up a bereavement counselling service at St Christopher's Hospice, making use of non-medical staff, established an important development in the field.

Two legacies of Freud's *Mourning and Melancholia* (1957) survive. The value of 'grief work' is still debated in the research community and the frequently heard admonition to 'let go and move on' is well established in Western culture, although as we shall see in Chapter 5 this has been challenged.

My historical exploration of grief theory stops here as detailed accounts of current models of grief and some of the stories behind them are the subject of Chapter 5. There is, however, a more important reason. Bowlby and Parkes set the foundations on which many bereavement models are constructed and on which counselling models of support are largely predicated. Even where this is not entirely the case, clients bring their attachment style to the counselling relationship. As I hope to demonstrate in Chapter 5, and this is borne out by my 13 years of experience as a practitioner, a client's attachment style will inevitably influence how they grieve. This will be an important predictor of the outcomes and duration of the counselling they need. Whatever the nature of the loss, or the client's relationship to the deceased, attachment theory will at some level have a part in the process. It is for this reason that the next chapter explores attachment theory in depth.

Notes for trainers

This chapter may make a reading assignment to be discussed at a later point, although it could form the basis of a PowerPoint presentation. Students may ask some quite searching questions and I would suggest that tutors need to be conversant with original source material, in particular *Mourning and Melancholia* (Freud 1957), Lindemann and Engel's articles (Lindemann 1944; Engel 1961), the articles by Inge Bretherton (1992) and Esther Shapiro (1996), the Milton Senn interview (that can be found online at www.beyondthecouch. org/1207/bowlby_int.htm) and the David Winnicott Memorial lecture 2004 by Richard Bowlby (Bowlby and King 2004). I would also recommend Colin Murray Parkes' 2002 paper 'Grief: lessons from the past, visions for the future'. In explicitly using original sources whenever possible, we impress on our students the nature of reliable knowledge. This is highlighted by some minor inconsistencies in some of the second-hand accounts that the astute reader can find.

Remember that all of these sources are protected by copyright and that there are strict laws about how these are made available to students.

Chapter 3

Attachment

In the last chapter we looked briefly at the life and work of John Bowlby and the people who came together to produce his enduring theory of attachment. In this chapter we will consider the meticulous work that Bowlby and his team devoted to an idea brilliant in its simplicity. Attachment theory continues to be researched and developed and continues to play a huge part in developing a better understanding of grief. It is important to theories of grief because time and time again, both in research findings and in the everyday experience of practitioners working with bereavement, we find that those individuals who experience complications in their grieving process are likely to exhibit attachment insecurity. Conversely, those people who are resilient in bereavement and who return to healthy function, tend to have secure attachment styles. Attachment theory is also the basis for the stage model of grief, which developed from the pioneering work of Bowlby and Robertson. The stage model of grief was refined in Bowlby's work with Colin Murray Parkes in the late 1960s and was published in 1970.

It seems likely that the germ of Bowlby's ideas originated when, in 1928 and 1929, he was teaching at a progressive school, an offshoot of A.S. Neil's Summerhill School, 'the original alternative "free" school'.[1] John Bowlby soon noticed that many of the most troubled children had experienced difficult childhoods. Perhaps his own experience of losing his nanny, Minnie, at the age of four was the catalyst that enabled him to make the link between emotional insecurity and disrupted attachment to a maternal caregiver. What we do know, from Milton Senn's 1977 interview with Bowlby (for the rest of this chapter referred to as 'the Senn interview') and from his son

---

1   www.summerhillschool.co.uk

Richard's conversations with his father, is that John Alford, Bowlby's mentor at the school, persuaded him to return to medicine so that he could pursue a career in the field of psychiatry so as to become better equipped to help children.

As part of his final work in becoming a doctor, Bowlby completed a thesis entitled 'Forty-four juvenile thieves: their characters and home-life' (1944). He concluded that there was a clear correlation between criminal behaviour and maternal separation. However, as every student researcher quickly learns, there is a huge difference between correlation and causation. If there was a causal link, Bowlby was going to have to find it if his work was to be taken seriously by his doubters and critics, many of whom, as we have seen in the last chapter, were fellow psychoanalysts. Encouraging support came from a colleague with a very different background from his own. In 1948 John Bowlby was joined at the Tavistock by James Robertson, a children's psychiatric social worker who grew up in a Glasgow tenement, one of five children in a closely knit working-class family, where his mother was at home looking after the family. Extra support for the family came from 'Grandma'. His father was always in skilled work, but with such a large family, money could be tight. As was normal for working-class families at that time, tenement life meant sharing some facilities with several families.[2] The sense of community we can imagine this engendered made his childhood very different from that of John Bowlby who had been raised by a nanny and who saw his parents for just a few hours each week, before being sent to boarding school at a tender age.

James Robertson, a pacifist, had gone to London in 1940 to help during the bombing of the Second World War. His wife, Joyce, joined him in January 1941 when they heard of 'a woman in Hampstead' who provided accommodation and a nursery for bombed-out mothers and children. The woman was Anna Freud, who had come to London to escape Nazi persecution. She opened The Hampstead War Nurseries. Joyce went there as a student, to look after babies. Joyce introduced James to Anna Freud, and she appointed him boilerman, handyman and fire watcher. All those working at the nurseries were asked to keep observation cards of the children's behaviour, and each evening Anna Freud would collect them (Lindsay 2013). Katherine McGilly,

---

2   I am indebted to James Roberton's daughter, Katherine McGilly, for her help and support in constructing an accurate narrative of his life.

Robertson's daughter (2013) makes the interesting point that his background was an advantage in the Hampstead War Nurseries because it enabled him to understand and communicate with the bombed-out East End families more easily than Anna Freud could. Robertson trained as a children's psychiatric social worker after this experience and both he and Joyce had long and productive careers in the field of childhood attachment and maternal bonding.

Bowlby appointed Robertson to make first-hand observations of young children during and after separation from the mother at the children's wards in local hospitals. Just as Robertson's background had helped him to communicate with mothers in the Hampstead Nurseries, it probably helped to secure the confidence of mothers before, during and after their children's hospital stays.

Today we take it very much for granted that when a child stays in hospital the parents will have open access to be able to stay with them. In the middle of the last century it was very different. Recently a client of mine who was experiencing difficulties in coming to terms with the loss of his wife, spoke of his confusion and surprise at the unremitting intensity of his enduring grief. A little exploration revealed that as a toddler he had spent two years in hospital, only seeing his mother once every two weeks, as was not uncommon hospital practice at that time. More than 60 years later he was still tearful when he recalled those visits, which he could remember vividly. As he talked about the complexity of his grief it was clear that this childhood experience had resulted in a lasting effect.

When he began this work, Robertson was unaware that young children in hospital presented a special problem, but within a few hours he grasped the essentials of a problem of distress that was not being acknowledged by the hospital professions (McGilly 2013). Although colleagues were interested in his reports, none were involved in the fieldwork and were preoccupied with their own projects. Another frustration, shared by Bowlby and Robertson, was that it was difficult to find hospital staff who would admit to children's distress on the wards. Bowlby also reported that his professional colleagues, where they *were* willing to recognize children's distress, believed that whatever factors were causing it bore no relation to maternal separation (Senn interview). How then, could Bowlby and Robertson change hearts and minds? Having read that visual communication does what words cannot do, Robertson decided to attempt a film record of a young child throughout a short stay in hospital. Everyone in a group would see the same scenes, while sequences could be viewed and reviewed in order to heighten perception and understanding without the intermediacy of the spoken word. Robertson made his film between July and August of the same year. Aware that critics may accuse them of selective editing in order to prove their point, he used a strict time schedule each day and included the ward clock within the picture whenever possible. When the film, *A Two Year Old Goes to Hospital*, was shown to The Royal Society of Medicine (Bowlby and Robertson 1953), the evidence was hard to deny, although some groups, notably the Kleinian and Freudian psychoanalysts, continued to believe that intrinsic factors rather than separation had caused the child's distress. As Bowlby said in the Senn interview, although there appeared to be an undeniable link, they still had no mechanism to explain what they had observed. More help was to come from another remarkable colleague, Mary Ainsworth.

Mary Ainsworth joined Bowlby's team in 1950. Before coming to England, she had worked in Canada using naturalistic means to study child behaviour. While at the Tavistock she developed an experiment called 'The strange situation'.

The strange situation experiment

Under laboratory conditions, an infant, typically aged about 13 months, is observed playing with the toys made available. The child's mother (or primary caregiver) is seated on a chair nearby. On another chair sits a stranger who initially does not engage with the child. The situation is observed by video camera or from another room concealed by a special mirror. After a short while, the stranger leaves her chair and attempts to play with the child. At first the mother stays close by but at a signal from the observers she quietly leaves the room. As one would expect, the child tries to follow the parent and protests with signs of distress. The parent soon returns to the room. The observers are now recording the behaviour of the child. In a second phase of the experiment, both parent and stranger leave the child alone for a short time and then return. Again the child's response is recorded. Mary Ainsworth noted that responses fall into three categories and from these varying responses she described three kinds of attachment style, that is, the style by which the infant is attached to her primary caregiver. Some children willingly allow their mother to pick them up. They are distressed for a short while but quickly calm down. These children are described as being securely attached and because this is the most usual behaviour, this is regarded as normal. Some children hardly acknowledge the mother's return or may ignore her completely. These children are described as insecure avoidant. A third group included children who would be distressed for longer, would sometimes fight against their mother picking them up, but alternate this with clinging behaviour. The attachment style of these children is described as insecure ambivalent and sometimes as anxious/ambivalent (Ainsworth *et al.* 1978).

Many years later, in the Senn interview, John Bowlby recalled that there were times when James Robertson and Mary Ainsworth were out in the world collecting data and he was fully occupied trying to make sense of it all. Although news of his team's work spread to the extent that the World Health Organization had enlisted his help in dealing with the children orphaned and dispossessed by the Second World War, Bowlby remained unsure of the function of attachment behaviour in the three styles Ainsworth had described. Melanie Klein had no such doubts. She remained adamant that the child possessed an aggressive drive towards the mother: an instinctual force driven by a fear that mother would take the breast away from the child. This drive was designed to ensure that the child was fed. Like Sigmund Freud, inbuilt drives rather than environmental circumstances were what mattered to Klein.

Harry Harlow's monkeys

On the other side of the Atlantic, Dr Harry Harlow was performing some intriguing, if distressing, experiments on baby monkeys (Harlow 1961; Seay, Hansen and Harlow 1962). Although it is highly unlikely that in a more humane climate these experiments would ever be repeated, they did add considerable weight to Bowlby's endeavours. Harlow removed newborn monkeys from their mother and placed them in cages containing crude model representations of a real-life monkey. One of the models was a bare wire structure with a monkey-like head. The structure included a rubber teat-like nipple from which the baby could suck milk. No nutrition could be obtained from the similar model monkey alongside, but this wire was covered in a warm, soft, fur-like cloth. Harlow timed and filmed the baby's time with each mother. To the surprise of many, the time on the cloth mother far exceeded the time on the wire mother, where the baby would go to satiate her appetite but then would immediately go to the soft cloth mother and cling on tightly. It seemed that nutrition was not the reason for the observed behaviour in primates, including humans, but that a need for closeness to a mother figure existed for another reason. Bowlby was still unsure just what this was.

The ethological perspective and the 'ghost of teleology'

It was only after Bowlby gained an interest and an insight into the emerging science of ethology (see Chapter 2) that he could see that the mechanism for attachment existed in the realm of biology, in particular evolutionary biology. It was clear to him that it did not exist in the old world of Freudian and post-Freudian psychoanalysis. At first, it has been reported (Bretherton 1992), Mary Ainsworth hesitated to follow Bowlby down this path. Perhaps because of the strength of argument against him from the old guard of Anna Freud, Melanie Klein and their loyal followers, he developed his case with good science and methodical reasoning. Following the series of controversial papers outlined in Chapter 2, he began setting out a detailed case in 1969 followed by a second book in 1973 and a third in 1980 (Bowlby 1969, 1975, 1980). In nailing his ethological colours to the mast in 1969, Bowlby was explicit that once and for all he was going to lay to rest the 'ghost of teleology'.

Teleology versus evolution

Teleology, a difficult concept to explain, is encapsulated in a belief in what is known as 'intelligent design'. This can be seen as an argument for divine creation that does not completely reject all notions of evolution through inherited characteristics. It is a middle ground that suggests that some kind of creative force allows functional features to develop in living things. A supporter of teleology could explain in these terms how a mole's fur came to be so resistant to soil and water and may explain thus:

> Moles have perfected a coat that shrugs off dirt and grime.

> Nature (or God) has gifted moles with fur that never gets dirty.

The first statement implies that moles have, with divine help, somehow deliberately and purposefully developed this fur for themselves to make it easier to live underground and the second statement that some intelligent designer had noticed the grubby plight of their ancestors and conferred on them soil-resistant coats. This is teleological thinking and is scientifically flawed. Scientists would claim that something very different happened for the mole's coat to evolve. Many millions of years ago a shrew-like creature would have begun to spend time underground hunting for earthworms. With damp fur they would have been susceptible to hypothermia and those with the wettest fur would likely have died first, before they had passed on their genes. Those with fur that stayed drier would have been at an evolutionary advantage. Similarly, fur that was susceptible to dirt would have harboured disease, placing those individuals with dirt-resistant fur at an advantage. Over many generations, these shrew-like creatures would have been most likely to breed if they had dirt- and water-resistant fur. With each generation the successful individuals could spend more and more time underground until they became a new species, the mole. It is this kind of explanation, based on the mechanics of evolution, that scientists have used to counter teleological argument.

In the 19th century and in the early 20th teleological explanations were rife even in the writings of some of the most eminent scientists, surviving in psychoanalytical explanations right into the middle of the 20th century and even beyond. Bowlby argued that the Freudians and Kleinians had no scientific explanation, or even evidence for their theory of psychic forces as a means of driving human behaviour. These were difficult ideas to challenge because at first they make intuitive sense. After all, if we are frightened we are likely either to hide or run. The difference between the Freudian position and Bowlby's new theory was this: Freud's belief was that emotion actually provided the energy for action whereas Bowlby argued that there was no scientific evidence for this notion of 'psychical energy'. Bowlby's case against psychic energy is scrupulously logical and meticulously recorded. To reinforce his case, Bowlby argued a logical proposition between cause and effect. He used the following example: glass is a brittle material and in certain circumstances it will break. However, to argue that a pane of glass breaks because it is brittle without providing a cause for the breakage is illogical. Likewise, to argue that a little boy bites his sister because he is jealous describes his emotional state but not the cause of his action. Jealousy does not, in Bowlby's view, logically explain the little boy's behaviour. Put another way, the emotional state, or 'affect' of jealousy does not *per se* provide the energy to cause the bite. Bowlby argued that affect is a phase in a more complex process of behaviour, a process that may include appraisal, choice and learnt experience before a decision is made about how to consciously behave in any given circumstances. In other words, even this small boy's decision to bite perhaps originates in a sisterly provocation and may, for example, be determined by remembering many instances of feeling upset by his sister and a recall of past reactions from his parents when he is aggressive.

Bowlby saw that it was time to start considering evolutionary mechanisms. In the first of his attachment trilogy, *Attachment* (1969) he drew his readers' attention to the concept of feedback mechanisms to explain how attachment behaviour could be explained without recourse to psychic energy. Bowlby used as his example the newly invented guided missile system to explain that, although the missile inevitably hits its target, there is no part of the missile imbued with consciousness and deliberation. The missile reaches its goal because of a carefully arranged system of electronics and mechanics that utilize the principle of feedback to determine an inevitable outcome. Similarly, Bowlby posited that seemingly purposeful animal behaviour has its genesis in random events and what starts out as an instinctive or hard-wired behaviour builds into more complex learnt behaviour. From this theoretical starting point, John Bowlby was able to explain how, given the right conditions and maternal attention, newborn mammals become attached to their mother.

Bowlby believed that there is no part of the newborn organism that consciously and deliberately seeks out the mother. Instead, a series of instinctive behaviours has an inevitable outcome that result in what we observe as bonding. This is not to say that young animals do not quickly learn about their main caregiver and then begin to take deliberate action, but it does mean that the first actions a living organism displays at birth can be explained in terms of biological feedback, for example the behavioural system of a newborn baby with regards to breastfeeding as soon as it emerges from the womb.

With the help of his colleagues in the field of ethology, Bowlby set about refining and consolidating his attachment theory by exploring many other behavioural systems in the animal kingdom, from the flight of a falcon in pursuing its prey to the behaviour of a honey bee collecting nectar. He realized that biological feedback mechanisms develop as an evolutionary process. Just as certain genetically determined morphological features such as beak shape or fur colour confer an adaptive advantage and make it more likely that this individual will go on to breed and pass on genetic material, so too are behavioural reflexes genetically transmitted by those individuals best suited to their environment. The bees most efficient in collecting pollen and nectar are those most likely to survive times of hardship and produce another generation. The advantageous behaviour that the parents displayed is passed on to their progeny. Indeed, evolution itself is a feedback process.

Of course, what John Bowlby was most interested in was exploring the behavioural system that attaches mother to child. Bowlby classified two main kinds of behaviour: behaviour that brings the mother to the child and behaviour that brings the child to the mother. The first category he called 'signalling behaviour'. In this he included crying, smiling and babbling, which he observed later developed into calling and gestural signals. All of these behaviours have the predictable effect of bringing mother closer to the child. He also noted different types of crying. A cry of hunger will induce attention from mother, but not with the urgency that a cry of pain will trigger, and smiling and babbling have the effect of reinforcing the bond between mother and child.

Now there was a mechanism to explain the findings of James Robertson, Mary Ainsworth and Harry Harlow. Furthermore, the work of Harlow suggested to Bowlby that the function of attachment was to keep the infant safe from predators rather than, as Melanie Klein had suggested, to ensure that the infant receives nutrition. If this was the case, then Harlow's baby monkeys would have stayed with their wire mother who provided all of their nutritional needs. What seemed to be demonstrated with Harlow's baby monkeys was instinctive seeking behaviour that ceased when the baby found the warmth and texture of fur.

Bowlby's phases in the development of attachment in children

Piecing together the work of his immediate colleagues and others in the field, Bowlby described four phases of development. The first phase lasting up to about 12 weeks from birth is the one in which the baby has a limited ability to discriminate one person from another, relying on hearing and a sense of smell. In this phase, the baby will track any nearby person, following their movements and responding with smiling and babbling. At the sound of a human voice the baby may stop crying. In the second phase, usually from 12 weeks to 6 months, the baby begins to discriminate, responding more positively to a mother figure than to others. In the third phase the baby's repertoire of responses towards the mother figure is extended. The baby will attempt to follow mother as she leaves and will greet her on her return. Once the baby can crawl or walk, the mother serves as a secure base from which to investigate the immediate environment. Responses to other people are no longer indiscriminate and strangers may be treated with suspicion, even alarm. However, the child may select one or two immediate family members to be additional attachment figures. This phase may begin as early as six months and extends into the third year. During phase three the child learns that the mother exists as a permanent and separate being. She may sometimes go away but the child accepts that she will return, although in this phase the child has no real understanding of what influences whether the mother is present or not, at any given moment. By phase four the child has learnt that there is some predictability in mother's movements and her patterns of availability. The child gains some insight into mother's feelings and motives and begins to understand that her mother has goals, interests and needs that are different and separate from her own and that must be taken into account. Phase four extends from the third to the fifth birthday, most commonly in the fourth and fifth years of life. Bowlby described this phase as a partnership between mother and child, a phase in which attachment is truly developed.

In response to a request from the World Health Organization, John Bowlby published *Maternal Care and Mental Health* (1951), which in Great Britain became a bestseller. In the Senn interview, John Bowlby reflected on the initial response to this book. He recalls that social workers took to his ideas enthusiastically. Psychoanalysts, he said, 'treated it with caution (and) curiosity'. To his great exasperation, he found that paediatricians 'were initially hostile but subsequently many of them became very supporting'. While adult psychiatrists showed total disinterest, child psychiatrists were 'pro; anything from strongly pro to moderately pro, but no hostility'. Two years later, together with colleagues Marjorie Fry and Mary Ainsworth, Bowlby published *Child Care and the Growth of Love* (1953). This book was embraced by social workers and subsequent editions were on the essential reading lists for student teachers well into the 1970s. The book conceptualized the idea of a secure base from which the young child, secure in her mother's love, is able to explore the immediate world and interact with the environment, including other children and adults, secure in the knowledge that should the world suddenly turn pear-shaped, mother would be there for her, to love, comfort and protect. Less secure infants would not have this certainty. Their base would not be so secure and they would not be so confident in their interactions with the wider world.

Attachment theory has continued to grow and develop through further research. You will recall Mary Ainsworth's three attachment styles from earlier in this chapter: secure attachment, insecure avoidant attachment and insecure ambivalent, sometimes called anxious/ambivalent attachment. Mary Main and Judith Solomon (1986) experimented with Ainsworth's 'strange situation experiment' and concluded that it was difficult to fit all children into these three groups. They discovered a fourth category that they called 'insecure disorganized attachment'. We will see later in this chapter how this has been used to understand grief reactions in adults.

In the mid-1980s, Cindy Hazan and Phillip Shaver (1987) became interested in applying attachment theory to adult behaviour. Based on the work of Mary Ainsworth and on John Bowlby's attachment trilogy, they theorized that the attachment styles adopted in childhood would endure into adult life. Adults, they hypothesized, would also demonstrate secure, or insecure/avoidant or anxious/ambivalent attachment. This they believed would have an effect on adult romantic relationships. They suggested that, if asked, adults should be able to recall their experience of maternal relationship that would match their attachment style. Hazan and Shaver designed what they described as a 'love quiz' (Hazen and Shaver 1987, p.513) and in July 1985 this was published in the lifestyle section of the *Rocky Mountain News*, a daily newspaper published in Denver, Colorado. Readers were told that the quiz was asking about the most important loved relationship of the reader's life. The reader was asked questions to elicit the details of this relationship, her feelings about this relationship and whether it was in the present or the past. Finally, there were questions about childhood in order to elicit readers' attachment history and attachment style. Fifty-six per cent of the readers classified themselves as secure with the rest split between avoidant (25%) and anxious/ambivalent (19%). The secure respondents tended to be positive about their relationships, which also generally last longer when compared to the insecure groups. The divorce rate was half that of the other two groups. The avoidant lovers demonstrated a fear of emotional intimacy, whereas the anxious ambivalent subjects experienced obsessional love, extremes of sexual attraction and jealousy. As Hazan and Shaver noted, a newspaper questionnaire is not the best way to conduct objective research. For example, there is likely to be a bias based on who reads and completes such a quiz. As a result, the same questions were asked of 108 college students. Surprisingly, the spread of attachment styles was almost identical to the newspaper result. Other results were very similar, differences being related to the age of students and hence the lack of relationship experience. They were also more likely to have a 'Hollywood romance' view of relationships.

It does seem then that childhood attachment styles do transfer into adult life. The messages about intimate emotional relationships learnt in childhood affect the way that the adult learns to love others. Earlier we have seen that Mary Main worked with Judith Solomon on investigating childhood attachment styles, where she discovered disorganized attachment. Main has gone on to work with other researchers and together they have devised the Adult Attachment Interview (1977) (George *et al.* 1985) as a means of assessing an adult's attachment style. If an adult's attachment affects how he or she relates to others it may also affect how adults cope with loss from divorce, separation and bereavement. It was the last of these, loss and grief, which was the subject of research carried out by Colin Murray Parkes described below.

In 2006 Parkes published *Love and Loss: The Roots of Grief and its Complications*. For many years both practitioners and researchers in the field of bereavement care have been aware, often anecdotally, that a subject's attachment style will almost certainly affect the way he or she experiences grief. It was Parkes' research that finally collected together, in a systematic form, what was known, or at least strongly suspected. It is this that links attachment theory to the theories and practice of working with loss and grief and it is hoped that this will help the reader to understand why this chapter appears in this book and why so much time has been taken to address the subject in detail. Remember too that it is primarily attachment theory that has taken grief theory away from the hands of the psychoanalysts with the historical emphasis on 'letting go' of the deceased. Remember that John Bowlby and Colin Murray Parkes were colleagues at the Tavistock Clinic for many years and that together they produced the first stage model of grief based on the stages of separation reaction expressed by an infant separated from her main caregiver. This was a model based on the ethological principles Bowlby had developed through his attachment, separation and loss trilogy.

Parkes asked 278 attendees at his psychiatric outpatients clinic to take part in the study, in order 'to test my clinical impression and evidence from (studies), that love and loss are intertwined' (2006, p.38). His research subjects were asked to complete a battery of 157 questions. Like Hazan and Shaver before him, Parkes was reliant on his subjects to assess retrospectively their childhood experiences and attitude to intimate relationships. His questionnaire sought to determine the subjects' experiences of being parented; how they viewed their childhoods, particularly in terms of vulnerability; significant events in their adult lives, including adult relationships and experiences of bereavement; their coping styles in dealing with stress; and finally the subjects' symptoms and emotional states at the time of completing the questionnaire. Drawing on the research of Bowlby, Ainsworth, Main, Hazan and Shaver and others, Parkes was able to formulate hypotheses as to the relationship between grief and attachment style in order to generate searching and meaningful questions. He was also able to use the fourth attachment style of insecure, disorganized attachment identified by Mary Main and added to the three styles previously described by Mary Ainsworth following her 'strange situation' experiments.

It will probably come as no surprise that Parkes found that, in general, secure individuals suffer less intense distress after being bereaved than their insecure counterparts. Yet, at the same time, many individuals with secure attachment childhood experiences still ask for support in their grief. These included loss through traumatic deaths, unexpected deaths and untimely deaths. Parkes suggests that '"perfect" parenting may not prepare the child for an imperfect world' (Parkes 2013b). In Chapter 1 we considered the value of little losses in preparing us for more serious life events. Parkes confirms this view, providing that a stressful experience 'does not cross an invisible line' (2013, personal communication). In Jeffrey Kauffman's edited collection, *Loss of the Assumptive World: A Theory of Traumatic Loss*, Therise Rando contributes a chapter entitled 'The "Curse" of Too Good a Childhood' (Rando 2002). I can think of clients who match this scenario, in particular when secure adults with blissful childhoods are bereaved by the premature death of a protective parent. A secure attachment style does not confer immunity to the pain of all types of loss.

But what of the results of Parkes' research into grief and insecure attachment styles? He found that both those with anxious/ambivalent childhood attachments and those who make dependent attachments as adults tend to experience enduring grief and remain lonely after a loss. The research did not, however, show that anxious/ambivalent children became dependent adults, rather that this group of children tended to have conflicted relationships when they reached adulthood. Parkes explains it thus:

> I believe that it takes two to tango, i.e. that, like relations with parents, insecure attachments are dyadic. Anxious/ambivalent people have a disposition to cling but they will only be able to form dependent relationships if their partner reciprocates and rewards their clinging. Most partners cannot stand being clung to and that leads to rejection and ambivalent relationships. (Parkes 2013b, personal communication)

It is this that can contribute to the loneliness and enduring grief of those with this type of attachment. It can also make it difficult for helping practitioners to successfully support her through her grief unless the client is prepared to enter into the counselling dyad.

What of avoidant attachments? Parkes predicted that those who developed this style in childhood would grow into adults with difficulties in expressing affection and maintaining relationships and that following a loss, this would tend to delay or inhibit grief. It would also mean that any psychosomatic illnesses associated with stifled emotions may rear their head at this time. These predictions were confirmed. Children who suppress their attachment needs because parents are emotionally unavailable grow into adults who continue to inhibit their own needs. Professionals working with this group are likely to need considerable patience with their clients and patients. These people need time to build up trust in a one-to-one relationship and the professional will need skilled human interventions to engender and foster this trust.

Finally, Parkes turned his attention to disorganized attachments. As children this group will often exhibit helplessness. When distressed they tend to try to deal with it without seeking attention. Parkes predicted that in adulthood and following bereavement, these people will turn inwards and tend towards depression, anxiety and panic. Again the predictions were confirmed. Disorganized attachment correlates with passive coping. Parkes discovered that when 'at the end of their tether' people in this group will often seek professional help. Those that do not appear to be at an increased risk of self-harm, even suicide. They may use alcohol and/or street drugs, which, because of the inhibition alcohol can release, increases the risk of self-harm. Because of the nature of disorganized attachment, it can contain features of avoidance and anxious/ambivalence. This group not only finds it difficult to trust others, they also find it difficult to trust themselves. Professionals working with this group need thorough risk assessment protocols in place, particularly a detailed suicide risk assessment, with clear procedures for keeping this client group safe. Clients in this group may miss appointments or cancel at short notice, particularly in the stage of the work before trust has been established. Like the avoidant attached, they are likely to need great patience and human care.

Attachment theory and the stages of grief

Although several authors have described stages or phases of grief, there seems no doubt to me that, historically, the credit for original thought should go to John Bowlby. Originally the stages of separation distress were applied to children. Robertson and Bowlby (1952) noticed three stages in the behaviour of a child grieving for a mother who does return within a short space of time. They named the three phases, 'protest, despair and detachment' (Bowlby 1969, p.xiii). Bowlby posited that this behaviour could be compared to a child or adult permanently separated by the death of an attachment figure and published a three-stage model of grief (1961). These stages were: 1. yearning and searching; 2. disorganization and despair; and 3. reorganization. When Colin Murray Parkes joined John Bowlby at the Tavistock Institute of Human Relations in 1962 they worked together on the study of adult grief in relation to attachment. This resulted in the recognition of a fourth, initial stage that they called 'numbness', so that the four stages were: numbness, yearning and searching, disorganization and despair, and lastly, reorganization (Bowlby and Parkes 1970). In 1964, when Parkes was engaged in the Harvard Study (see Chapter 2) he met a young trainee called Elisabeth Kübler-Ross, and discussed with her his work with Bowlby on the stages of grief (Parkes 2002). When, in 1969, Kübler-Ross published her book *On Death and Dying,* Parkes very generously wrote the foreword to the 1970 British edition. As Parkes has recalled in the journal *Mortality*, her claim in *On Death and Dying* to have discovered the 'stages of grief' makes no mention of the work of Robertson, Bowlby or Parkes (Parkes 2013a, p.95). *On Death and Dying* went on to become an international bestseller. Perhaps it is for this reason that I meet many people who have come to believe in the originality of the Kübler-Ross stages.

Notes for trainers

I have not found Bowlby's attachment trilogy (1969, 1975, 1980) easy to read, although you may do. As fascinating as it is, there are some complex ideas inherent in the theory. However, I firmly believe that it is important for tutors of attachment theory to have read the literature in the field and this includes Bowlby's complete works. (In addition to the printed books, I also have all three as digital editions, which makes the text far easier to search.)

When I teach attachment theory I use pictures of my own children and grandchildren in order to bring the theory to life and by doing this I avoid copyright restrictions. Another way of bringing the topic to life is by making use of video clips. A computer connected to a projector and to an internet terminal will enable you to show your students examples of Mary Ainsworth's 'strange situation' experiment. There are several good examples to be found on YouTube. This is also a good source of some of the original film from Harlow's monkey experiments. James Robertson's film *A Two-Year-Old Goes to Hospital* is another good source.[3]

It is available in two versions – an abridged version of 30 minutes in length or a full version of 45 minutes – at the same price from Concord Media. They will send you the abridged version unless you specify the full 45-minute version.

---

3 Available as a DVD for £70 plus tax and postage from:
   Concord Media
   22 Hines Road
   Ipswich
   Suffolk
   IP3 9BG
   UK
   email sales@concordmedia.org.uk

Chapter 4

Basic Counselling Skills

Theory into Practice

A model of counselling for loss and grief

The bereavement practitioner helps facilitate the emotional, cognitive and behavioural processes of grief in bereaved clients, by his theoretical knowledge, non-judgemental attitude and counselling skills. As well as knowledge of models and theories of grief, the effective practitioner will also possess understanding of human development, cultural issues and family dynamics, particularly in relationship to grief.

Such practitioners have the ability to form a working relationship with their clients and negotiate a contract that will be regularly reviewed. They work under supervision. They are taught to be able to differentiate their own needs from those of their clients. It is my firm belief that a client-centred approach, in which the bereaved person is an empowered participant in the counselling work, is central. This is epitomized by the work of Carl Rogers.

The life of Carl Rogers

I include a brief biography here because Carl Rogers is such an influential figure in the development of the counselling profession. The other reason is because I want to continue the theme that what makes each of us unique is the narrative of our life. Rogers is an example of the observation that our ability to help others is linked irrevocably to our past.

Carl Ransom Rogers was born on the outskirts of Chicago on 8 January, 1902, the son of a civil engineer. His parents, particularly his mother, were devout Christians and Carl received an early religious education. He studied agriculture at the University of Wisconsin when he was 17 and gained an MA in history from the same university in 1924. In the same year he joined a seminary. However, perhaps because of an interest in the scientific method, he found it hard to accept faith without questioning, something his religious training did not encourage. He eventually left the seminary and studied education at Columbia University, gaining an MA in 1927 and a PhD in 1931.

In 1928 he was employed as a child psychologist at The Rochester Society for the Prevention of Cruelty to Children in New York, becoming Director of the society's Child Study Department in 1929. From 1935 to 1940 he taught at the University of Rochester and published *The Clinical Treatment of the Problem Child* in 1939. In 1940 he became Professor of Clinical Psychology at Ohio State University, publishing *Counseling and Psychotherapy* in 1942. By this time Rogers had begun to establish the notion of 'client-centred therapy'.

In 1945 he was appointed Professor of Psychology at the University of Chicago where he opened a counselling centre. This enabled him to conduct studies in order to develop his client-centred ideas and to evaluate the effectiveness of his methods. From this work came the 'core conditions'. In 1951 he published *Client-centered Therapy* and in 1961 perhaps his best-known and most influential book, *On Becoming a Person.*

In 1964 Carl Rogers joined the staff of the Western Behavioral Studies Institute at La Jolla, California. In 1980 he published another influential work: *A Way of Being.*

In 1987 he fractured his pelvis in a fall. Although an emergency operation was successful his heart began to fail and he died on 4 February 1987.

The core conditions

To share something that is very personal with another individual and it is not received and understood is a very deflating and lonely experience. I know that when I try to share some feeling aspect of myself which is private, precious and tentative and when this communication is met by evaluation (judgement), reassurance, and distortion of my meaning, my very strong reaction is 'Oh, What's the use!' At such a time, one knows what it is to be alone. (Rogers 1980, p.14)

In *On Becoming a Person: A Therapist's View of Psychotherapy* (1961), Carl Rogers reported the findings of his research into the conditions that best bring about therapeutic change. He said that when three core conditions are met in the therapist's behaviour and attitude towards the client, their effect is greater than any effect due to the therapist's technical skill and knowledge.

Congruence
The first he described as congruence, so named because it is a measure of the extent to which words match feelings. Congruence in the therapist is sometimes described as genuineness. It concerns opening one's awareness of your clients and engaging with them with no façade of clinical professionalism behind which the real person hides. If you are congruent you do not take a role, you present as yourself.

Unconditional positive regard
The second he named unconditional positive regard (UPR), which he described as 'non-possessive' caring for your clients. Sometimes the expression 'prizing the client' is used. It means being warm, positive and accepting of the way that your client is, without passing judgement on him. Rogers described UPR as 'an outgoing positive feeling without reservations' (Rogers 1961, p.62).

Empathy
The third core condition he described as 'empathic understanding'. This requires the therapist to enter fully into the feeling and meaning of another person to the extent that he comes to see the world as the client does. If you get this right, Rogers said that this becomes so complete that you lose all desire to judge the client. He added that in grasping the client's inner world it is important not to lose one's own identity in the process.

Deepening your empathy for others
In a 1975 paper entitled 'Empathic: an unappreciated way of being', Rogers described empathy as a 'complex, demanding, strong yet subtle and gentle way of being' (Rogers 1975, p.4). He acknowledged that

there were levels of empathy and that we should always be striving for deeper levels. With practice and experience deep-level empathy is a skill that most of us can learn and use, although there will be no substance to it unless it reflects our usual way of being with the client.

Some key references to Carl Rogers

Rogers observed that behaviours of organisms (including individuals in therapy) move in the direction of maintaining and enhancing themselves. To explain this idea, he posited the idea of a tendency for individuals to self-actualize in order to reach full human potential. The basis for all of his thinking about therapy, human development, personality and interpersonal relationships (1959) was the actualization tendency (1963). He stated:

> In client-centred therapy, the person is free to choose any directions, but actually selects positive and constructive pathways. I can only explain this in terms of a directional tendency inherent in the human organism-a tendency to grow, to develop, to realize its full potential. (Rogers 1986, p.127)

Rogers (1980) uses the metaphor of the potato sprout growing towards the tiny source of light in the dark cellar to clarify his point. He said:

> The conditions were unfavourable, but the potatoes would begin to sprout – pale white sprouts, so unlike the healthy green shoots they sent up when planted in the soil in the spring. But these sad, spindly sprouts would grow 2 or 3 feet in length as they reached toward the distant light of the window. The sprouts were, in their bizarre futile growth, a sort of desperate expression of the directional tendency I have been describing. They would never become plants, never mature, never fulfil their real potential. But under the most adverse circumstances, they were striving to become. Life would not give up, even if it could not flourish. (p.118)

Transference

Not all schools of counselling recognize the concept of either transference or countertransference. In Chapter 5 of *On Becoming a Person*, published in 1961, Carl Rogers describes his 'warm interest' that allowed him into one particular client's life as 'certainly not (a phenomenon) of transference and countertransference' (Rogers 1961, p.81). Rogers believed that the warm closeness that can develop between therapist and client in person-centred counselling is part of a genuine relationship rather than an unrealistic, even unhealthy, event implying that those who label therapeutic closeness as transference are uncomfortable with the intimacy that such warmth evokes.

In Chapter 6 of his book *Psychodynamic Counselling in Action* (1988), Michael Jacobs defines transference as 'where the client treats the therapist or counsellor as if he or she were a parent or lover' (p.94). Jacobs goes on to cite Sigmund Freud who, in Jacob's words, saw transference 'as a way of seeing past relationships come to life in the context of the therapeutic relationship' (p.94). Put another way, it involves a client transferring feelings and behaviours from a significant person who is or has been in his life, and directing these feelings towards somebody else. Because this is a largely or wholly unconscious process, and because of the intimacy of the counselling relationship, sometimes a powerful transference develops, to which the counsellor responds. The counsellor's response is called countertransference.

At first Sigmund Freud saw this phenomenon as a contamination of the therapeutic relationship and tried to avoid it by sitting out of his patient's sight. Other therapists began to make use of the transference and, from this, psychodynamic counselling was born. Psychodynamic practitioners sometimes go to great lengths to allow an unfettered transference to develop. They keep their counselling room and any part of their house that the client will see free of personal objects such as family photographs. By doing this they hope that each client's view of them is based on transference rather than reality. Neither do they disclose anything of themselves such as family, hobbies, interests and past losses.

When I was a student counsellor I wrote in my learning journal that transference was like love: one could define it but could not understand it before experiencing it. What the psychodynamic and psychoanalytic schools recognize as transference and countertransference can be very powerful parts of the counselling relationship. Once we identify such events and explore them with our supervisor then we can begin to understand the relationship that has developed.

Take, for example, a client who I will call May. When I met May she had recently lost her husband of more than 50 years. He had been a kind, hard-working, sober and sensible man who had treated her well. Although at first May was loyal in what she told me about him, it transpired that her husband had in her view lacked passion and a sense of humour, two qualities May had in abundance. Part of her request for counselling was to address her guilt for not loving him like she believed she should have done. Her biggest secret was that for nearly 60 years she had 'held a candle' for a previous fiancé, by her account the unreliable but charming, funny, impulsive and loveable rogue she still wished she had married.

Although in our sessions we explored May's guilt, she would often regale me with amusing stories from her younger days, all quite unsolicited. I grew to look forward to our counselling sessions and over the weeks we reached the point when there was far more laughter than sadness in our bereavement counselling, as her stories got more and more outlandish. I began to wonder when the grief work was going to be done and of course took this to supervision. With my supervisor's help I came to realize that the positive relationship, which some would attribute to transference and countertransference, was the work that needed to be done. In the next chapter we will meet Thomas Attig's concept of 'relearning the world' as being part of the process of grief. At age 80, May was relearning the world of her youth, and rediscovering the attractive, quick-witted and funny woman she thought she had lost for ever. The last I heard of May was ten years ago, when she had befriended a widow of her own age and they were going on holidays and day trips together and having the time of their lives.

Was my mutually warm relationship with May genuine as Carl Rogers would have us believe, or a psychodynamic phenomenon based on the unconscious actions of client and counsellor? The reader must decide. For my part I valued May for who she was. I was genuine, warm and empathic towards her and whatever process took place there was a good outcome.

Putting counselling theory into practice: active listening and how it compares with social listening

Active listening differs from social listening in many ways. In social listening we tend to hear the other person and acknowledge what he says with an example from our own life. For example, if somebody tells us about his holiday we will probably tell him about our holiday.

Also if someone tells us their problems and difficulties we are very likely to give some kind of advice even without thinking about it. Sometimes social listening takes place when we are busy with something else, such as driving or doing housework. This means that we are very likely to be distracted and are certainly not making eye contact. Another feature of social listening is that two people may be bursting to tell the other their news or gossip.

Active listening is very different from this. As the active listener your whole focus is on the person you are listening to. You are there to meet the other person's needs, not your own, as opposed to social listening when two people's needs are being met. You are focused not only on the words but also on the person's tone of voice, posture and facial expressions. How they speak is as important as what they say. Equally, *how* you hear is as important as *what* you hear. You are listening not only with your ears but also with your eyes and your mind. You should also be listening to your own responses and have an awareness of your emotional reactions to what you are hearing.

For active listening to be really effective it is important that the other person can tell that you are listening carefully. It is important that he can sense your undivided attention. This means good eye contact, open body language, tone of voice and receptive verbal cues to indicate that you are listening.

A checklist

- **Seating:** There may be times when you have no choice but to actively listen when both of you are standing up. If it's at all possible then take the person to a confidential space where the two of you can sit down. Most people find it best if the chairs are at an angle to each other rather than facing head-on since this allows the other person to avoid eye contact if they need to.

- **Eye contact:** Think of this as having your eyes available to your client whenever they look at you. This doesn't involve staring, looking intently or trying to attract his gaze.

- **Body language:** Adopt an open and receptive posture. Distance from your client is also important: not too close and not too far away. Leaning towards them both reduces the distance between you and shows you are listening. Remember to smile if this is appropriate but be aware of responding inappropriately when the client is telling you something distressing with a smile on their face. The last thing you want to do is to collude with a defensive smile.

- **Mirroring:** As you become more relaxed you may begin to notice that you and your client are sitting in the same posture. This is an indication that you're likely to be effective in your active listening.

- **Tone of voice:** If you remain feeling calm and relaxed the tone will take care of itself. Don't try too hard: you could come across as the stereotype of a concerned person, which can seem false.

- **Verbal cues:** These are effectively nods with sound. Unlike silent nods, which are also important, nods with sound show that you are listening even if your client is finding it difficult to make eye contact. 'Uh-huh', 'mmm', 'OK', 'yes' and so forth are all good ways of showing your attention.

Difficulties with listening

- Active listening is hard but gets easier with practice. It is made more difficult if you are trying to think of what to say to your client in reply. If you are relaxed then and you will listen far more effectively.

- It is also difficult to listen if what he is telling you is distressing, particularly if what he is saying echoes your experience.

- If there is something particularly striking about your client's appearance you may find this distracting.

- If what he is telling you makes it hard not to judge him then you will find it hard to give your client your full attention.

- If you are tired, cold, hungry or if you need to go to the toilet then you are unlikely to give your client your full attention. Dwelling on a row with one of your family, feeling affected by a difficult journey to work or fretting that you've left the iron on won't help either.

Active listening techniques

Summarizing

The first skill to learn is that of summarizing. This is an extremely effective way of showing that you have been listening and it also has another very useful function: that of introducing a helpful break in the narrative. Sometimes when clients get into full verbal flow you find they are providing you with so much information that it is difficult to process it. As soon as you can find an appropriate moment it is helpful to summarize what they have been saying. You may even need to interrupt them, gently saying something like, 'Can I stop you there? What I've heard you say so far is... (summary).'

A good summary does not repeat what your client has said verbatim but it brings together all of the main points of what he has told you. It is important to be aware of a temptation to edit what he has said by summarizing only the things you have personally found interesting or have judged to be important. It can also be tempting to interpret what he has told you and to introduce new material into your summary. While an assertive client may point out to you that you're putting words into his mouth not everyone has the confidence to do this. A good summary focuses both speaker and listener. It ties up loose ends by bringing together what has been said so far. It can be used at several points in the session or at the end of the session or last week's summary can be used to introduce this week's. Either the listener or the client can summarize.

A shorter variation of the summary is the paraphrase.

Paraphrasing

A good paraphrase involves rephrasing the client's words without any change in their meaning.

Example

Client: I'm all over the place. I just don't know where I am any more.

Helper: You're totally disorientated and feel lost.

Offered tentatively, the paraphrase allows the helper to check if he understands the client. Perhaps more importantly it allows the client to re-hear what he has said; it offers feedback on his emotional state. Of course it also shows the accuracy of the helper's listening skill.

Like the summary, the paraphrase should neither add nor subtract new material.

Making effective use of silences

Novice students of active listening often find silences difficult, just as many of us do in social settings. Remember, however, that in an active listening setting your client may be processing some very difficult emotions and struggling to find the right words. Your client may need space to stop, think and feel. When you are a novice a short silence feels very long. It is unlikely to feel as long to the client as it does to you. You may be tempted to jump in, usually with a question, which to the client can feel like an intrusion on their thoughts. You may need to learn to be comfortable with silence. And you may need to learn to trust yourself with this space in the helping relationship. If eventually you need to break the silence then it is probably better to do this with some kind of reflection than it is to ask a question.

Stella (a fictitious case study): extract from her first session

Skills demonstrated:

- arranging the room
- summarizing and paraphrasing
- making use of silence.

Stella had been referred to me by her GP. From the referral letter I gathered that her son Daniel had gone on a Mediterranean holiday with his mates and while there had died in mysterious circumstances. I was meeting Stella in the GP consulting rooms at her practice and had time to arrange the room before she arrived. I arranged two identical chairs well away from the doctor's desk at an angle to each other and at a comfortable distance apart. I put a 'please do not disturb notice' on the door and went to fetch Stella from reception.

Stella greeted me with a smile and was still smiling as she sat down in front of me. Quietly and gently I asked her if she could tell me what had brought her to the surgery. For a moment she hesitated. The smile vanished and her face began to crumple.

'My son... He... died in Ibiza,' she replied and began to cry quietly. I kept my eyes focused on her but remained silent for a while sensing that she needed a little space to compose herself. After a few minutes she apologized for getting upset.

'There's nothing to apologize for,' I replied.

I invited her, in her own time, to tell me the story surrounding her son's death. Stella had received a garbled message from one of Daniel's mates saying that something terrible had happened to him. Stella and her husband had got to Ibiza as quickly as they could and had found Daniel in a hospital mortuary. Everything after that, up to and including the funeral, had been a blur. Stella's husband Des was drinking heavily and was refusing to talk. Daniel's sister Emma had taken to shutting herself in her bedroom and spending hours on Facebook. Stella was feeling very alone.

I was aware that I was getting a lot of information and was beginning to feel overloaded with it. I said to Stella, 'Can we just take a moment for me to check that I heard you right?' Stella agreed. I began tentatively, 'As soon as you found Daniel you felt numb and everything seemed unreal. You got him back to England but his funeral is a blur. Now your husband drinks every evening and will not talk about what has happened. Your daughter shuts herself in her bedroom. You feel isolated and alone. Is that right?' Stella nodded and began to cry again.

'It's just so surreal. I can't take it in. Some evenings I expect him to walk through the door as if it's all been a huge joke.'

'It just feels unreal and unbelievable,' I said. Stella nodded.

Reflecting

The purpose of reflecting is to bring your client into awareness of his emotions. We do this by holding up to him a metaphorical mirror in which he can see himself. We will only do this effectively if we have been listening to him with all our senses and with an awareness of what we are experiencing at an emotional level. The form of the mirror is our verbal response. For example:

Client: 'I still expect her to walk through the door as if she's never been away. I just feel so totally bereft.'

Some possible reflections are:

'It sounds as though you haven't really accepted her death.'

'It feels a very lonely place that you're in.'

'I notice you fight back tears when you say that.'

'You look so sad and lost right now.'

Sometimes the most effective reflection is simply to repeat a single emotive word back to the client: 'Bereft'. Say the single word and then give your client the silent space to respond.

Sometimes your reflection will miss the mark. At other times your reflection will be inaccurate but the client will not feel safe enough to respond emotionally. Always be tentative and be prepared to back off until the client is ready.

Stella: extract from her second session

Skill demonstrated:

- reflection.

Stella's welcoming smile faded as she sat down in front of me. She frantically fanned her face with her hand and exhaled as if blowing out a candle. Her eyes filled with tears.

'I promised myself I wouldn't cry this week. That didn't last long,' she said, and laughed. I smiled back gently, managing to make eye contact. She wiped her eyes. 'I've been thinking about what we talked about last week,' said Stella. 'I tackled David, my husband, about not talking. He said that he is trying to be strong for me because there can't be two people in pieces.' She paused thoughtfully for a long time. Twice she drew breath as if to speak but each time went silent again.

'I'm wondering what it is you're struggling to say,' I said.

'For weeks now this has all been about me. I refuse to feel guilty about that 'cos I'm Daniel's mother. But there are two other people in the house who are hurting as well.' Stella began to chew her bottom lip and I sensed that she was fighting back angry tears.

'I can see your sadness but suddenly you look angry as well.' Stella's right hand made a fist and she banged on the arm of the chair. She tried to speak but the words wouldn't come. 'I wonder if you are beginning to be angry with Daniel,' I offered tentatively.

'I can't be angry with him. He didn't mean any of this to happen. But some nights I look at his photo and tell him how stupid he's been and how much trouble he's caused.'

Clarifying

Effective use of clarifying questions and statements is an important skill in active listening. Sometimes the need for clarification is ours because we are seeking to be clear about what the client is telling us. At other times this intervention helps our client to be clear about what they are trying to express. Sometimes clarifying questions may be appropriate:

'How old was your mother when she died?'

Although this is a closed-ended question, that is, a question that limits the respondent in his choice of answer, it is still appropriate to seek this kind of clarification. Usually, however, open-ended questions are better:

'What was it like to get such terrible news when you were out of the country?'

This is an open-ended question. It gives the client an invitation to explore thoughts and feelings.

An alternative to the clarifying question is the clarifying statement:

'I find myself wondering what it must have been like to receive this news.'

Clarifying statements are generally gentler than questions.

Further questioning skills

We began by comparing active listening with social listening. With social listening, questions play an important part in the conversation. Whether it is holidays, wedding plans, relationships or just juicy gossip, we love finding out and generally people enjoy telling us.

In the helping relationship it is important that the client is able to tell us his story. However, we want to put him in control as much as possible by avoiding asking surplus, intrusive questions. We also need to be clear who will benefit from our questions. Do we really need to know or are we just being 'nosy'? Too many facts can get in the way of the client having the space to address his needs.

As with clarifying questions mentioned above, other forms of questions can also be open-ended or closed-ended.

Closed-ended questions

These require a short and very limited answer: for instance, yes or no, a number, the name of a place or a date. In our work with clients we may sometimes need such specific information. However, open-ended questions give the client a much greater chance to explore what is going on for them.

Open-ended questions

Open-ended questions typically begin with words such as 'Can', 'How' and 'What'. 'When', 'Where' and 'Who' will have more limited answers (time, place and person, respectively):

> 'Can you tell be about…?'

> 'How did you manage?'

> 'What happened when he came out of hospital?'

Remember that open questioning statements can be gentler:

> 'I'm wondering how you coped.'

The dreaded 'Why?' question

A rule of thumb is to try to avoid 'Why?' questions. This is because the answer will invariably be a justification. This can feel threatening to the client and leave him on the defensive:

> 'Why did you stay in bed when everybody else in your family went to the funeral?'

If you have to know why then try to phrase it as a questioning statement:

> 'I'm wondering why you didn't go to the funeral.'

For the client this probably wouldn't be much better. More tentative would be:

> 'I wonder if you would find it helpful to explore your difficulties in going to the funeral.'

Stella: extract from her sixth session

Skills demonstrated:

- clarifying
- questioning.

Since we last met, Stella had received Daniel's post-mortem report. She said that in some ways it had helped to read it but in other ways it hadn't.

'What is it about the report that has helped?' I asked.

'Well having an answer about why and how Daniel died feels better, even though it doesn't tell me anything definite,' Stella explained.

'Do you feel able to tell me some of what it says?' I asked.

'They found a very high level of alcohol in his blood stream. There was a wound on his head and vomit in his lungs. So it could be that he banged his head by falling and drowned in his own vomit or it could be that somebody attacked him.'

'I can see how it helps to know some of why Daniel died. And I'm wondering in what ways it hasn't helped,' I said.

'Well it hasn't helped that I will never know for certain whether or not he was attacked. But the main thing is that having his death down in writing makes it all the more real. Now it's much harder to pretend it hasn't happened.'

'Mmm, I can see that,' I replied. We spent some time exploring Stella's reaction to the harsh reality of the post-mortem findings.

Later in the session I asked, 'So would you say that both you and your husband accept the findings of the post-mortem?'

'I think it helps having an opinion from two different sources,' Stella replied.

'Two sources?' I queried. 'You mean the Spanish authorities and the British?'

'Yes. The Spanish authorities took a blood sample and I have his medical notes from Ibiza. Then there was a full post-mortem when we got him home.'

'How has your husband taken the report?'

'He's angry with Daniel but more angry with himself for persuading me to let him go on holiday. He knew I didn't think Daniel was mature enough.' Stella sobbed.

Challenging

A challenge in the helping relationship involves pointing out discrepancies between aspects of your client's behaviour.

Sometimes it is important to challenge clients. For example, you may feel that the client is not aware of his strength and resilience and because of his low self-esteem he may tend to put himself down repeatedly. In these instances it may be helpful to challenge in order to point out to the client that he is doing better than he thinks.

Client: I'm useless, I'm just not making any effort.

Helper: I don't experience you as useless.

There may be challenging moments in the here and now, for example you may say to a client:

'I know you say you're okay but I notice a tear in your eye.'

There may be other times when the client's words do not match his body language and you may feel it is helpful to point this out to him.

Sometimes the client knows what needs to be faced and what needs to be said but you sense that he is avoiding the issue. If this avoidance continues then there may come a time when you feel that a challenge is appropriate.

As with all interventions any challenge needs to be made tentatively and sensitively. Some clients will be more open to challenge than others. You need to be sure of your relationship and your levels of trust with the client before you challenge.

Remember that the purpose of the challenge is *always* to help the client and that it is *never* about you or your needs.

Stella: extract from her eighth session

Skill demonstrated:

- challenging.

When Stella arrived she tried to smile but kept looking down at the floor and was not making eye contact.

'Are you OK?' I asked. Stella bit her bottom lip and nodded. Her eyes welled up with tears. 'You don't look OK,' I said tentatively.

'I wonder if I ought to stop coming here,' said Stella with a strained look on her face.

'Tell me more Stella,' I said.

'I'm just being a wimp,' replied Stella. 'I'm fed up with myself. I need to be strong and I need to stop wasting your time.'

'I guess sometimes it must seem forever since Daniel died but actually it's seven months and that's no time at all to recover from what you've been through.'

'I need to be strong for my family,' said Stella.

'I wonder if you're seeing coming here and getting upset as not being strong – as being weak. "A wimp" I think you said.' Stella nodded through her tears. 'It takes a lot of strength and courage to face a loss like this. It's not weak to get upset.' There was a long silence. Stella looked pensive. I waited a long time before speaking to give her time to process her thoughts and feelings. Eventually she looked at me and I decided she was inviting me to speak. 'I don't feel that you're wasting my time. I think you're working very hard and I'm full of admiration for your courage and bravery.'

Empathic communication

As we saw earlier, empathy is one of Carl Rogers' core conditions. It is about establishing a mind set in which you put yourself in your client's shoes and begin to feel what it's like to be him. For most people it takes a lot of practice but it does seem to be something that most of us can learn to do. However, all the empathy in the world is not going to help our clients unless we *communicate* it to them. Sometimes this communication is made with facial expression, body language and even the odd tear. Mostly it is communicated in words.

Empathy works at different levels: from a primary level when you first meet your client (and perhaps because you are inexperienced), to a deeper level that comes with practice, experience and with getting to know your client intimately.

Empathy is not an intellectual exercise; it concerns the heart and the gut. It is not about *knowing* what your client feels; it is about *feeling* what your client feels. Always be gentle and tentative with your empathic responses. If your empathy turns out to have been inaccurate then quietly accept your client's reply whatever your heart tells you: it may be that he is not ready to face the emotion that you have accurately contacted in him:

Helper: You're angry with him for dying and leaving you.

Client: How can I be angry at him? He didn't want to die.

Empathic responses come from good active listening but also with your congruence. This means listening to your client and listening to your own thoughts and feelings as he talks. You may find that as he is talking an emotive keyword forms in your head. Here are some examples:

- anger

- frustration

- despair

- confusion

- exhilaration

- hope

- nervousness.

Once you are sure of the keyword then you can communicate your empathy:

'I can sense real frustration with the care your husband received.'

'You seem really confused and unable to make sense of what is happening to you.'

'It feels really exhilarating to have had some recognition at last.'

If you empathy is accurate then you and your client will move emotionally closer together.

Stella: extract from her tenth session

Skill demonstrated:

- empathic communication.

'My family is not speaking to me and I'm not speaking to them. I'm sick of the lot of them. I just feel like getting on a train and leaving them, the house, the job, everything. Running away. Never coming back. Being somebody else.'

Saying this seemed to calm her and she began to smile. She fixed me with a stare that would melt steel. 'And don't you cross me else you'll be next in the firing line,' she added, with a smile that told me that she was at least in part joking. I smiled back to share the joke but I didn't want to lose the feeling behind her initial statement.

'Would it help to tell me what has happened for you to feel like leaving home and never coming back?'

'Where do I start?' asked Stella. 'Emma does nothing at home. She treats the place like a hotel. She takes her meals up to her room. If I'm lucky she puts her dirty pots in the sink but usually I find them mouldy under the bed. Her room's a tip. She expects me to do all her washing but just leaves her dirty clothes on the bedroom floor and then moans when she has nothing nice to wear. Yesterday I tackled her about it. All she could say is, "whatever". I just hit the roof. She told me to "get a life", stormed out of the house and banged the door. I was in pieces. Right then I needed the support of my husband and do you know what he said?' I shook my head. 'He told me not to be so hard on her, to remember that she had lost her brother and that she was depressed. Where do you go with that one? I just lost it. I can't remember exactly what I said but I reckon I said some pretty hurtful things. Now he's not speaking to me.' Stella fell silent. I waited to give her the space to gather her thoughts and feelings.

'I get up. I go to work. I come home. I hoover round. I sort out the dishwasher: all three of them [I assume she was including Daniel] seem to think it stacks and unstacks itself. I cook. I clean. I go to bed. I get up and it all starts again. Well I'm sick of it.'

I felt that it was important to communicate a deep empathy and in my head went through a number of key words to try to match what Stella was experiencing: anger, frustration, irritation, despair... All these were close but what felt to be the best fit was the word 'missed'... By which I mean not noticed and taken for granted and seen as the wife of Des and the mother of Emma, not as a deeply grieving human being. The word 'missed' felt just right but I still offered my empathy tentatively to see if Stella agreed.

'You feel unnoticed, as if nobody can see what you're going through. Because you're always there for them Des and Emma think that you are strong enough for the whole family. They are missing what you are going through, not seeing you for you. That must feel very frustrating but also very lonely.' As I spoke Stella was nodding and the recognition on her face encouraged me to go on. 'You must feel like shouting at the top of your voice, *"what about me?"*'

'Yes,' said Stella, 'that's exactly right.'

Working in the here-and-now: immediacy

Many years ago just after I had trained in bereavement counselling, I was given my first client. Looking back on the experience I am really not sure that I was of very much use to him. Week after week he showed up and he was always on time and eager to start. He would launch into an account of his week, including all the events that had left him stressed and anxious. In other words, everything he explored was 'out there' rather than in the room with me engaged in a dialogue. The account of his week would last an hour, at the end of which he would thank me and leave. In my inexperience and my misunderstanding of what 'client-centred' really meant, I believed that in time he would get something from being there and talking. I had been taught that client-centred counselling was non-directive. I seldom challenged him by bringing him back to the present moment. On the rare occasions when I did intervene with anything more than a nod he would look puzzled, give a cursory answer and continue his story. This meant that his thoughts, feelings and actions seldom or never got explored.

Only by encouraging and challenging our clients to reflect on their thoughts, experiences and behaviours is any change likely to take place.

Clients will, quite understandably, find this challenge difficult. In normal conversation we do not relate to each other in this way, so that counselling interventions that invite the client to stop and reflect could easily feel threatening. For this reason we learn to be sensitive and empathic. We need to be open and willing to share what we too are experiencing in these here-and-now moments of relationship. All of our invitations to immediacy need to be tentative and delivered from a sense of collaboration with our client, rather than from a superior place of believing that we know what is best for him. It is this way of being alongside our client that makes our work 'person centred', rather than practice based on a misguided faith in non-directed listening.

Immediacy: some interventions with Stella

Usually when I collected Stella from reception and walked with her to the counselling room she would make some small talk. Today she was silent. When we got to the room and closed the door I asked, 'I notice you are unusually quiet. What is going on for you?'

'I nearly didn't come today,' replied Stella.

'And now that you are here?' I queried. There was a long silence. Eventually Stella smiled with her mouth but not her eyes.

'Just ignore me. I'll be alright in a minute.'

'I'm wondering what you're angry about.'

'Who said I'm angry?' she asked.

'Well are you?' I enquired.

'Irritated, frustrated, fed up, pissed off. Life just feels so pointless.' Stella began to weep. I passed her a tissue but did not speak.

'Thanks,' she said, but this time smiling with her eyes.

Working at this level of immediacy requires respect for the client and mutual trust. There is also an intimacy involved that can be emotionally draining for both client and counsellor.

Practising the theory: working in triads

The usual way that counsellors try out what they have learnt in training is to practise in groups of three called triads. Three chairs are arranged in a triangle so that the observer is not in the line of sight of the other two but can observe both of them. One trainee takes the role of counsellor, one the client and one the observer. The observer watches the session and takes responsibility for keeping the trainee counsellor to time. At the end of the counselling session, which is usually timed to last for 10 and 20 minutes, the counsellor reflects to the other two how they felt the session went: what they felt went well and what they would do differently in hindsight. Then the client gives feedback on the experience, after which the observer, who has had the luxury of being able to take notes, gives more detailed feedback to the counsellor. When this is completed all three move round. The observer becomes the counsellor, the counsellor becomes the client and the client becomes the observer. The reason for doing it this way is to avoid a situation where a client who may have stirred up some personal emotions does not have to immediately sit in the counsellor's chair, where he could be distracted and ineffective.

Giving feedback to your peers

'I can only know that much of myself which I have had the courage to confide in you.'

John Powell (1999, p.14) *Why Am I Afraid to Tell You Who I Am?*

If done sensitively, giving and receiving feedback can be an effective way of learning about ourselves. It teaches us to reflect on the effect that our behaviour has on those around us and to glimpse how others see us. This allows us to choose what we change about our way of being and what we reinforce. It can help us to become more effective communicators.

Feedback can be uncomfortable. None of us likes to hear negative things about our actions, especially if they are our best attempt. Some people even find it uncomfortable and embarrassing to hear nice things about themselves. For this reason we often avoid giving our friends and colleagues feedback of any kind, which is a shame.

Giving helpful feedback is an important skill that we can learn, even *must* learn in order to be effective helping practitioners. There are some important guidelines to be acquired. Before you consider giving feedback, check with yourself that you are offering it helpfully, rather than to gain some advantage, settle a score or some other less than honest reason. This kind of feedback will say more about you than your interlocutor. Similarly, always own the feedback and never claim to be speaking for others, as in, 'Several of us in the group find you a bit overbearing at times.' Once you have checked your conscience, it helps to ask directly, 'May I give you some feedback?' It also helps if you can invite the person to say how the feedback has been received.

Offer your feedback in a supportive frame of mind. It helps considerably to start with something positive: 'I liked the way that you were able to welcome your client and the way that you enabled him to feel relaxed.'

Examples should be specific and framed in plain language: 'Five minutes into the session I felt you gave the client an abrupt response,' is more specific than, 'There was a general air of anger and sarcasm in your approach to that session.'

Only offer feedback on behaviour that can be changed. For example, if you are giving feedback to somebody with a stutter or a speech impediment it would be unhelpful (and cruel) to refer to it.

If you think that the person would have been better to take a different action, try to provide an alternative: 'Towards the end of that practice session you asked the client if they could try a weekend without binge drinking. I wonder if it would have been better to ask how they intended to address their alcohol use.'

There is a limit to how much feedback we can take on board at any given time. Try not to overload your peers. The most effective feedback is immediately after the event you are talking about.

Receiving feedback

Receiving feedback to your best advantage is an acquired skill, too. It is helpful to hear what is said rather than what you think has been said. As an example from the past I recall saying to my daughter Sarah, 'This bedroom's a mess.' Sarah began to get angry. I calmly said, 'Just wait a moment and hear what I actually said.'

'You said my bedroom is a mess.'

'And what did you hear?' I asked.

'I heard, "You're a terrible person, Sarah,"' and she smiled. Peace was restored.

Just because one person feeds back one piece of information does not mean it is either true or has to be acted on. The best piece of advice I ever received on planning and revising a course, came from an experienced trainer who cautioned against responding to every student evaluation with kneejerk revisions. Only make changes if the same feedback crops up several times. A wise counsellor once told me this ancient proverb:

> If one person tells you you're an elephant, that doesn't make you an elephant.
>
> If lots of people tell you, then it's time to pick up nuts with your trunk.

Sometimes we need to be brave enough to ask several people we trust for feedback about an aspect of our behaviour.

Notes for trainers

Working with triads

My colleagues and I, who have taught many bereavement counsellors at Saint Catherine's Hospice in Scarborough in collaboration with York St John University, are aware that many trainers advise using role play in practice triads. However, experience has taught us that the situation is made far more meaningful if students are asked to present their peers with real-life situations. This poses a responsibility on students to present issues that are not too demanding for their novice counsellors. It also demands of trainers a duty of care to make sure that no heavy emotional loads are placed on trainees. We interview each course candidate at recruitment to make sure that any past losses have been adequately resolved and that no student is actively grieving a recent loss. We are aware of the possibility that some people will seek a place on such courses as a way of meeting their own emotional needs and our interview procedures are designed to guard against this.

We believe that the best practice requires two tutors working side by side during skills teaching sessions. We are able to demonstrate the use of active listening techniques before students split off into triads. We have a responsibility to sit in on triads to ensure student's affective wellbeing and safety, to make sure that trainees use practice time wisely and to be sure that everyone is participating appropriately, with no unhelpful interpersonal dynamics becoming established. When with the groups we will model giving feedback and at times model the use of counselling skills. In some situations we would reserve the right to intervene: to highlight particular strengths and to prevent mistakes being reinforced. Students are also aware that tutors meet between sessions to discuss students' progress and flag up any concerns.

At the beginning of the course we establish the rule that what is talked about in each triad stays within that triad and is not discussed in the larger group. We have experimented with mixing students into different triad combinations over the duration of the course but have found that students generally prefer to stay in the same group of three throughout. That way trust builds and students become confident with one another.

We produce a checklist of active listening techniques for our students. The observer ticks when the technique is observed and writes a comment on how effectively it was used. This is signed by the observer and given to the student who was observed to leave a written record of triad practice observations. A tutor who is present also completes the written feedback checklist.

We provide each triad with a digital recording device. We recommend those small battery-operated devices that can download the recorded sound file onto a computer via a Universal Serial Bus (USB) socket. This allows us to listen to all of the practice sessions and to email each student their recorded session to listen to at his leisure and the recorder is left running during the observer's and tutor's verbal feedback so that each student can build a complete practical record of his skills development.

Each round of listening and giving feedback is given 30 minutes, so a triad works for 90 minutes, usually with a break after the first or second round.

SKILLS AND QUALITIES CHECKLIST

You may wish to use this chart as a checklist when acting as observer in your triad.

SKILLS AND QUALITIES OBSERVED	Yes	Practice needed
1. body language: eye contact good		
2. body language: relaxed and attentive		
3. body language: welcoming posture		
4. uses encouraging nods		
5. appears to be listening closely		
6. appears to be interested in what the client said		
7. appears to be searching for understanding		
8. uses prompts gently and appropriately		
9. uses paraphrasing appropriately		
10. reflects back appropriately		
11. clarifies appropriately		
12. summarises appropriately		
13. uses questions appropriately		
16. appears to accept client and their world		
17. appears congruent and alongside client		
18. appears empathic		

I completed this chart for: date:

Name of observer:

Figure 4.1 Skills and qualities checklist (as used for counselling skills training at Saint Catherine's Hospice)

Chapter 5

Working with People Experiencing a Loss

In Chapter 1 we looked at the nature of grief and in Chapter 2 considered theories of grief that were developed over the course of the 20th century. We concluded Chapter 2 with an exploration of the work of John Bowlby and Colin Murray Parkes and in Chapter 3 considered the research that developed attachment theory and related it to loss. In Chapter 4 we considered the theory and practice behind the development of humanistic counselling: the style of counselling usually used by counsellors and other helping practitioners who work with loss. In this chapter we will explore the models of loss and grief that are currently used by practitioners working in this field. It is true that most of these models are generally employed in helping people experiencing the effects of bereavement. However, many of these models have a place in working with other forms of loss.

Working in a humanistic or person-centred way involves a joint endeavour between the client and the helping practitioner. It is a collaborative process. Both anecdotal evidence, gleaned from talking to practitioners, and empirical evidence, collected from careful research point to the fact that certain preconditions are necessary for person-centred counselling skills to be effective. We will be discussing assessment procedures in detail in Chapter 8 so what follows is a brief introduction to that. Think of the person experiencing a loss and asking to be helped in terms of these three questions: is she ready to change? Is she willing to do what it takes to make this possible? Is she able to think of herself in psychological terms?

Ready. Many years ago, when I was very new to this work, a young woman was referred to me. Two days before I met her she had suffered a traumatic and devastating bereavement of someone very close to her. I immediately offered her the space to tell the story of what had happened and sat quietly with her when she cried. Together we created a dialogue in which she could try to find meaning in something that seemed to make no sense at all. In the first week I saw her twice. Just before the fifth appointment I saw her approaching the front door of the building where I worked and went to the door to let her in. She did not ring the doorbell but an envelope dropped through the letterbox. A carefully handwritten letter thanked me for what I had tried to do, but explained that she needed to stop the work because it was doing a very good job of convincing her that she would never see her loved one again and she was not ready for this. The people we work with need to be truly ready to face the outcomes of bereavement support. If it is a recent bereavement and they are not ready to face the reality of the death, then I suggest that a counselling model of support should be delayed.

Willing. When a person is supported professionally following bereavement, it is common for her to experience a rollercoaster of emotions, many of them painful and difficult. I often say to clients, by way of preparation for what is to come, that bereavement support may make them feel worse before it makes them feel better and that they need to be prepared for this possibility. In any eventuality, counselling can be hard and tiring work, certainly for the client and often for the counsellor. If the work is to be effective it must be entered into willingly.

Able. Counselling psychologists and researchers have used the concept of 'psychological mindedness' (see for example, Cooper 2008, p.74) in order to assess the likelihood that counselling will be effective. What this means in a nutshell is that the client can step outside of herself in order to observe what she does in any given situation and reflect on her motivations for doing it. If you could give a detailed answer to the question, 'How would your best friend describe you in terms of your strengths and your areas for growth?' then this would indicate that you have a high degree of psychological mindedness. Psychologically minded people are aware of their needs and desires and of how these influence their actions. They also have good understanding of cause and effect: 'If I do x, then it is likely that y will happen.'

In the ten years since experiencing a devastating loss, Jayne had spent nine of those years living life on the edge. She had become a user of street drugs and had abused alcohol. She had lived through many abusive relationships and in her view had damaged the relationship with her family. Then at the end of the ninth year she made the decision to turn her life around. She went 'cold turkey', quitting all street drug use without professional help, although she continued to use alcohol. Not unexpectedly, now freed from the anaesthetizing effect of substance abuse, she began to experience the pain of grief fully for the first time. After trying to go it alone for 12 months, she finally presented for counselling. When she described the circumstances of her loss and the guilt that she had carried for so many years, I anticipated that we would be working together for many months and I shared this with her. To our mutual surprise and delight, the counselling was completed in six sessions. Between the fifth and sixth session Jayne went away on her own to perform an ending ritual of her own choosing. When she returned for a final session she was at peace with the world, at peace with her loss and had begun to build bridges to her family. Jayne heaped praise and gratitude on me. She said that what she had gained from counselling was 'better than winning the National Lottery'. I pointed out that it was her, not me, who that had done the hard work, but that if she wanted to thank me in a way that may help others, was she willing to let me tell her story in a book?

Jayne was *ready* to change: quitting all street drugs had shown that. She was *willing* to face some challenging interventions from me as her counsellor, as I reinforced the fact that her loved-one was dead and never coming back. She was *able* to take responsibility for her actions and to make sense of her destructive behaviour in relation both to her denial of reality and her guilt surrounding the circumstances of the death.

Models of grief

Once we have met our client and have made the mutual decision that we can work together, it falls on the practitioner to make appropriate use of the models of grief that have been developed by practitioners and researchers. The decision at the end of a formalized assessment, to proceed with counselling, is almost always mutual. There may, however, be very rare occasions when the practitioner deems a person-centred approach to be inappropriate and, in all likelihood, to be of limited success. In these circumstances the practitioner may not offer counselling even though the client is requesting it. This is discussed in Chapter 8. None of the models described below are mutually exclusive. Some share features with one another. Counsellors tend to be a pretty pragmatic lot, upholding no deference to academia, but simply picking and mixing what works. Of course, what works with one client may not work with the next. For this reason it is helpful to have a good working knowledge of each model of grief and to question where currently used models of grief originate from and how their usefulness is assessed (see the journals and organizations listed in the Further Reading section at the end of the book). If we think of the roles of helping practitioner as being to create a safe environment, foster a trusting relationship and listen actively, we must add an expertise in this area of work. With experience the practitioner comes to anticipate which grief models are likely to be appropriate for each client. Remember that these models do not exist for us to take our clients where they do not wish to go. Think of them as possible paths on a map of the client's journey through grief. There is no one pathway through grief. At a talk to the Bereavement Research Forum in 2009, Neimeyer described 'multiple, qualitatively distinct pathways through grief that call for greater understanding both of complication and of resilience' (Neimeyer 2009a).

The six perspectives for looking at grief appear in no particular order and, as we will see, many of them overlap to some extent.

1 Assumptive world theory

In Chapter 3 we saw how much of Colin Murray Parkes' work is based on attachment theory. However, his psychiatric work with amputees led him to develop a second theory of grief. Parkes noticed that amputees go through a process that is akin to grief and that involves accommodating the new world the amputee finds herself in. This is more than learning to manage practically; it involves adjusting to a new body image and self-image. Parkes was puzzled by the grief reaction since it could not be attributed to attachment theory. After all, the amputee does not love the lost limb in the same way that a bereaved person loved the lost loved-one. Parkes came to realize that the amputee's grief is for a personal world that has been radically changed by the surgery and that a new assumptive world has to be created in order for the grief to be resolved. You can find a more detailed account of this in Parkes' 2006 book, *Love and Loss* (p.30). Each of us lives in our own unique assumptive world that can be challenged by sudden and disastrous life events. Bereavement not only shapes our attachments, it also turns our assumptive world upside down. Grief resolution from an assumptive world perspective depends on the grieving person's ability and willingness to accommodate new assumptions. Indirectly this may still be affected by attachment style since secure adults can find it easier to embrace change.

In her book *Shattered Assumptions: Towards a New Psychology of Trauma* (1992) Ronnie Janoff-Bulman has developed assumptive world theory to apply it to any traumatic loss. She sees our healthy world as being made up of three basic assumptions: the world is benevolent, the world is meaningful and the self is worthy. After a traumatic event we ask ourselves why it happened. Why did it happen to us? What bad thing have we done to make it happen? We may get angry because of our assumption that bad things should only happen to bad people. If our world suddenly ceases to be benevolent towards us, if it suddenly stops making sense, we are thrown into uncertainty and confusion. We expected our world to be always benevolent and meaningful and expected to feel worthy of living in such a world. A catastrophe that suddenly surrounds us takes away all these assumed certainties of meaning past and present. We only get our equilibrium back once we make sense of our new world and adapt to the changes and challenges it presents.

My own belief is that the possession of a personal assumptive world can be seen as a successful evolutionary adaptation. It makes our world familiar enough to survive in. If it changes suddenly we are threatened until we relearn our environment and assimilate the changed circumstances. I would go as far as to say that all mammals possess, to a greater or lesser extent, an assumptive world that they acquire from their parents and that equips them to survive. Familiarity may be what keeps animals to their own territory, thus reducing conflict and competition with neighbouring groups of the same species.

Implications for our practice

If we listen carefully to our clients we will hear them describe the world they once knew and the world they find themselves in. In doing so, they will effectively be describing their shattered assumptions without having the language to describe their confusion in these terms. From an empathic place we can paraphrase what they tell us with this concept in mind. We can encourage them to describe the two worlds: pre-loss and post-loss. In comparing the two and recognizing the differences, they will be more able to identify what they need to do to move forward.

Case study: Mary

After the sudden and unexpected death of her husband, Mary resolved the worst of her grief much more quickly than she had expected. In one of our last sessions we reflected on her successful journey and tried to pinpoint the reasons for this. Many aspects of her assumptive world had remained unchanged: she still had children to look after; she still had her parents and her in-laws living close by; she had been, and remained, the primary breadwinner in the family; her work gave her a sense of purpose and a source of self-esteem; and she had a large circle of friends independently from her husband. Although she missed him and mourned for him, she was quickly able to restore many aspects of her life and felt able to end counselling support.

Case study: Morag

Morag and Harry had retired to the coast five years before Harry died. Morag said that Harry had been everything to her. Because as a couple they were so self-sufficient they had never made friends in the area and had never joined any of the many clubs and societies available locally for retired people. Their two children had jobs 200 miles away and Morag had never learned to drive. There was little public transport from her isolated village.

If you contrast the life of these two widows (Morag and Harry are fictitious characters based on real examples) you will see that Morag's assumptive world was changed beyond all recognition, save for her house and possessions, although even her home now lacked its most important feature, Harry. Morag did her best to hold on to her old assumptive world. An urn of Harry's ashes was buried in her garden. Framed photographs of Harry dominated her living room. Morag became reclusive, clinging to the safety of her home as best she could.

2 Meaning-making theories

We saw in the last section how bereaved people try to make sense and find new meaning in their post-loss assumptive world. Many researchers and other commentators on the grief process have noted the human need to find meaning and make sense of loss, including loss through bereavement. Thomas Attig, a philosopher, effectively links assumptive world theories with meaning making. He writes of grief as the relearning of a complex world through the interplay between meaning making and meaning finding. The relearning involves how to be and act in the world without the person we loved. We come to terms with our shattered assumptions and reconfigure our interactions with others:

> As we grieve we seek and find ways of making a transition to lasting love. We do not want to stop loving those who die. We rightly resist those who say we must... In our lasting love we give them symbolic immortality. (Attig 2001, p.46)

Thomas Attig goes on to say that following the death of a loved-one, not all is lost if we can allow ourselves to develop and foster a *symbolic*, lasting and loving relationship. This means facing the reality of the physical absence first. My own professional experience supports this view. Many clients seem afraid to abandon a desperate kind of clinging to a pretence that their deceased partner is still alive. Their partner's dressing gown still hangs behind the bedroom door and the wardrobe remains full of their clothes. It is common for a client to feel that if she abandons this behaviour she will lose her husband forever. In fact, for most clients, once the painful reality is finally accepted, a new enduring love is free to grow. We will explore this more fully when we look at 'continuing bonds' theory.

Other researchers have explored the concept of meaning making in coming to terms with loss. Janice Nadeau (2001) explored this when working with bereaved families. Sometimes the family members talked about what the death did *not* mean. Sometimes they agreed that no sense could be made of the loss and that the death was unfair or unjust. Family members talked about an afterlife, and elicited religious, spiritual or philosophical meaning. A family will usually try to make sense of how the person died and of the attitude to death that had been expressed by the deceased. They are likely to want to explore how the family has been changed by the death. Finally, they will want to explore the deeper and wider questions: what lessons they feel they have learnt from the experience and what truths have been realized. Anybody who has worked with bereaved people will recognize these themes. In fact, I and many other experienced bereavement counsellors would argue that an important part of our work, be it with families, couples or individuals, is to listen for these themes and offer support as they are worked through. Janice Nadeau concluded that paying attention to the family's meaning making helps practitioners to track individuals' progress and focus the work.

On more than one occasion I have worked with individuals whose deceased loved-one's death was reported in the media, either as a news item or as an obituary. The fact that a life and death is acknowledged nationally is invariably a comfort.

In a study of caregivers bereaved after a long illness, Christopher Davis (2001) identified two processes of meaning making: making sense of the loss and finding benefits. He suggested that where people could not make sense of the loss, finding a benefit may compensate to some extent. For example, it is hard to make sense of the death of a young person in any circumstances. If a child's illness involves incapacity or chronic pain, some parents may say that at the least their daughter is no longer suffering. On the other hand, if the bereavement is the result of the sudden death of an apparently healthy child, what sense can possibly be made of that? However, given time some parents will report that the tragic loss has brought them closer together as a couple, has made them less likely to take life for granted and has made them more caring and empathic to others. Although this may be inadequate compensation for the loss of a child, such changes can all the same be seen as benefits found as a result of the loss. I have noticed in my work with bereaved parents that where they can find no meaning in the death, they can sometimes find meaning in the life of the child, as the following story demonstrates.

Case study: Holly

Holly was a remarkable woman whose firstborn child Amy died before she reached her fourth birthday, having spent many months of her short life in hospital. Although Holly could make no sense of why her child had to die, she found meaning in Amy's life, as a 'little ray of sunshine' with a cheerful nature that lit up the lives of the medical staff and the other children on the hospital ward.

Parents who can find no meaning in either the life or death of their child will sometimes find meaning in their own lives, as fundraisers for charities or as campaigners for changes in a law so as to prevent other children dying in the same way. It would be of no surprise to me if parents who lost a child in a shooting incident became vigorous campaigners to change laws relating to gun ownership.

One of the leading research practitioners in the field of meaning-making research is Professor Robert Neimeyer. At the 2009 Oxford conference (Neimeyer 2009a) he referred to 'the storied nature of human life'. He believes that our life is accompanied by a continuing self-narrative, by which we organize our understanding of (and reactions to) day-by-day events. When we experience significant loss or trauma it has the effect of disrupting our self-narrative process so that it may become totally disorganized. In some circumstances a grieving person may even dissociate from their self-narrative. At other times an unhelpful self-narrative about the loss may dominate, leading to rumination and depression (Neimeyer 2009a).

Together with his colleagues, Robert Neimeyer has attempted to quantify the importance of meaning making. In a study of 157 bereaved parents, Nancy Keesee, Joseph Currier and Robert Neimeyer (2008) found that by far the most important factor in grief resolution (including cause of death and time since the loss), was the ability to make sense of the loss, although 45 per cent of the cohort struggled with making sense of the loss of their child. The most common sense-making theme involved spiritual/religious interpretation. Parents who could make little to no sense of their child's death were more likely to feel more intense grief. Frequent benefits of making or finding meaning involved altruism to others, a greater appreciation of life and personal growth.

In a paper published in the journal *Death Studies* (2000), Christopher Davis and colleagues questioned the assumptions behind typical decisions made by practitioners working with grief, in particular that 1. clients will inevitably search for meaning, 2. that they will usually manage to find a meaning that ameliorates grief and 3. that finding meaning is essential if resolution is to be found. Davis and colleagues' sample was 124 parents bereaved of a child and 93 adults mourning a spouse or child in a road traffic crash. What they found was that many people do not search for meaning, yet appear to adjust relatively well. Less than half reported finding any meaning in their loss even after a year or more. It did appear, however, that those seeking and able to find meaning are better adjusted than those who search and find none. However, even those who find meaning will continue to search as keenly as those still trying unsuccessfully to make sense of the loss. Of course it may be that those who never began searching for meaning had either concluded that such an attempt would be pointless, or it could be that some of this group have quietly and privately made sense of the loss – perhaps from a religious or spiritual perspective.

Implications for our practice: helping our clients to make sense and find meaning

When I read the published research and view it alongside my own observations, my experience suggests that many clients can be helped to find meaning in the death of the deceased. If this is not possible the rumination that follows the hopelessness of the quest can lead to complications. It is at this point that they may, like Holly in the story above, find meaning in the life of the deceased.

Another possibility may be that the bereaved person explores new meaning in her own life. As in benefit finding, this is likely to be a long and slow journey. Whatever the outcome and the process, an important part of the helping process is in the space to explore the territory if the client so desires. It is often from this point that bereaved people become fundraisers for hospitals and hospices, or campaigners for other charities. However, and this is important, there may come a point when your client needs gentle support and encouragement to abandon the search for meaning. I have had a client express her appreciation of having been 'given permission' to stop the fruitless search for why her husband had to die at a young age, leaving a young family behind. My own personal experience of a devastating bereavement involved six years of tormented questioning. I found peace when one day I stopped asking, 'Why?' and answered, 'Why not? These deaths happen for no reason.'

3 Grief and growth

If there is one model of grief that captures my students' imagination more than any other, it is what has become known to many as the 'fried egg model', but that the author of that model, Lois Tonkin (2007), refers to as the Circles Model of grief. I think that this model appeals to us because intuitively we understand at a personal level our potential for growth as a result of adversity and we can empathize that this is also true for our clients.

This way of thinking about grief was described to Lois Tonkin by a mother bereaved of her child in New Zealand where Lois lives and practises. This mother felt totally consumed by her grief, morning noon and night for weeks and months. She thought that in time her grief would diminish; people told her it would. In fact what happened is that her grief remained fairly well the same. However, and this is the part of the story when my students' eyes light up in delight and recognition, the woman found that her life grew around her grief, so that in effect she became a bigger person as the result of her loss.

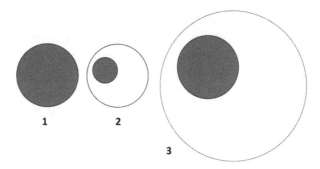

Figure 5.1 Lois Tonkin's (2007) Circles Model of grief

Figure 5.1 shows the Circles Model in graphic form. Circle 1 represents the mother completely filled with grief, which she thought would diminish, as in circle 2. What actually happened is that her grief remained the same, but the mother's life grew larger around her grief, making it a proportion of the whole self, as in circle 3.

Lois Tonkin points out that, at times, especially around anniversaries, the circle representing one's life may shrink again temporarily, but that, as time passes, the anniversaries get easier and the circle gets larger again more quickly. Thomas Attig, whose work is associated both with assumptive world theory and with meaning making, has also noted the growth potential of painful bereavement: 'We had no choice about what happened, but we can, and often do, grow positively through experience. We find new strength of character. We grow in self-understanding and self-esteem. We become more sensitive and responsive to others' (Attig 2001, p.43).

Lois Tonkin has noted that the helpfulness of the Circles Model applies to other losses and life-disrupting events that do not involve bereavement. Another important point she suggests is that people not only grow around their grief but that 'the loss becomes part of who they are. It stays there, as well as new engagement with the world happening around it' (2013, personal communication). I wholeheartedly embrace this idea, not only in recognition of my own research and teaching, but also from my personal experience of losing a child. What Lois Tonkin emphasizes also accords with Robert Neimeyer's idea of all life experiences being assimilated and accommodated as part of our life narrative.

Case study: Rita's story

Every other case study I have used in this book involves pseudonyms or composite fictional accounts based on true events. Rita, however, has asked that her real name and the name of her son be used as a memorial to him. I first met Rita in a professional capacity following the tragic death of her son, Gary, one of four who died in a road traffic crash in 2001. It takes little to imagine Rita's numb and distraught state in the weeks and months following Gary's death. The next time we met I was a tutor on a counselling skills course that Rita had signed up to in preparation for eventually training as a psychotherapist. Rita was still very sad but she was able to smile and I felt that a large part of her study was to find meaning in her own life and to make some positive meaning from Gary's apparently pointless death. Now Rita is a qualified and experienced psychotherapist and has become a colleague who volunteers as a Bereavement Supporter in the service where I work. Anybody who knows Rita will still recognize her enduring grief, but around it has grown a large circle: a warm approachability, a deep empathy and a compassion for supporting others tragically bereaved of loved ones.

4 Finding a balance

There are several ways of coping successfully with grief that I have grouped together under this heading. I will begin by describing Margaret Stroebe and Henk Schut's Dual Process Model of Grief, followed by Terry L. Martin and Kenneth J. Doka's model of Instrumental and Intuitive grief, before concluding this section with Linda Machin's Range of Responses to Loss (RRL) model.

The Dual Process Model of Grief

We saw in Chapter 2 how at the beginning of the 20th century psychoanalysts such as Karl Abraham and Sigmund Freud thought of grief as an introject that acted as a block to healthy living.

They suggested that in order to live healthily again it was essential to 'let go' of the deceased. Other theorists and practitioners picked up on this idea. Erich Lindemann, whose work we met in Chapter 2, was still basing his practice with traumatically bereaved patients on ideas born of Freudian psychoanalysis. Although as we saw in Chapters 2 and 3, John Bowlby largely rejected classical psychoanalytic ideas by the 1960s, the idea that it was necessary to confront one's loss in order to recover continued to be prominent in mainstream academic thought. Grief came to be seen as a task to be worked through and J. William Worden, in his classic book *Grief Counselling and Grief Therapy* (2009), outlined four tasks of grieving: by implication, necessary work to be undertaken before grief could be resolved. Failure to do so was seen as maladaptive behaviour. It follows from this argument that bereavement counselling was for a long time thought to be about helping bereaved people to do their 'grief work' (Stroebe 2002, p.169). In a workshop at St Christopher's Hospice in London in 2011, Professor Margaret Stroebe defined grief work as: 'The process of emotionally confronting the reality of the loss, of going over events that occurred before and at the time of death, and of focusing on memories and working toward detachment from the deceased.'

Margaret Stroebe has been critical of the concept of grief work. She has said that, apart from the 'lack of conceptual clarity' engendered by the term and the lack of rigorous scientific evidence that grief work is effective, it overlooks the evidence that that are other ways of successfully managing grief and the possible 'benefits of denial'. She points, for example, to the people of Bali. In a book entitled *Managing turbulent hearts: a Balinese formula for living* cited by Stroebe (2011), Unni Wikan (1990) described how the Balinese exhibit very minimal grief for only a short amount of time. The assumption that grief work is essential has with this example alone been shown to be flawed. Camille Wortman and Roxane Silver have also demonstrated from their research that grief work is, of necessity, neither essential nor universally beneficial (Wortman and Silver 1989).

If models of grief based on grief work alone prove to be inadequate, where, asked Margaret Stroebe, do we look for a model that takes into account both the need for grief work and the need to take time out from the pain of grief? Together with her colleague Professor Henk Shut, Margaret Stroebe developed the Dual Process Model of Grief (see Figure 5.2). Although the model was brilliant in its originality, like all advances in psychology it owes something to the legacy of earlier research – in this case to the work of Richard Lazarus and Susan Folkman (Folkman and Lazarus 1980; Lazarus and Folkman 1984; Lazarus and Folkman 1987) who spent many years investigating strategies for coping with stress. In addition to citing Lazarus and Folkman, Stroebe and Schut (1999) have cited Mardi Horowitz (1986) who described how stressors from traumatic events will either intrude into our life or will be avoided.

Figure 5.2 The Dual Process Model of Grief
Source: Stroebe and Schut (1999, p.213). Reproduced with permission from the authors.

The Dual Process Model (often shortened to DPM) has proved enduringly effective and is frequently referred to by practitioners. The larger, outside oval represents the bereaved person's everyday life. The two smaller ovals represent two possible grieving styles: 'loss-oriented' and 'restoration-oriented'. It has been found that people who make the most successful adaptations to their loss spend some time in each grieving style, while those who spend all their time either completely dwelling on their loss or completely avoiding thinking about their loss, are more likely to experience long-term dysfunction. Note that the zig-zag, oscillating lines, indicating alternating jumping between styles, sometimes stop in the everyday life place, thus allowing 'time out' from grieving. Margaret Stroebe has suggested that in time the two inner circles may shrink as grief diminishes.

I use this model with many of my clients quite openly and proactively. At the first session I will often show a client this model if what she has told me suggests that finding a balance in her grieving style could be helpful. As the work develops in the succeeding weeks and my client tells me how they are behaving, I will use the model again. For example, if a client does little but dwell on her loss, venturing out of the house on few occasions and spending a lot of her time in isolation, I may encourage her to explore the idea of pursuing some more restorative activities. On the other hand, some clients keep busy to avoid going too near the pain of their grief. We have seen here how some people do not need to actively pursue 'grief work'. Nonetheless, with experience one comes to recognize in some clients a mismatch between their body language and the words they choose to describe their feelings. Such instances suggest that they are suppressing feelings in order to control an overwhelming sense of loss and heartache. These clients can be helped by providing the counselling space to share their grief (loss-orientation) with encouragement perhaps to do the same with friends and family they trust.

Two case studies that illustrate very different ways of coping with loss illustrate the DPM. I will call these clients Margot and Marion.

Case study: Margot

Margot's husband died after a long struggle with cancer. Margot was devastated. She was also a very practical, confident and independent person. Once the funeral was behind her she threw herself into her career. She applied for, and was given, significant promotion at work. She remodelled her garden to a more low-maintenance design. She moved out of the marital bedroom and turned it into her study and converted what had been a study into her bedroom. She joined various social groups that allowed her to make new friendships and I am sure that most of her colleagues and friends would have been amazed at how well she appeared to be doing. Each week she would arrive to see me, would greet me with a smile and would tell me that she was 'OK'. Within minutes she would be weeping and recalling the tragedy of her husband's last weeks. At the end of the session she would take a deep breath, dry her eyes and return to the outside world with a smile. You will see that most of Margot's week was spent in a restoration-oriented frame, but that the counselling space was a time she could orientate towards her loss.

Case study: Marion

Marion also lost her husband to cancer. In our early sessions together she volunteered that she had never been confident on her own and that her husband had been her whole life. She told me that since he died she spent a great deal of her time crying at home, that she talked to a husband as if he was still there and that she cried herself to sleep. As the weeks passed nothing seemed to change from Marion and eventually her doctor put her on a low dose of antidepressant. This appeared to give her enough emotional energy to try new things. She joined a support group for people affected by cancer and she joined a local social group where she made new friends. Marion had moved from a place of almost total loss orientation to a place where some of her time was spent in restoring her life to some semblance of normality.

There is a small coda to Stroebe and Schut's work. In a book chapter entitled 'Meaning Making in the Dual Process Model of Coping with Bereavement' (Stroebe and Schut 2000) they concluded that we need to see grief as a process of reconstructing a world of meaning and restoring coherence to the narrative of our lives. Interestingly, they have explored the part played by meaning making in the grieving process in the context of this model. They reviewed literature pertinent to this process, and concluded that *facing up to* the reality of the loss can for some prove helpful, while others do best if they *avoid* the reality. Now you may quite reasonably ask how both can be true. What they have concluded is that for people who can only find negative meaning in the loss, to face it and continually ruminate on the pain is *unhelpful*. However, people who discover a positive meaning from the loss are more likely to *be helped* by facing the reality. Rumination is the process of going over and over the same thing, often something that happens when lying awake at night. Following a bereavement it has been described as 'persistent, repetitive and passive focus on negative emotions and symptoms' (Stroebe *et al.* 2007, p.462).

Depressed people can end up in an endless cycle of rumination, with each cycle taking them more and more out of control. Some forms of meditation, such as mindfulness, can help individuals get out of the loop.

Instrumental and intuitive grief

A detailed description of instrumental and intuitive grief appears in *Men Don't Cry... Women Do: Transcending Gender Stereotypes of Grief* by Terry Martin and Kenneth Doka (2000). They have researched the field of grief theory very thoroughly and have produced a thoughtful and very readable book, central to which is the authors' discovery of two grieving styles that they name as 'intuitive' and 'instrumental' grief. I have included descriptions of these grieving styles here as although Martin and Doka do not suggest that grieving people move between them in the same way that Stroebe and Schut describe oscillation in DPM, there are striking similarities between the descriptions of intuitive grief when compared to loss-orientation and of instrumental grief when compared to restoration-orientation.

The authors begin their book with a challenge to many of the classic assumptions of grief work and in this they are in accord with the views of Stroebe and Schut. They see grieving as a process of adaptation to the new circumstances of a post-loss world in which the bereaved person is required to reformulate their definition of who she is and what she lost. This is an idea we have already visited both in assumptive world theory, in meaning making theory and in the relearning principles of Thomas Attig. Crucially in Martin and Doka's view, this adaptive process may not necessarily manifest itself as painfully expressed emotions or distressed behaviour. In other words, it is acceptable *not* to cry. In my own professional work I have lost count of the number of times that clients have worried about not shedding tears, believing in some way that this is a sign that they have yet to grieve. Martin and Doka go on to describe the adaptive strategies grieving people are observed to employ. These may include making sense of events by thinking and talking; expressing feelings and emotions; being open to spiritual and religious experience; and engaging in activities that help one to come to terms with the loss.

Grief, according to Martin and Doka, releases a huge amount of what they refer to as 'psychic energy'. The concept of 'psychic energy' owes much to classical psychoanalysis and was discussed in Chapter 3. Some would question its validity. In truth, I would include myself in this. Like John Bowlby (see, for example, Bowlby 1980), I can accept the phrase as a useful metaphor, but the idea of a physical force being generated by emotion is not an idea that scientists would recognize, and, as Bowlby concluded, it is not a helpful concept for developing a sound theory of grief. That said, it is true that many people do become very energized in their grief – almost as if they are driven to be active in search of a resolution to their discomfort. Perhaps it is this frenetic activity that Martin and Doka are referring to and that they say must be dissipated through the process of adapting to the loss. By observing client behaviour and by piecing together relevant theoretical evidence, they have concluded that there are distinct major patterns of adaptation that they have called 'intuitive grief' and 'instrumental grief'. Intuitive grief is characterized by intensity, tears, painful feelings, expression of distress shared with others and a feeling of being out of control. Psychic energy they say, is channelled into feeling, not thinking. Extremes can lead to disorientation and exhaustion (Doka 2002). You may notice as you read this, the similarities with Stroebe and Schut's loss-orientation category. On the other hand, instrumental grief has much more of a cognitive focus: grief 'in the head'. Clients may exhibit a reluctance to discuss feelings. They may become engaged with problem-solving activities: recall the case example of Margot who remodelled house and garden in response to loss. Efforts, in other words, go into a *restorative* process. Psychic energy is channelled into thinking not feeling. Extremes of this grieving style may lead to 'cognitive dysfunction' (p.53). Although grieving patterns can exist along a continuum, with perfectly blended grieving being in the middle, they suggest that individuals tend towards one style of grieving, although this may vary with age, life stage and relationship to the deceased.

The subtitle of Martin and Doka's book is *Transcending Gender Stereotypes of Grief* and this takes us to the heart of their argument: that complications arise when individuals feel hooked into grieving as they feel they should be grieving, rather than expressing what comes naturally to them. As the title of the book suggests, many individuals feel bound to their gender. In other words, women tend to feel they should grieve intuitively, and men that they should grieve instrumentally. Individuals stuck in what is the wrong style to meet their needs, display *cognitive dissonance*. As Martin and Doka succinctly put it: 'These grievers are not only expressing grief differently than it is experienced, they are truly at war with themselves' (p.58).

Dissonant responses are defined as responses that do not fit with the individual's style of grief (intuitive, instrumental or blended). In some cases these responses can be seen as a sign of complicated grief. Such responses may typically involve the suppression of feelings, something seen as particularly risky for intuitive grievers trying to be instrumental grievers.

Case study: Gerald

Gerald was, on his own admission, a man who once would have dismissed a depressed person as 'somebody who just needed to pull themselves together'. He told me that he never expected that counselling could help. For many months he had tried to present a public face of determination and fortitude following the death of his mother. He developed a way of talking about his loss that was completely at odds with his inner feelings. His need was to be an intuitive griever, but the outward expression of his emotional state left him in a state of dissonance. Persistent incongruity between his inner experience and his outward expression was complicating his grief. Only when he trusted himself and his counsellor could he express his emotions as he needed to and thus he was able to reduce his stress and grieve healthily.

Conversely, Martin and Doka coin the phrase 'penitent griever' to describe the naturally instrumental griever, who believes that she (for it is more often a woman) should behave far more tearfully than is the case. Whereas intuitive grievers frequently criticize themselves for controlling their grief, 'penitents' are grievers who condemn themselves for not having feelings to hide. Some penitents even use alcohol to conjure up such feelings, while suppressors may use alcohol to hide them. I have met many women who feel that something is wrong with them because faced with a bereavement they have cried hardly at all, while those around them are mourning in a more 'acceptable' fashion. On these occasions I will point out that maybe they don't need to grieve in this way.

The Range of Responses to Loss model

In 2009 Linda Machin published *Working with Loss and Grief: A New Model for Practitioners*. This book is the result of many years of work with bereaved people combined with careful first-hand research. I cannot do the book justice in the space available here so would encourage you to read it in full.

As Machin makes clear in Chapter 5, the Range of Responses to Loss (RRL) model came from attending carefully to the coping styles of grieving clients. Hence the model is grounded in real, first-hand experience. As an experienced practitioner with a good grasp of theoretical approaches, she could make sense of what her clients told her in relation to other theories. She noticed that what clients expressed could be grouped into three categories; categories, which, we shall see, were validated by their relationship to other models of grief and personality. The three categories she identified are *overwhelmed, resilient* and *controlled.* We will explore each in turn.

Overwhelmed clients, as the term suggests, find the experience of loss overwhelming. They feel that they cannot deal with this loss and may in general find change difficult. As a result they may be consumed by their changed circumstances and may see their loss as being far worse than the losses of others. Contrast this with the resilient client who will voice a belief that 'I can deal with this, even if it is difficult.' Resilient clients will recognize the support of others and will in turn compare the grief of others as similar and equal to their own. Meanwhile, controlled clients believe that with diversion from the reality and distraction from their pain, they can effectively manage their grief by keeping a firm lid on it. Controlled individual's response to the losses of others is to avoid recognition and to expect others also to control their grief.

As a result of new research, there will be a second edition of Machin's 2009 book, due for publication in 2014. She now defines the overwhelmed/controlled spectrum in terms of *reactions* to grief, in contrast to the coping spectrum of vulnerability/resilience in terms of active *grieving.*[1] In the second edition of *Working with Loss and Grief,* vulnerability is scored by adding together overwhelmed and controlled responses and deducting the resilient responses, and the new edition includes a grid to arrive at this score. There is also an additional chapter that relates the Range of Responses to Loss model with a pluralistic approach to bereavement counselling (Machin 2013, personal communication).

Machin is clear that comparisons can be drawn between Stroebe and Schut's DPM. Overwhelmed people are analogous to loss-orientation and controlled people to restoration-orientation. The resilient are, as Stroebe and Schut also pointed out, those who oscillate successfully between the other extremes. Machin also acknowledges the stress theory of Horowitz and colleagues (Horowitz, Wilner and Alvarez 1979; Horowitz 1986), comparing intrusion and avoidance with

---

1   Note Machin's new distinction between *grief* and *grieving,* a distinction I defined in Chapter 1.

overwhelmed and controlled respectively (Machin 2009). Importantly, she also records her observation that early in developing her model, there was an observed connection with attachment styles: anxious ambivalent and avoidant being at the extremes, with the securely attached individual being resilient in approaching loss and change (p.75). Machin also mentions that the RRL model parallels Martin and Doka's descriptions of instrumental and intuitive personality types. All of this can be found in detail, and illustrated by tables, in Chapter 5 of Machin's 2009 book. Like me, she uses the metaphor of 'balance' and there are many diagrams involving balances and see-saws throughout the book. The text is well supported by real examples from case study research.

I have introduced many of my clients to the RRL model. In the appendices of Machin's book are a number of questionnaires and scales that allow client and counsellor to determine the client's response to the loss, in terms of being overwhelmed, controlled or resilient. The nature and intensity of the response to loss is determined by the Adult Attitude to Grief (AAG) scale that Linda Machin originally developed to test the validity of her RRL model (Machin 2009). This questionnaire can be legitimately photocopied from the book to use with clients. There are also record sheets to map a client's journey in her grief, where Machin reminds us of the uniqueness of each person's route through this. What my clients and I have found particularly useful is Appendix 4. This form invites clients to comment on the reason for their responses to the AAG scale. I will illustrate its usefulness with a case example.

The new Vulnerability Rating Grid, which Linda Machin has kindly shared with me, is a useful assessment tool and will appear in the second edition of *Working with Loss and Grief* (2014).

Case study: Hilda

Hilda's completion of the AAG scale following a death in a close-knit family revealed that Hilda was both overwhelmed and controlled. She strongly agreed with Statement six: 'For me, it is important to keep my grief under control.' When invited to explain this response she explained her belief that as the head of the family she had to be strong for the sake of everyone else, because she felt responsible for all her children and grandchildren and didn't want to upset them with her tears. Once such a belief is voiced it allows both the client and counsellor to explore it. Of course in Hilda's case there were more explanations she could give for the extremes in her responses. As we will see below, Linda Machin identifies the overwhelmed and controlled clients as being particularly vulnerable.

Mapping the range of responses to loss

Each of the nine statements that comprise the AAG scale are answered by one of five possible client responses ranging from 'strongly agree' to 'strongly disagree' with 'neither agree nor disagree' in the middle. Researchers refer to this design as a Likert scale, named after the inventor Rensis Likert. Now the aggregate AAG scores on the Likert scale can be plotted along a horizontal straight line, with overwhelmed and controlled as mirror images of each other like the East–West points of a compass. If a resilient versus vulnerable scale is plotted on a verticle line, the 'map of responses' appears like the other two points of a compass, with vulnerable and resilient in place of North and South respectively (see Machin 2009, p.98).

When you read Linda Machin's book you will see that the AAG scale needs no statements to map vulnerability. The reason for this is explained on pages 96 and 97 of the 2009 edition. Vulnerability arises from the tension of being unable to reconcile the extremes of being both overwhelmed and controlled, as in my example of Hilda (see too Machin 2009, p.97, Figure 6.3). Vulnerability is an absence of resilience. Resilience comes from willingness and an ability to find the strength to face loss and change and to oscillate effectively between overwhelmed and controlled states, as in Stroebe and Schut's Dual Process Model (see above). The focus of grief therapy, in Linda Machin's words, is to 'facilitate a move from the limitations of vulnerability to the possibilities of resilience' (p.112). Four more points can be added to the compass. Hence a client may be mapped as 'overwhelmed/vulnerable', 'controlled/vulnerable', and so on. (Machin 2009, p.100). The beauty of the AAG scale is that the client can periodically complete it afresh and hence map the progress of her journey.

Notes for trainers

Implications for practice

The idea of helping our clients to find a balance in their cognitive, affective and behavioural response to their grief brings home the importance of accepting each client's uniqueness and working in partnership alongside her in the journey. Acceptance of the client's position is not, however, about being a passive player in the therapeutic dyad. Grieving people can be in a temporary state of diminished capacity to help themselves. They may need to be gently guided in a helpful direction, perhaps away from a loss-orientation and towards more strategies involving restorative activities. Perhaps they will need a gentle challenge to their vulnerable self-image and an encouragement in their tentative steps towards resilience. While I was writing this chapter I had a client who I had previously challenged for her tendency to find an excuse not to pursue new opportunities presented to her. She reported that she had found my challenge helpful and that after she tried some restorative strategies she felt better. Her vulnerability decreased as her resilience increased. This was not about 'advice giving' on my part; I gently pointed out my congruent frustration towards what she told me were her typical responses to, for example, friends asking her to join them for social events. I pointed out that she tended to respond to every invitation with the equivalent of 'Yes, but…' Between one week's challenge and the following week's counselling she had chosen to accept a social invitation, had enjoyed the occasion and was planning to go again. She also began some other restoration activities of her choosing and is getting back some control in her life.

For further case examples of Linda Machin's RRL model I would urge you to explore her book.

5 Continuing bonds

In 1996 Dennis Klass, Phyllis Silverman and Steven Nickman edited a book entitled *Continuing Bonds: New Understandings of Grief*. They also wrote a substantial part of the book, drawing on other researchers and practitioners with expertise in the field to provide examples of the central thesis. In essence the book suggested that, in many instances, a person's grieving never ends. Instead it goes through a lifelong process of adaptation and change. Klass and colleagues' claim was that we cannot look at bereavement as a psychological state that ends and from which one recovers. They proposed that rather than the emphasis on 'letting go', a concept that we have seen occupied the predominant thinking from Sigmund Freud to John Bowlby, the emphasis should be on negotiating and re-negotiating the meaning of loss over time. They presented evidence from case observations that the bereaved remain involved and connected to the deceased and that the bereaved actively construct an inner representation of the deceased that is part of the normal grieving process. Memorializing, remembering, knowing the person who has died and allowing them to influence the present, are active processes that seem to continue throughout the survivor's life.

The book immediately struck a chord with practitioners who, from experience, had found that many clients do not relinquish their attachment to their lost loved-one and have no intention of doing so, yet at the same time appear to find that the pain of grief diminishes over time in spite of the continuing attachment. For many years prior to the publication of *Continuing Bonds*, my colleagues and I had discussed the fact that clients did not as a rule 'let go' as the classic theories had said they would, and indeed should. Klass and colleagues were explicit that a continuing bonds model of grief did not mean that grieving people would in some way begin to live in the past, denying the reality of the loss, but that bereaved people could come to recognize that the loving bonds formed during life can inform how we go forward in living a new life in the present and future. This is a model of accommodating change, rather as Thomas Attig suggested as part of assumptive world theory and his reference to new meaning making: 'In our lasting love we give them *symbolic* immortality' (Attig 2001, p.46; my italics). This to me seems to be the key to successful and healthy continuing bonds. The continuing bond to which this model refers is one that first requires a cognitive and affective acceptance of the reality of the death before the grieving individual can successfully negotiate a symbolic immortality and a new lasting and loving relationship with the loved-one they have lost. This can take time, and it is a journey that not every client is willing and able to take, preferring instead to go on pretending that the deceased is just away temporarily and will come back. Clients sometimes say to me, 'I *know* he is dead. I just don't *feel* that he's dead, and maybe I don't want to.' As practitioners we can help our clients both to accept the reality of the death and to develop a new, post-loss relationship. In her inspiring book *Talking with Bereaved People: An Approach for Structured and Sensitive Communication* (2009), my colleague Dodie Graves includes many ways of achieving this, based on many years of working in this field. This book is another that should be on every practitioner's bookshelf.

My own position is that although a continuing bonds model has validity, I do not believe that it entirely negates observations that some bereaved people *do* become stuck in grief. We can, for example, look at Bowlby and Parkes' stages of grief (1970). They identified an initial phase of numbness, which eventually turns to yearning and searching. Only when the bereaved individual accepts that the deceased will never return does the yearning and searching stop. Experience will sooner or later teach everyone who works with bereaved people that some clients will get stuck here, whatever opposing theorists have to say. My own interpretation of Klass and Silverman's introductory chapter of *Continuing Bonds* is an inference that clients do not have to move away from this yearning attachment to the deceased, that such continuing attachment is healthy, natural and to be encouraged. I cannot agree. I accept that a continuing bond with the deceased is often something the client wants and it is something the bereavement practitioner can help them develop. However, for this continued bond to be helpful to the deceased, it must go through a transitional stage of acceptance before it can become symbolic. In fact on page 142 of *Continuing Bonds*, one of the contributors, Kirsten Tyson-Rawson, makes just this point. In the conclusion of Chapter 8, Tyson-Rawson refers to the need for the bereaved to construct 'a new working model of attachment'. Such a revised representation of the deceased, she says, will determine how significant relationships will be experienced in the future, in terms of thoughts, feelings and behaviour.

Case study: Betty

It was ten years since Betty's husband had died when she was referred to me by her GP, where she had presented at the surgery with depression and thoughts of suicide because life appeared to have become pointless. Her GP, who she had seen for many years, correctly identified a delayed grief reaction. In the decade from bereavement to being referred for counselling, Betty said that she had coped well and hardly gave her late husband a thought. When invited to talk about him she was dismissive and dispassionate about him. Although I had no way of being certain about this, I suspected that she had suppressed her grief and her yearning to the point at which it became a habit. I also suspected that if Betty could develop a healthy, re-negotiated bond with her husband she would be able to bring the happiness of her marriage into the present and into a more optimistic future. Fortunately, Betty's husband had been an amateur potter and Betty still had some of his creations at home. I asked her to bring one or two pots and bowls to her counselling. As she talked about the pots she recalled her husband's workshop, which she said was chaos to her, but he seemed to know where everything was and she was forbidden to clean or tidy it. She began to be able to laugh at this account and at his other quirks and foibles as she saw them. Effectively we were bringing him 'back to life' and Betty became able to talk about him and to recall the happy memories she had apparently blocked out. Her dear husband's memory and the fun they had shared became part of Betty's present and her depression lifted. Six years after the counselling completed, Betty was able to let me know that the change was lasting and that she was continuing to enjoy life.

Dodie Graves's book *Talking with Bereaved People* (2009) is an invaluable resource for finding appropriate ways to develop a helpful continuing bond and I cannot improve on the 'Six Elements' for working with the bereaved that she outlines in her book. All I would add is to reinforce once again that a helpful continuing bond is not one where the client clings desperately to a lost attachment in the hope that the deceased can magically return one day. Healthy lasting bonds appear to be based on acceptance and symbolic transition. At the beginning of this chapter I gave as an example of readiness for support a client I have called Jayne. An attempt to keep her close relative 'alive' by denying the death had left Jayne in an unhappy place for ten years. By the end of her counselling she had developed a healthy continuing bond. In our last session she recalled what she saw as the most significant moment of our work together. She remembered a tearful session when I had said to her, 'He is dead, and he's not coming back.' I recalled how she had sworn and gasped.

'That's hard John.'

Yet only by facing the harsh truth did she feel able to move forward.

Implications for practice

In the service where I work, at the initial assessment we find it helpful to ask our clients where they feel their loved one is now. The answers tend towards three categories. Some mention the deceased as being 'in my thoughts', others say 'in my heart' and a third group will believe that the person continues to exist in another dimension, for example, 'in heaven watching over me'. We are then able to use what the client says as a starting point for the support we offer her.

6 Bereavement and biography

No account would be complete without a mention of Professor Tony Walter's work on biography as a model of grief (Walter 1996). Since 2011, he has been Director of the Centre for Death and Society based at the University of Bath, UK, and Walter's model is sociological rather than psychological. However, Dodie Graves (2009, pp.136–137) describes how she uses the client's story therapeutically, and the case example of Betty, above, also indicates the value of such an approach.

Implications for practice

I find that inviting the client to tell the story of her life with the deceased is often a way to encourage a nervous client to talk. Sometimes she will recall a humorous incident that offers momentary respite from her tears. I believe that biography is an important part of accommodating a new assumptive world, a pathway into finding meaning and making sense, the beginning of new growth and a means of orienting on the loss. As we have seen from Betty's story, it can also foster a continuing bond. Story telling is, in other words, central to the relearning process of grieving.

Specialist interventions

These interventions are no less important than the six approaches already described. Indeed, in cases of PGD, other forms of complicated grief and grief in which the client has also been traumatized by events surrounding the loss, specialist interventions may be the preferred option. An appropriately qualified counsellor or psychotherapist could do this work, but it calls for training beyond what an introductory training would equip counsellors to do.

Shear's treatment of complicated grief

In 2005 Katherine Shear and her colleagues reported the results of a randomized controlled trial of a treatment for complicated grief. Ninety-five clients, all diagnosed with complicated grief, were split randomly into two groups. One group of 46 clients received interpersonal psychotherapy and the other group of 49 clients received specific treatment interventions. The practitioners working with both groups all had either a master's degree or a PhD in clinical practice, a minimum of two years' experience and a commitment to the treatment protocols. There was a manual for the complicated grief intervention and the treatment included discussion of the loss, a focus on personal life goals, procedures for retelling/revisiting the story of the death and exercises to help the client confront avoided situations. The revisiting exercise was sound-recorded and clients were given the recording to listen to between sessions. Clients were also encouraged to have 'imaginal conversations' with the deceased, guided by the therapist. Although both treatments produced improvements, the complicated grief treatment helped 51 per cent of the sample, compared to 28 per cent of those who had received interpersonal therapy. Response times were also better for the complicated grief treatment group.

Eye movement desensitization and reprocessing (EMDR)

Nearly ten years ago a client was referred to me for a recent and traumatic bereavement. My client had escaped unharmed from a domestic accident, but another family member had died by his side in very distressing circumstances. The client was severely traumatized by the experience and I referred the client back to his GP to see if it was possible to access EMDR. It so happened that one of the mental health practitioners at the surgery had recently completed EMDR training. The treatment was successful and the client reported that he was now able to cope with his grief without bereavement counselling. Scientists would say that single accounts such as this are anecdotal and prove nothing, which is true, and it doesn't even show that EMDR *can* work, because other factors in the process, such as the relationship between client and practitioner, or the practitioner's skill in relaxing the client, may have made the difference. However, the apparent success was enough for me to investigate EMDR as a treatment for clients who are both traumatized and bereaved. My clinical experience leads me to conclude that bereaved clients will sometimes have been traumatized by the experience of the death or even in some cases from viewing the body of the deceased. I would also suggest that to watch somebody you love become emaciated and physically changed by cancer can also be traumatizing. The comorbidity of complicated grief and post-traumatic stress disorder (PTSD) is discussed by Jan van den Bout and Rolf J. Kleber (2013) and in the same book by Raphael, Jacobs and Looi (2013).

EMDR as a treatment for PTSD was pioneered by Francine Shapiro, who discovered in 1987 that she could reduce her own stressful feelings by moving her eyes from side to side. She published the results of her PhD on the subject in *The Journal of Traumatic Stress* in 1989. EMDR involves the client recalling the traumatic incident while following the therapist's hand as it moves in different trajectories, across the client's field of vision. Of course this is an oversimplification, and the properly trained practitioner goes through several phases of assessing and preparing the client before the desensitization exercise, and then further phases in consolidating the treatment. A colleague well qualified in the technique pointed out to me that clients will often spontaneously move their eyes from side to side as they process difficult memories, and I have since noticed that this is true. Some researchers, while accepting that the treatment as a whole is effective, have questioned whether the eye movements are a significant part of the treatment. However, a recent independent study and fresh analysis of previous research (Lee and Cuijpers 2013) has concluded that EMDR is evidence based, and that the eye movements do have a significant effect. There is very specific training to become an EMDR practitioner.

Cognitive behavioural therapy (CBT) for complicated grief

One of the leading experts in this field is Paul Boelen from Utrecht University in the Netherlands. In 2008, at a conference at St Christopher's Hospice (Boelen 2008a) I heard him give an interesting account of working with a client bereaved of a son and displaying prolonged grief disorder. This client was eventually helped using CBT. Boelen (2008b) concludes that complicated grief is developed and maintained when the client is unable to integrate the loss into her existing biographical narrative. These clients also maintain unhelpful thinking patterns and avoidance behaviours that lead to anxiety and depression. All of these unhelpful processes can be targeted by CBT using interventions such as exposure, cognitive restructuring and behavioural activation. These are standard techniques in the toolbox of the CBT practitioner.

So do specialist treatments have a place in person-centred bereavement counselling? I and others (see, for example, Shear and Frank 2006; Shear, Boelen and Neimeyer 2011) would argue that there is a place for working eclectically. I believe we should be adaptable practitioners. The ability to work flexibly according to our client's needs comes with practice and confidence, and sometimes I will use more cognitively inspired interventions with clients who are drawn to work more in their head than with their emotions. Remember, however, that it is always unethical to work beyond one's competency and to work with any technique without adequate training and experience. Readers of this book drawn to any of the three specializations mentioned above should access appropriate training before putting them into practice.

Conclusions

From the uniqueness of each person's grief there emerge patterns. By observing these patterns, practitioners and researchers have been able to describe the ways that real people are seen to grieve. I believe that in order to be effective, the practitioner needs an understanding of each of these models. As we listen attentively to our client, she will lead us towards the model(s) she intuitively leans towards. For example, if a client talks about how different life is since her loss, the focus may well be on her assumptive world. The client who is trying to make sense of what has happened can be helped by finding and making new meanings. The client who dwells on the loss can be encouraged to explore new activities, while the client who actively avoids her grief by pursuing frenetic activities may gently be invited to talk about the deceased. I find that photograph albums brought to the counselling session can be a helpful starting point. Clients who punish themselves for not grieving 'correctly' (for example, by gender stereotype) or who are in a state of dissonance may need encouragement to pursue whatever grieving style they naturally feel drawn towards. A continuing bond with the client can be developed through talking about the lost loved, particularly about fond memories and lessons learnt from life with the deceased. Dodie Graves' book, already mentioned, contains the starting points to introduce such conversations. To me, grief counselling is both a science and an art. Each client will bring her own unique needs to us and we can use our knowledge, skill and compassion to support her in the best ways we know how.

Notes for trainers

When my colleagues and I teach the models of grief covered in this chapter, we devote two mornings of our eight-day course to cover it. That is about six hours of class contact excluding breaks.

It goes without saying that trainers need sufficient knowledge of these models of grief to lead a discussion on the topic and to be able to answer students' questions. The competent trainer will have read the core literature and in many cases this requires access to original journal articles. Journals do eventually appear online but access is usually through subscription. This is much easier for trainers working in partnership with universities and colleges than for those working independently. It may, however, be possible for training organizations in the charity sector to find ways of accessing online material for free. In the United Kingdom, for example, hospice staff can access the NHS online library that gives access to the electronic versions of the leading death, grief and mourning journals. Remember, too, that authors are generally happy to be contacted for copies of their original articles. Some publishers give their authors a number of free electronic copies of even the most recent articles, which can be legally downloaded for private study purposes. Be aware of copyright laws that are likely to restrict photocopy distribution to student groups.

In producing teaching materials, including PowerPoint presentations, it is important to reference your sources correctly. Not only does this avoid any accusations of plagiarism, it also models good practice for your students.

Case examples to support your teaching may come from your own caseload. Such examples bring the theory to life and are valued by students. This, however, places on you the responsibility to get informed consent to talk about your clients. Even then it is good practice to heavily disguise the case in order to render the client unidentifiable. This is harder than you may think, especially if you practise and teach in a small community. For this reason, some case examples, particularly those following a recent, high-profile and unusual death cannot be used. It is also good practice to have in place a contract with your students that materials shared in the teaching space remain in this space and are not talked about outside. You may of course find that students share examples from their own caseload.

Chapter 6

Families and Grief

This chapter invites the reader to explore the part that the family plays in affecting how individuals grieve, rather than the very difficult and skilled task of working with a grieving family. There are many resources available for helping professions work with families, including grief in the family context. The most important book on the subject in recent years has been *Family Focused Grief Therapy: A model of Family-centred Care during Palliative Care and Bereavement* (Kissane and Bloch 2002) and I have no intention of writing a chapter on working with families so long as such excellent resources exist. That said, there are times when talking to clients on a one-to-one basis it soon becomes very clear when that at least one other family member is present in the therapeutic relationship. In a metaphorical sense, these clients bring other family members into the therapeutic space. I remember many years ago a young woman who had married into a family deeply affected by the sudden, traumatic death of a family member. The family believed that the death was a result of manslaughter, but there was insufficient evidence for this and there was no prosecution. The bereaved family felt embittered that there had been no justice for the loss. My client had no emotional connection to the deceased and she had also tried to take a balanced view of the death. The family members accused her of being disloyal, and were vocal in criticizing her, making it difficult for her and for her husband who had tried to defend his new wife. Much of the first counselling session was concerned with the behaviour of one particularly embittered in-law.

Sometimes individuals suppress grief in the interests of the family. For example, one young woman grieving her father deliberately isolated herself from other family members. Fearful of upsetting her mother, who after all was grieving a husband, she hid her tears when they were together. When she told me this I suggested that it was likely that her mother was hiding her tears, too, and the client reflected that this was probably true. In such situations, elaborate collusions develop. Personal grief that could be a shared and supportive family grief is so easily driven underground. Sometimes a client will tell me of resentment towards siblings, because they have not been sufficiently supportive either in illness or in bereavement. Unspoken resentments fester and can complicate the grieving process. Since almost nobody grieves in total isolation, I often find it helpful to explore with my client his place in the family system. Once I have an understanding, I can try to hold an empathic awareness of the positive and negative influences the family will have on the client's grief.

One way of understanding the effect of the family on the client is to invite him to talk about his family and how others are grieving. In this context it helps our understanding of the situation if we view his family as a complex system of inter-related individuals, each operating in ways that will have an effect on everyone else in the family, including our client. As he talks about his bereavement and his grieving, we listen for clues about the family context, perhaps asking open questions if this feels appropriate. Gradually this allows us to build up a picture of the client's grief in relation to the family system.

Case study: Amanda

When Harry died I began to work with Harry's 28-year-old maternal granddaughter Amanda. Amanda and Harry had been very close, perhaps since she was the only female grandchild. Amanda's grief was compounded by her grandmother's grief reaction. Outwardly, maternal grandmother Hilda appeared not to grieve much. Indeed it seemed to Amanda as if Hilda had found her husband's death something of a relief, not because Harry had ceased to suffer, but because it seemed Hilda was enjoying the freedom of no longer caring for Harry. Even worse for Amanda and Amanda's mother, it felt as if Hilda could turn on her grief 'to order', that is, whenever she felt she was being watched. To Amanda this did not look or feel genuine, and Amanda's mother agreed. Amanda and her mother grew closer but felt that they had moved away from wanting to be with Hilda. In her counselling Amanda reflected that Harry had been the hub of the family, a pacifier who could defuse tensions. He was a generous man – with time, love, money and gifts – whereas Hilda had, it transpired, always been far more reserved and careful with money – a characteristic that Harry's actions had covered up. With Harry gone, the aunts, uncles, nephews and nieces were less likely to visit Hilda. Harry, for all of his physical problems, had been warm, cheerful and welcoming, so that all of his children and grandchildren regularly went to visit Harry and Hilda's house. Hilda noticed the lack of visits now that she was alone. Understandably she began to complain and to express her grief loudly. While this made her family feel guilty it did nothing to make any of them feel like visiting, apart from out of duty. Amanda had to deal not just with her grief, but with the apparently changed character of her grandmother, her mother's distress at this, and the lack of regular contact with the extended family. Although in this family system only Amanda was my client, it was easy to imagine the bereavement needs of others in this family.

What do we mean by 'a system'?

A system is an organized collection of component parts that operate together to perform a task. The components may be physical, like those that are a central heating system or a domestic hot water system. They may be living creatures, like as one present in an ecosystem. They process. Alternatively, they may be abstract, like as one present in an office management system or factory process, or the system may comprise of individual human beings, like as one present in a team or a family. As you can see from the case study above, if one part of a system behaves less than optimally then it will have an adverse effect on all of the other parts. A blockage in a pressurized system plus the failure of a safety valve can have catastrophic results. Systems are often conceived as being greater than the sum of the component parts: for example, a symphony is more than musical notes played by musical instruments.

What do we mean by 'a family'?

The traditional, Western nuclear family of mother, father and their children is just one form of family. To this may be added grandparents and other relatives living under the same roof or living so close by that childcare arrangements are shared. Extended families under one roof may be more common in some cultures than others. In some instances the female partner may go out to work with the male partner taking the day-time childcare role. Home working is in any case increasingly common in the West. Many couples cohabit rather than marry, and same-sex couples may have children. Two partners may have had children by previous relationships, some, but not all of whom may live together. There may be half-siblings in the family as well as what traditionally would have been called stepchildren. All this may seem obvious but I mention it to make the point that invariably it helps to ask bereaved clients to talk about their family in a very broad sense, especially if this appears to be a factor in the grief reaction. It is important not to make assumptions about your client's family. In cases of particular complexity, I have sometimes found it helpful to construct a genogram with the client, more of which appears below.

Theories of family systems

A good overview of family system theory in relation to loss and grief is found in Chapter 7, *Family Systems Theory and Models of Family Bereavement*, in Esther R. Shapiro's book *Grief as a Family Process: A Developmental Approach to Clinical Practice* (Shapiro 1994). Shapiro argues that any understanding of bereavement within a family is incomplete without family systems theory as a conceptual framework. She emphasizes the interdependence, to greater or lesser degrees, with all the other family members. Death in a family generates a cascade of responses. The nature, intensity and effect of these responses, Shapiro argues, will be due to the family structure and interdependence of the family members. Such responses will be unique to each family, and will be determined as much by the nature of the family system as by the nature of the death. This does not mean that the nature of the death is insignificant. Anticipated deaths following a life-limiting illness will have a different effect to sudden deaths, particularly if the death was also violent. A suicide may result in spoken and unspoken recriminations and guilt and in replaying events within the family. We cover this in detail below when we look at the work of John Rolland.

Bowen's family system approach

From his extensive work with families in the latter half of the 20th century, Murray Bowen (1976) observed that family stress fuses a family together, causes mutual emotional reactions and results in overly rigid family structures with no opportunity for individual needs to be met. Bowen went on to discuss how family equilibrium is disrupted by death. Inter-relationships change. New alliances in the family may be formed, but often difficult relationships are exacerbated by the intensity of grief that permeates the family. Families where individuals are able to differentiate from one another, communicate freely and honestly, and value the family's ability to adapt to change, are far more likely to adapt to change than families with poor communication, an unspoken adherence to conformity and rigid family structures. Bowen has also noted what he called the shock wave that can ripple through a family when a significant family member dies. This may be a matriarch or patriarch. It may be a child who had united family members in a shared appreciation of her qualities, for example academic successes or caring nature.

Family and homeostatic equilibrium

One way of understanding the process of disruption and recovery following a family death is to utilize the physiological concept of homeostasis. Homeostasis is the process by which living things strive to exist in a state of balanced health. For example, if we become too hot we perspire and the energy used in evaporating sweat from our skin cools us down. Lorna Bowlby-West (1983) suggested that death puts the family into a state of homeostatic disequilibrium. The family members will employ whatever means they have at their disposal to try to regain the normal state. Remember, however, that the place in which family members will most likely have learnt what to do will be from other members of the family. In this way a family culture develops, which passes through the generations. For example, a client will often describe his family in terms of how physically demonstrative they are with one another. He may contrast his family with his partner's family. Some families deal with grief by trying to avoid one another's emotions, while other families are far more open, tearful with one another and generous with hugs. Whatever the family style, the usual goal is to try to get through the loss and return to some semblance of self-regulated homeostatic normality.

Families and attachment style

Families in which there is a history of attachment insecurity and disturbed relationships are particularly likely to attempt to maintain stability by behaving in rigid ways. Just as change threatens emotionally insecure individuals, the changes brought about by bereavement are frequently seen as overwhelming and threatening to the family stability. The responses of the family members tend to be rigid and controlled. A secure family will react differently. It is more likely to adapt to the loss of a family member and regain a sense of stability and continuity without resorting to the rigid behaviour of the insecure and disturbed family (Shapiro 1994, Chapter 7). Jordan and colleagues (Jordan 1990; Jordan, Kraus and Ware 1993) have looked at phases in family life-cycles, with a natural oscillation between centripetal (turning inward) and centrifugal (turning outward) forces. Jordan has suggested that family bereavement is best understood as a crisis of attachment in which loss turns the family inwards and fuses members into rigidity.

Differences in family attachment style appear in different forms. Shapiro (1994) describes what she calls 'enmeshed' families. Enmeshed family members demand great conformity of one another, to the extent that a client's sense of independent identity can get lost. Individuals who try to behave outside of rigid family expectations will be sanctioned, as in the example of the young wife I described above. At the opposite extreme is the family system where individuals show little involvement or engagement with one another. The identity and stability of the enmeshed family may be threatened when individual members think and behave independently. However, a client from a disengaged family may sometimes feel unsupported and cast adrift. Only in the security of the adaptive and flexible family does a grieving client have the best chance of feeling safe. The client from this background is likely to feel that similarities and differences are respected and tolerated and that thinking and behaving independently are no threat to the continuity and coherence of his family.

The family and differential grief

In a paper engagingly titled '"We've had the same loss, why don't we have the same grief?" Loss and differential grief in families', Kathleen Gilbert (1996) takes an approach that conceptualizes individual grief, while recognizing the influence of the family. Gilbert is clear that '[f]amilies do not grieve. Only individuals grieve' (p.273; original italics). As she explains, family members may well use one another to test a new, post-loss reality, but, ultimately, our reality is personal, unique to us and evolves from both within and outside of the family environment. Earlier in the article she expresses her discomfort at the concept of shared belief as a family phenomenon. In her view, and it is a view I share based on clinical experience, as we grieve we make new meaning in our loss and in our grief. In doing so we reconceptualize what is real to us. This reality may or may not reflect the dominant family position. One very common example of this, which I meet regularly, is the competitiveness with which family members may express grief. A husband and father dies. His wife claims to the daughter that her grief is unbearable because her husband of 30 years has died. She points out that her daughter still has a husband to go home to at night. The daughter replies that she has lost her daddy and her best friend, and he can never be replaced. Mothers and daughter-in-laws get into similar conflict. If these words are not actually said to the other person, they are certainly said to the bereavement counsellor:

'I have lost a son I can never replace, but my daughter-in-law can remarry eventually.'

'I have lost the love of my life. My mother-in-law still has a husband for comfort, but I go home to an empty house.'

In other instances, stories may grow up around the deceased, with very different perceptions. All family members may believe that their reality about the life and character of the deceased is objective, yet some may criticize, even vilify him, while others virtually sanctify him. I have talked to mothers who have described their dead son in forgiving and adoring terms such that he would be quite unrecognizable even to the rest of the family. Tensions and jealousies between siblings of the deceased will sometimes arise at this point.

Gilbert sees grief as more than a psychological and emotional response to a loss. She argues that in reconstructing a new normality we regain order and stability in a world changed, both by the absence of the deceased and the realignment of family relationships. She adopts the term 'differential grief' to describe the contrasting styles, differing issues that have to be dealt with and varying speeds and trajectories of grief exhibited by individuals. Gilbert is explicit that family members need to recognize and respect individual difference, rather than nurse an expectation that all family members should and will grieve in the same way. All bereavement counsellors value the importance of helping clients to accept the varying ways in which others close to them will need to grieve.

Rolland's Family Systems-Illness Model

There are times when family bereavement is preceded by a long period of chronic, life-limiting illness, perhaps punctuated with periods of remission and restored hope and optimism, which ends in disappointment and despair. It is always important for the bereavement counsellor to understand the story of the death as well as the client's relationship to the deceased. In cases where chronic illness and disability have preceded the death it is also important to understand the effect that this has had and continues to have on the client as he attempts to come to terms with grief. Professor John Rolland MD (1988, 1994, 2005) has for many years studied families overshadowed by illness and has devised the Family Systems-Illness (FSI) Model that we can use to better understand what bereaved clients bring to us. He, too, takes a systemic approach to the family, perceiving the family unit as a potentially supportive resource for its members. The FSI Model is conceptualized in three dimensions: 1. the type of illness or disability, 2. the developmental natural history of the illness and 3. the key variables in the family system, such as belief system and culture. The chronic illness is viewed as an unfolding process that imposes psychosocial demands on the family. The degree to which family members successfully meet these demands will depend on the resilience of the family. The value of the FSI to clinical practice is that it gives practitioners a conceptual framework on which to hang both the family's identified psychosocial demands and the strength of its coping strategies in guiding the family through the vicissitudes of the illness.

Types of illness

By way of further explanation we will look more closely at chronic illness. Rolland identifies the possible courses an illness can take: *progressive*, in which the condition gradually worsens over time; *constant*, in which a disabling condition is stabilized over a long period of time; and *episodic*, in which periods of comparative health are interrupted by relapse or acute debilitating symptoms. Examples of progressive disease includes metastatic cancer or some neurological diseases. The family is typically worn down and exhausted by the unrelenting progress of the disease. Roles in the family are likely to change as the illness leads to increasing incapacity and pain. A spinal injury is a constant condition that will affect the family in stable but semi-permanent ways, although family relationships and roles will be affected. Because of the unpredictability, episodic conditions such as asthma and some cases of cystic fibrosis cause great strain on families. Resilient families learn to cope with flexible responses needed when a condition can flare up at any time.

The complexity of many illnesses means that they do not fit neatly into the three categories of progressive, constant and episodic. Progressive cancers may include alarming episodes of crisis, such as infections and lymphedema. Stroke symptoms may initially improve over time before stabilizing, although the family could remain braced for a second stroke or series of 'mini strokes' (transient ischemic attacks). Episodic illnesses may eventually lead to progressive deterioration and death. I have worked with a woman bereaved of a sibling with cystic fibrosis who was deeply affected by the unpredictability of the relapses, the progression of the disease and the final traumatic death. All the time she, her sibling and her family were hoping for a lung transplant. My client was also affected by the coping styles of other family members including her sick sibling.

The effect of chronic disease on grief

As Rolland suggests, a chronic disease will significantly affect the family if death is the final outcome (2005, p.2586). Just what effect that will be will depend on the nature of the death. Sudden deaths, such as from haemophilia, may be a shock tempered by the family's shared and accepted truth that this was always a possibility – a biological time-bomb waiting to go off. On the other hand, a cancer with a reasonable prognosis and a statistically high chance of survival, but that then has a fatal outcome, can leave the family feeling cheated and confused. Where a disease progresses through a long period of pain and incapacity such as metastatic cancer, or cognitive impairment such as dementia, the family may see the death as a relief from suffering, particularly where it concludes a long and what was otherwise a fruitful life. Against this are similar trajectories in younger patients with dependent children. In these cases grief in surviving family members may be prolonged and complex.

In many cases the bereavement will have been preceded by a long period of incapacity and high dependency on other family members. Dealing with incontinence and limited mobility can become a way of life for family members, who following the death of somebody they have cared for over many years, grieves not only for the deceased but for the lost lifestyle. Clients will often say that as tough as 24-hour caring could be, life without the dependent spouse, parent or child seems purposeless. Some families may have discussed the progress of the disease and its outcomes with one another and with the affected family member. In some instances family sub-groups collude to protect those in the family who they judge to be vulnerable. Young children are often protected in this way. In many cases of working with individuals, the dying family member would not discuss what was happening, in spite of the best efforts of palliative care professionals. Shared anticipatory grief, in which the family members are able to be open and honest with one another, can and does frequently mitigate the effects of bereavement. The benefits of counselling family members in the palliative care setting are difficult to assess empirically, since this would be a sensitive and difficult area in which to conduct research. Nevertheless, counselling interventions can be evaluated by 'customer satisfaction' style questionnaires. In the professional setting where I work,[1] such evaluations by family members are generally positive. The counsellor may work either one-to-one with the person with a life-limiting illness, with one or more family members, or with several members of the family. Because of the nature of palliative care settings, counselling in this context has to be flexible and creative, although it must remain boundaried by the same ethical standards as more conventional forms of therapeutic approach.

The developmental natural history of the illness
According to Rolland, the extent to which family members will have been prepared for the death will be reflected in the way in which the family adjusted to the development of the illness. An important part of the bereavement counselling involves the client's telling, and sometimes repeated retelling, of the narrative preceding the death, including the family's psychosocial management of the illness. Rolland sees the illness placed on a time-line in three phases. The first is the crisis phase, which begins with the emergence of symptoms, proceeds to diagnosis and concludes with adjustment to the shock. When my clients recall this time they invariably describe the reaction

---

1   The author is not involved either with the practise or evaluation of palliative care counselling in this or any other setting.

to the diagnosis as a violent metaphor 'like being punched in the stomach' or 'like having a door slammed in our face'. Lory Clukey, in her research into anticipatory grief in palliative care settings, made a similar observation (Clukey 2007). The crisis phase involves considerable adaptation and the accommodation of new realities, changes that family systems theorists would expect to be much easier for the secure, adaptive family to cope with, compared to the more rigid, inward-looking family.

From the crisis phase the family moves into the chronic phase, which Rolland (2005) refers to as 'the long haul'. This phase can last many years, and families get used to the illness, the hospital visits and the working relationships with health professionals. The nature of family relationships, including marital relationships, changes in this phase. As one husband movingly said in a carers' support group, 'I used to be her lover. Now I'm her carer. Life used to be spelt F-U-N. Now it's spelt C-R-A-P.' Sometimes the understandable resentments silently harboured in this phase emerge as guilty thoughts during the bereavement counselling, a phenomenon that Rolland notes (p.2587).

From the chronic phase, the illness progresses to the terminal phase. I would suggest that individual family members move into this phase sometimes out of step with one another, since it begins when, in Rolland's words, 'the inevitability of death becomes apparent and dominates family life' (p.2588). My experience of working with many bereaved clients who have lived through this phase is that some come to this point before others, some are quietly accepting and others rage against the reality. Sometimes family members, including the person who is dying, resist facing the reality until so close to the end that goodbyes are not said and emotional business is unfinished. It almost goes without saying that secure and open families adapt best to this final transition and in nearly all of these cases, grief takes a normal course. It is often clients from families who did not cope well with the course of the illness and whose family did not 'pull together' during life that present with complications after the death.

Family belief system and culture

Rolland emphasizes to clinicians the importance of understanding the part played by family culture and belief systems in charting how the family copes with chronic, life-limiting illness. He suggests using illness-focused time-lines and genograms to explore with the family the key events, moments of transition and the strategies that were developed to cope with the illness. This will include current and past stressors on the family as well as coping styles and communication styles.

Case study: Teresa

Nigel was a successful bank manager and family man, with an emotionally dependent wife, Liz, and two daughters, Teresa and Janice. Liz had come to her marriage to Nigel from an insecure childhood and they had married when quite young. The marriage had been successful and Nigel doted on his three 'girls'. He did everything for them, practically, emotionally and financially, including all the shopping and a significant part of the cooking and housework. To the outside observer it could look as though he had cultured this high level of dependency on him. He was also the peacemaker in sibling rivalry and smoothed tensions between mother and daughters during the teenage years. Teresa's career path took her towards self-employment. Her father was emotionally and financially supportive of the venture and kept a professional eye on the finances.

At 60, Nigel was diagnosed with bowel cancer. In an attempt to protect his family he hid his symptoms and prognosis for as long as he could. At 61 he was admitted to a hospice where he died.

My professional role was to work with Teresa, aged 38. Even into the terminal phase of her father's illness she hoped for a miracle, retaining a strong denial that her father could die. Her grief became prolonged and it was 12 months before she could engage in counselling, by which time she had developed a range of somatic conditions that her doctor attributed to grief reaction. She acknowledged that she, her mother and her sister found it very hard to cope. Without her father's calming influence they had fallen out with one another on a regular basis, even becoming competitive with one another in their grief. It took a great deal for Teresa to face the reality of her father's death. Her counselling took place over 12 months, with a gradual increase in the time between the sessions. Teresa acknowledged that much of the work focused on growing up enough to realize that she could face the world and be successful without her father constantly by her side.

Rituals

A ritual is a purposefully undertaken event or activity imbued with a symbolic meaning. Every culture marks the end of a life with symbolic action, and archeology reveals evidence of prehistoric ritual surrounding death going right back to Neanderthal Man (Solecki 1977). Funerals perform several functions, including acknowledging the death, saying 'goodbye', celebrating a life and honouring the deceased. They are an opportunity for shared memorializing and recollection. In the best of circumstances, a funeral will draw family members together. Any experienced bereavement counsellor will be familiar with exceptions to this, such as cases where families have been unable to agree on arrangements and on the disposal of the remains. When this happens, family conflicts appear and existing schisms are widened. There is huge power in symbolic meaning, which helps to explain why grief rituals that can heal can also do harm and can complicate grief.

Case study: Helen

Helen had lived with Maurice for seven years. Although they never married, they saw each other as husband and wife, and were very much in love. Both had grown-up children from previous relationships. When Maurice died after a long illness, Helen was distraught, but managed to carry out his funeral wishes. Maurice had told Helen that he had lost his faith and wanted a secular funeral and a cremation. His daughter Kerry did not accept this. She believed that her dad should have had the funeral of his birth religion followed by a burial. Maurice had a brother, Dennis, who had emigrated to Canada and who came over for the funeral. He was happy with the cremation and asked Helen if she could scatter the ashes before he went home, in the woods where they had played as boys. Helen said that she was not ready to part with the ashes, and that when her time came, she wanted her own ashes to be mingled with those of Maurice and scattered on the moors where they had walked together hand in hand. Dennis returned to Canada upset and Kerry stopped talking to Helen.

This case study is fictitious; it would be unethical to commit such a true story to print. I wish I could say, however, that stories similar to this are rare. Fortunately, professional experience has also taught me that a funeral that to family and friends captures the essence of the deceased and that celebrates the life *as the deceased would have wanted it celebrated* can be of tremendous comfort to the family members. However, by the time a bereavement counsellor meets the bereaved client, the funeral is usually in the past and it has either been experienced as a unifying occasion or as a divisive one. Our clients will often seek our help in finding a personal or shared family ritual that they can perform, sometimes to ameliorate what the client feels has been missing. This may be to memorialize, for example by tree planting, fund-raising, or organizing an event, be it religious or secular. In recent times, having a tattoo has become a secular form of permanent memorial. Sometimes a client seeks a ritual to unblock a feeling of 'being stuck'. Commonly this concerns difficulties in visiting a grave. I may work for several weeks helping a client find the courage and opportunity for this. Similarly, the client may have difficulties in burying or scattering ashes. To many clients this means a symbolic farewell they find hard to bear. Clients may want to mark anniversaries. Lighting a candle is a traditional memorial ritual, so are flowers. Near to where I live, for ten years now, roadside flowers have appeared afresh on the anniversary of a road death. Sometimes family members and friends meet for a shared memorial ritual that celebrates the hobbies and interests of the deceased, perhaps a football game or a music night. At times the ritual is about symbolically 'letting go' and, to this end, one client put a message into a glass bottle, threw it into the sea and watched it float away.

My own position is not to be directive about rituals and not to give advice. It may help your client to discuss and reflect on possibilities; the message in a bottle came out of such discussion. There are books of ideas, one of the best being *Good Grief Rituals: Tools for Healing* (Childs-Gowell 1993). The charity Winston's Wish provides resources for children to support them in finding rituals that can heal.

Working one-to-one with the family in mind

With each client, we work to build a trust in which we learn the unfolding story of individual and family loss. I believe that we help the client more effectively if we understand his loss in relationship to his family. How free is he to grieve as he feels he needs to? How may the family be supporting (or impeding) his grieving process? What disloyalty to the family may he feel if he shares with his counsellor matters that he is unable to share with family members, particularly if he is critical of others he loves, living or dead? A client may find it easier, for many reasons, to talk to his counsellor than to members of his family. However, the family willingness to share thoughts and feelings will be central to coping with loss and returning to an even keel. Conversely, as Shapiro (1994) points out, if family members deliberately choose not to talk, to consciously hide thoughts, feelings and decisions from one another, there will be just as much of a cascading effect through the family as when members deliberately choose open communication. An important part of one-to-one bereavement counselling is to help the client better understand his family relationships and to help him communicate his needs to those close to him. As we see from Rolland's FSI Model, we need to listen carefully to our client's narrative of the progress of the illness, gleaning from this the family coping strategies, belief systems and communication style. From Gilbert's meaning-making model we need to recognize our client's personal reality in the context of the family narrative. When you hear your client's story – and he may need to repeat it several times – remember that he too is hearing new aspects of the narrative with each retelling, as he constructs new understandings of his grief and grieving. This brings us to the practicalities of gathering information: genograms and the button exercise.

Genograms

Children do not stay in their birth family forever. In most cases they eventually set up home with another person and may start another family. Each partner at the head of this family will of course bring their own self-with-others relational style, traditions and beliefs into the new family. Differences between each partner's response to a triggering event may be thrown into very sharp focus following a bereavement. Monica McGoldrick and Randy Gerson were responsible for standardizing the genogram, which they described as 'a graphic depiction of how different family members are biologically and legally related to one another from one generation to the next' (Gershen and McGoldrick 1985, p.9). We now look at the basics of drawing a genogram. Women are represented by circles and men by squares (see Figure 6.1). Deceased family members have a cross drawn through the circle or square (see Figure 6.2). Married partners are linked by a line (see Figure 6.3) and cohabiting couples by a dotted line (see Figure 6.4) and two dashes on the line indicate a divorce or separation (see Figure 6.5). A pregnancy is marked with a triangle (see Figure 6.6) and stillbirths are marked as deceased, with the diagonal line. Twins are joined at the parental line and identical twins also have a horizontal line joining them (Figure 6.7).

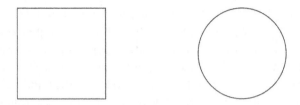

Figure 6.1 Symbols for male (left) and female (right)

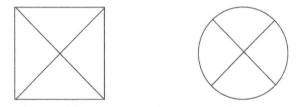

Figure 6.2 Symbols for deceased family members

Figure 6.3 Married partners

Figure 6.4 Cohabiting partners

Figure 6.5 Divorced or separated

Figure 6.6 Pregnancy

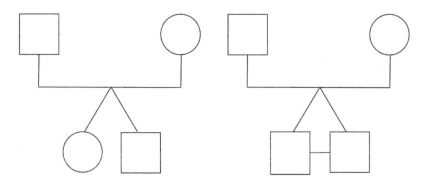

Figure 6.7 Fraternal twins (left) and identical twins (right)

The buttons exercise

Genograms provide us with the structure of the family and the interconnected relationships, but they do not tell us much about the nature and strength of the family bonds. An exercise with buttons is sometimes useful, both for the client, who can use buttons to explore family connections, and the practitioner who can use this as an opportunity to familiarize himself with the client's family.

The object of this exercise is to help your client reflect on his relationships with others in the family. It enables him to explore the closeness of different family members and to identify alliances and conflicts in the family system. This can facilitate new choices the client can make. It helps if you have the chance to practise this with friends and colleagues before working with a client. With a newly bereaved client this can be an emotional experience. If I believe it could be helpful I usually suggest that we carry it out in the next session. I want there to be plenty of time to complete it and I want to allow the client time to process the more difficult emotions before the end of the session.

The exercise requires a large dish of assorted buttons, such as you may acquire from a household auction, a car boot sale or an obliging relative. The greater the variety of sizes, textures and colours the better. Invite your client to choose a button that represents him. When he has chosen, invite him to explain his choice.

Next, invite him to choose buttons to represent his close family members. With each button, invite him to explain what it is about the button that represents his family member. In addition to his choice of buttons, he must decide how to group them in relation to one another and to himself. For example, he may place his button and his dad's button almost touching each other while his mother's button, although close by, is slightly further away than the space between him and his dad. I have known clients to position mother's and father's buttons touching each other, but with the children some distance away and some distance apart. Gradually, on the table in front of you both, family relationships are revealed. As your client works encourage him, using open-ended questions, to talk about his family members and his feelings towards them. Aunts, uncles and cousins can be added, as can members of stepfamilies. The exercise ends when the client feels he needs to do no more. A great deal of emotional material can be revealed during this exercise and the client may learn things he didn't know before.

Implications for practice within an organization

Within some bereavement services there may be occasions when different counsellors within the organization are each working with a member of the same family. If the bereavement service has a policy of shared confidentiality within the team, then special care is needed to maintain the confidentiality of individual family members. In contracting with clients we should be clear at the beginning of the work where it is our practice to share information about clients within the team, and our reasons for doing so. For example, in the service where I work, we employ a coding system for clients who have expressed suicidal ideation. This means that if a client telephones our service in the absence of his counsellor, we can refer to his notes and take measures to keep him safe. Within a family system, however, each family member needs to know that he can talk in confidence to his counsellor without other family members knowing what has been discussed. It is important to respect this confidentiality. If we and our client feel that the family would benefit by two counsellors discussing the processes of their respective family members, then we must only do this with the informed consent of all parties. I have been in the position of supporting a mother alongside my colleague supporting her child. The support for each has been helped by a shared professional awareness of the family dynamics, but only with the expressed permission of mother and child, in ways that never exceed the boundary of confidentiality any more than they need to. Nothing was ever discussed with my colleague unless I had my client's expressed permission.

The family sculpting exercise

Much of this chapter is highly theoretical. There is, however, a role-play exercise that helps students to get to grips with grief and family systems theory, not only at a theoretical level, but from a place of emotional understanding. As in any exercise in bereavement counselling training, trainers need to be explicit that students can opt out of any exercise and can take time out if it becomes too emotionally difficult. This activity can evoke a range of emotions and trainers have a duty of care to keep their students safe. It is particularly important to make sure that students come out of role at the end of the exercise. The exercise relies on having enough students each to role-play a member of a fictitious family, plus one or more observers of the process. Students who are taking part are issued with a self-adhesive label on which is written the name of the person they are role-playing. When the family is assembled, the students are asked in turn to read from a card that contains a short narrative of the character they are playing. When all the characters are revealed, they are invited to form a 'family sculpture'. Based on what they have heard from each character they put themselves into positions of distance and closeness from one another. This is quickly revealed to be a dynamic process that with family discussion (each player should remain in character throughout), eventually stabilizes into a pattern of relatedness. The observers are then invited to comment on what they have noticed, and the family members are invited to discuss how they've come to be standing where they are.

Now the trainer breaks some 'bad news'. One of the 'family sculpture' has died suddenly. The student role-playing this part is asked to leave the sculpture and sit down. The family players are invited to move in relation to their role-played needs. The dynamic process resumes as the players, watched by the observers and the 'deceased', group into new configurations in response to the death. Again they are invited, in role, to express their emotions, their changed needs and their motivation for moving into new family relationships. The observers are invited to reflect on what they see.

This activity is always powerful. Even when students are given the same scenario it configures in a different pattern every time. Allow plenty of time for everybody involved to say what they need to say. I would expect the activity to take at least 40 minutes and would allow for the possibility of an hour including discussion after everyone has finished the sculpture. At the end of the exercise be explicit about coming out of role. I invite students to remove and screw up the character name badge and to say out loud, 'I am not (name of character), I am (student's name).'

Below you will find the scripts of eight fictitious characters I have used several times, and Figure 6.8 provides a genogram of this family.

Family sculpture: the characters

Please feel free to use these scripts. You may wish to change place names to make the places more relevant to your setting. In my family sculpture it is David who dies.

Alfred

I'm Alfred, a time-served motor engineer from the days when engines meant British quality! I've lived in Malton all my life. I moved to this bungalow after the wife passed away, but I do OK, all things considered.

We had a boy and a girl. Our David married a lovely lass he met at university, had a kiddie by her, then ran off with his secretary.

And our Alison – the least said the better – I can't understand why she doesn't meet a man and settle down. She says that will never happen. Sometimes I think their mother's illness was due to all her carrying-on.

The only one I get on with nowadays is young Luke. He's got his head screwed on right – got himself a decent education and a job making British cars!

Mary

I'm Mary. I live just outside Leicester. Ron and I just had the one child, Jenny, who met her husband David while they were both at Sheffield University. When he left her Luke, their son, was little more than a toddler – bless him! Me and Ron, God rest his soul, had to give Jenny a lot of help. She was heartbroken. I love little Luke like I was his mum. Mind you, he's not so little now!

Alison

I'm Alison, sister to David. I tried not to take sides when David separated from Jenny. He had neglected her and Luke, but on the other hand she could have listened to how stressed he was. I liked Jenny, though. It's a shame that since she moved back to Leicester I've seen so little of her. I've regularly seen Luke though on the occasions when he came to stay with his dad and I've always tried to be a good auntie. Visits to see my dad, the cantankerous old so-and-so, are more difficult, but I do always remember him on birthdays, at Christmas and on the anniversary of mum's death. I don't think Dad will ever understand my sexuality. I live near York.

David

I'm David. I live between Malton and York and run my own agricultural supplies company. I've always worked long hours, perhaps that's what caused Jenny and me to start arguing so much. Amanda was my secretary, and was prepared to work long hours to support the company through lean times. Meanwhile all Jenny did was nag and whinge. I know looking back she was bringing up Luke with little support from me. But Amanda seemed to really care about me and the business. We just fell in love.

Just lately I've been getting headaches and chest pains. I haven't told anybody, even Mandy; I reckon it's just stress and indigestion.

Jenny

I'm Jenny, David's ex-wife. I live near my mother in Leicestershire, and work in a library. I've never remarried, although I have had a couple of longish relationships since David dumped me for that woman. When I've had a drink I will admit that I've never really stopped loving David. Luke and my mum are my life now.

Amanda

I'm Amanda, David's wife. I watch what I eat and go to the gym regularly so as to keep well enough to support my family. I still keep the books for the family business but otherwise I'm a full-time wife and mother.

Luke

I'm Luke. I've recently completed a mechanical engineering degree and I'm working for a company in the Midlands producing specialist car engine conversions for racing and rallying.

As devoted as I am to my mum, at times I have found her attention a bit claustrophobic and smothering. I've stayed close to my dad for all the time I grew up. Amanda, Dad's second wife, has always been great fun, and I rate her far more than I could ever admit to my real mother. I'm also pretty fond of Josh, my half-brother. I'm also very grateful to grumpy old granddad, Alfred. It was his shed full of car parts and vintage motorbikes that first gave me this enthusiasm for cars and bikes.

Josh

I'm Josh, I'm 11. When I leave school I want to play for Manchester United.

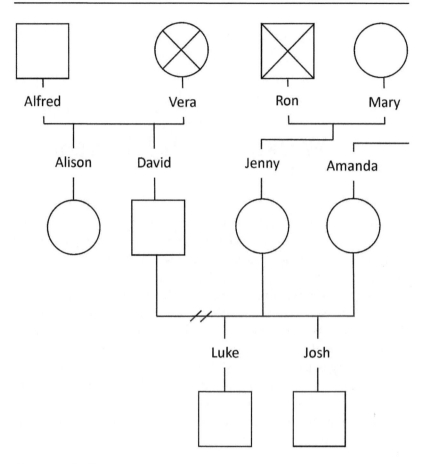

Figure 6.8 Family sculpture genogram

Chapter 7

Working with Difference

This was without a doubt the most difficult chapter for me to write, and it would not have been possible without my good friend, professional colleague and teacher Golnar Bayat, whose workshops I would recommend without reservation. Her contact details appear at the end of this chapter. I take full responsibility for what you read here, but the text has been overseen by Golnar and for this I am deeply grateful. Golnar is not only an expert in this field, with far more knowledge than I will ever have, but is also from a different culture to mine.

As caring practitioners we all have a duty to work with difference in ways that are moral, legal and ethical. In the UK the British Association for Counselling and Psychotherapy (BACP's) Framework for Ethics requires counsellors to practise with a sense of justice that promotes good actions and prevents harm to others. This requires that its members educate themselves and develop good practice in working with difference. Other professional bodies will expect similar standards from the membership. The onus is squarely on the individual to take this area of practice seriously.

Why it is so important to take culture into account?

When we meet a newly bereaved person it is both ethical and moral to take as little as possible for granted, and to use the first and subsequent sessions to glean what we can about the beliefs, values, customs and general approach to life this client will wish to communicate. Remember that she may be distressed and that she will be dependent on you to ask the right questions and make an accurate assessment of need. Recognize that clients will not approach their grief in isolation, but in the context of their culture, life experience and relationships, current and past. If, as will inevitably happen sometimes, you catch yourself making an inaccurate assumption, do chastize yourself, but learn and record it as a useful learning experience.

What do we mean by 'culture'?

The Oxford Dictionary defines 'culture' in terms of ideas, customs, behaviour and attitudes. We may also add values and beliefs to this broad meaning. The boundary of a culture is determined by the group that share these features, and in our childhood we learn about our culture by example more than through deliberate teaching. Perhaps each and every one of us takes our own beliefs, values and customs for granted and attributes 'culture' to others, rather like it is easy to see other people as having an accent or dialect whereas our pronunciation is the 'correct' one. Although most of the values and beliefs we grow up with have never been formally taught to us, they can bond us together as a social group. I would argue that important cultural differences even exist within what at first glance appears to be a homogeneous group. For example, in my early 20s I moved from the largely affluent South of England to industrial Yorkshire, at that time dominated by the coal and steel industry. I noticed subtle differences compared to my native culture, epitomized by the commonly used phrase, 'You have it to do.'

This phrase is usually added to the end of a conversation by one person telling another about the stressful tasks of daily living. It encapsulates the quiet acceptance by which traditional working-class communities approach life with an almost cheerful sense of resignation, since to do anything else would only raise false expectations and ultimately make things worse. I had experienced no equivalent sentiment in my early life. Now I have moved to a more rural part of Yorkshire and although I am only 50 miles north of my former home, I no longer hear this phrase. Even in this small geographical area I notice as I work with bereaved clients, clear differences in the cultures of rural farming Yorkshire, the cultures of the local market towns and the cultures of the coastal communities. The point I wish to emphasize is that cultural awareness is not something with limited relevance in geographical regions of limited ethnic and religious diversity; it is important everywhere.

Case study: Janet

Janet's adult daughter died following a riding accident. Janet was the wife of a farmer with a small dairy herd and with sheep on the higher ground. Janet had been born into farming, having left her own family farm when she married. From birth she had learnt the role and expectations of a traditional farming wife. Yorkshire family farming means a wide network of acquaintances who meet up at markets and auctions, but a tight-knit family circle who care for their own and expect little help from outsiders. After her daughter's death her sons and husband busied themselves outdoors, sometimes from dawn to dusk. Janet felt lonely but to turn to professional help felt disloyal. She felt herself growing apart from her husband but to discuss this with a stranger was an even greater taboo than seeking bereavement support. An extra complication was the matter-of-fact way that farming communities approach death as part of the cycle of life. Janet was confused that traditional acceptance that living things die when their time comes did not feel appropriate when her own daughter had been taken. Janet's husband, born of a long line of farmers, held the belief that feelings are best kept under wraps and certainly not talked about. He maintained the stance that after a death you put it behind you and move on. This belief was not helping him, but the effect on his wife was even more devastating. Only when she presented to her doctor with a severe grief reaction did she reluctantly agree to a bereavement counselling assessment.

Janet came to me for the initial assessment. My understanding of Yorkshire farming culture was limited to what I had learnt from counselling other members of this community. However, I had enough understanding to be able to ask questions and from a place of empathy anticipate the likely beliefs, behaviours and attitudes that were making her reaction so complex. I was able to reassure her and listen to her concerns about family loyalty without dismissing or minimizing them, so that she was able to make a choice about whether to take up the offer of counselling. An assurance of strict confidentiality was important. In the event she did agree to counselling. Her husband brought her to sessions, although he waited outside in his truck. Janet reported that he was relieved that she was getting help.

Greater cultural differences

We have explored subtle cultural differences as part of traditional white English culture. As vital as these differences are to the unique individual, differences based on sexual orientation, disability, ethnicity, gender and religion present other challenges, partly because we are very likely to make uninformed assumptions and display unhelpful prejudices about cultures very different from our own. In order to understand our personal and professional behaviour, we have a responsibility to learn to work with difference.

What is 'working with difference'?

We need to be clear about what is meant by 'working with difference', a chapter title that incidentally I have shamelessly plagiarized from one of Golnar Bayat's workshops. I believe that each word in the phrase carries its own vital importance and suggest we look at each word in turn.

Working

In this context 'working' implies deliberate, purposeful action taken through conscious choice, as opposed to automatic or reactive action taken without thinking it through. Part of the professional journey in becoming a caring practitioner involves being aware of our feelings, behaviours and actions. This is part of what Carl Rogers (1961, p.270) called 'congruence' and it is through engendering a sense of self-awareness of how we are in relation to others that we stay on course on this lifelong journey. Working with difference is hard work. We never stop learning how to do it and we never complete the journey.

With

This suggests a reciprocal process between us and others who, in this context, we regard as different from us in some way. Working *with* has the effect of positioning two people in equal relationship, as opposed to a one-up position, as, for example, was commonly assumed by anthropologists and missionaries in less enlightened times. I was struck recently by the judgemental tone of the child development scientist Jean Piaget, his ideas recorded in a 1929 translation of his classic book *The Child's Conception of the World*. Here he refers to 'primitive people' when describing tribal belief systems. It compares dramatically with the more respectful approach of Dorothy and David Counts in 1991. Interviewing members of the Kaliai people from Papua New Guinea about customs and the traditional expression of grief, they referred to one of their interviewees as a 'consultant' (p.193).

In the field of counselling, humanistic practitioners embrace the idea of working *with* clients rather than delivering treatment from a position of expert superiority. The value of working with clients as opposed to treating them is explored in a book by Arthur Bohart and Karen Tallman entitled *How Clients Make Therapy Work: The Process of Active Self-healing* (1999). The theme is also picked up in Mick Cooper's book *Essential Research Findings in Counselling and Psychotherapy: The Facts are Friendly* (2008).

Difference

Difference is usually conceptualized under what at first sight are clearly definable headings. We would have to live on a desert island not to be familiar with the differences that anti-discrimination legislation has brought into common awareness: ethnicity, gender, disability and sexual orientation are perhaps the most familiar. As we will see as this chapter unfolds, such conceptualization can complicate rather than clarify our view.

Practising legally, ethically and morally

If you and I were face-to-face at this point you may reasonably ask, 'What is the problem?' You would perhaps tell me that you are not racist, homophobic or in any other way discriminatory, and I would have no reason to disbelieve you. In fact it is very unlikely that you would be reading this book if you were overtly oppressive to others. However, if I gently suggested that you may nurse certain prejudices of which you are unaware, I wonder how you would react? I will stick my neck out here and say that each and every human harbours a host of prejudices and assumptions about those stereotypically different to themselves. Before you throw this book down in disgust and denial, allow me to illustrate my point with a real example.

Shortly after I had trained in bereavement counselling I was asked to provide support for a man bereaved of his partner. His address was a residential home and his date of birth, provided on the referral information, indicated that he was 93 years old.

The man I met left me feeling shamed about the prejudices I had nursed as I had driven the five mile journey to meet him. He was an educated, intelligent man, immaculately dressed and showing no sign of disability. Before he retired he had been managing director of an international British-based company.

As I drove back to my office I reflected that my expectations of a 93-year-old person were based on other nonagenarians I had met, including my infirm grandmother. I also realized that I had made a judgement about my new client based on his address. The point I am making is that I can be guilty of making assumptions about others often using tenuous information. Such judgements are unhelpful, to me and more importantly to the person I am attempting to relate to. Consider if such behaviour is, or ever has been, true for you, too.

The concept of 'difference' is a social construction

When any of us write about difference we must recognize that inevitably we write from a perspective that is socially and culturally determined. I write as a white English male with a level of education that breaks from my family tradition. My ancestral roots are firmly in the servant classes of Victorian and Edwardian England and in the rural labouring traditions of the 18th century. My ancestry, particularly as it affected my parents' and grandparents' values, has affected my own narrative perspective more than I would sometimes like to admit. I note this because I invite readers to reflect on how their own past affects their own personal constructs. Our ethnic and cultural background will affect both how we think and the meaning we construe in the words of others. Few if any readers will read what I think I have written, since the sense you make of the text will be determined by each reader's unique history and worldview. While some will read these words and nod in agreement, others will react less positively, yet the words you read are the same. The American academic Professor Bill Stiles has written eloquently about this phenomenon in a paper entitled 'Signs and voices in psychotherapy' (Stiles 1999).

Language also imposes a structure on our personal narrative. It affects how we think and feel about the world. Some years ago I sat next to Golnar in a university lecture and noticed, as one may expect, that she was taking notes in her first language. Then I noticed that although intellectually I should not have been surprised, it had actually aroused my curiosity, given her eloquent command of English. At tea break I asked her if she thought in English or in her first language, to which she replied that she could think in either language but always cried in her first. Any language has its limitations, regardless of our own familiarity with it. In English, for example, notice how few words there are to describe bereaved people: 'widow', 'widower' and 'orphan'. Historically, this suggests that other losses, such as losing a child, were so commonplace that they were not considered to have the importance of being specifically named. In traditional Chinese picture language, powerful meanings arise from the symbolism of this language form. In a chapter in *Spousal Bereavement in Late Life* (Carr, Nesse and Wortman 2006) Robert Neimeyer describes the traditional Chinese characters for widow, pronounced *mei mon yan* in Cantonese or *wei wan ran* in Putonghua (Mandarin). They translate literally as 'not yet', 'die', 'person' or 'she who is not yet dead'(Neimeyer 2006, p.233 citing Chan and Mak 2000), reflecting the traditional Chinese view of the value of widowhood. In reflecting on the cultural interface of the East and West in a Hong Kong bereavement counselling service, Brenda Koo and colleagues (2006) have reported how the label 'widow'(寡婦) can create a sense of shame and inferiority through loss of role identity and of the relationship of self to husband. Counsellors working with a widow from any culture would be wise to explore any meaning, implicit or explicit, in the client's perception of her changed status.

What model to use in approaching 'working with difference?'

Kai, Spencer and Woodward (2001) concluded that although health educators and trainers are keen to develop diversity training, they may have in the past received limited training themselves and they may have limited experience of delivering such training. As a result, although the subject is seen as important, many approach it with considerable uncertainty. Perhaps this explains the range of approaches I have observed first hand over the past 15 years. The titles I have given to each of the approaches below are my own and serve to illustrate the points I wish to make. In most chapters of this book the notes for trainers are limited to a discrete section of each chapter but here both trainers and students may wish to consider which of these approaches will best serve their purpose.

The deficit model

One approach is based on what I would term a deficit model of teaching and learning. This assumes an audience of people who belong to a majority group and who are deficient in their knowledge of a minority group defined by the exercise in hand. One example may be a tutor teaching about disability, with the assumption that through ignorance or maleficence the audience may unwittingly or deliberately discriminate against people with a disability. Of course, the tutor has no way of knowing how her words will be received. If she meets her audience in a workshop she could remain quite unaware of hidden disabilities such as dyslexia, epilepsy and hearing loss. Some of her audience could be members of a minority group and she risks patronizing them in her attempts to help. In other words, a deficit model risks the trainer making unhelpful assumptions about the audience, including an underlying, implicit assumption that many of the members are overtly or covertly oppressive and are in need of prescriptive correction.

A more political version of the deficit model involves the prefix 'anti' such as anti-racism and anti-discrimination. These models abound on the internet, with definitions, politically correct terminology and commonly the formula:

Power + Prejudice = Racism

I was first introduced to this formula in 1995 in a workshop very much based on a deficit model. My personal experience of this model, with its emphasis on combatting anti-discriminatory practice, is that many audience members are antagonized by what they see as an assault on their integrity. Such training can leave audience members with a sense that in spite of their best efforts they are by their own sins of omission guilty of discriminatory practice. That perception may be considered by some trainers as an unreasonable and defensive position taken by a privileged majority. In some instances overt racists and homophobes may well shelter behind crocodile tears of protest at this kind of training. I need to make it clear that I am in no way opposed to its aims; it is the mode of delivery and presuppositions I struggle with.

The 'celebration of difference' model

Unless this phrase is carefully defined we may all be left with little more than a warm fuzziness but no conceptual clarity. There is also the danger that the word 'celebration' can imply patronizing tolerance of difference rather than genuine acceptance of the benefits to a society that cultural diversity can bring. Acceptance demands respect for the values, cultural norms, beliefs and rituals of others. Most importantly it demands a personal and professional commitment to lifelong learning. Diversity is not just a feature of groups other than ours. We are all diverse and our uniqueness is cause for celebration.

The reader may find it helpful to construct a personal definition of the phrase 'celebrating difference'. Trainers may wish to turn this into a workshop exercise. To help the process, here are some key words:

- embrace, respect, unique, understanding, richness, open-minded, nurture, values, appreciation.

It is arguable that all organizations and institutions have a duty to take the celebration of diversity beyond the theoretical definition and towards actively pursuing its celebration. Schools, for example, are ideally placed to do this. Exploring practical ways of celebrating difference is outside of the scope of this book but this does not lessen the contribution that this approach can offer.

The 'starting with myself' model

This way of working with difference recognizes the uniqueness of each and every one of us. It invites us to explore the ways that our uniqueness affects us in relation to others, in particular those aspects of our difference that may not immediately be apparent. Very often we take our own differences for granted until our interactions with others bring them into relief. It can be tremendously helpful to explore this for ourselves using real examples from our own lives. With a little thought we can all recall times when somebody made a judgement about us based on a stereotype or false assumption. Once we begin to become aware of the assumptions we find others making about us, we will recognize the assumptions we make about others. This can set us on a personal and professional journey in exploring the nature of assumptions and the taken-for-granted perspective of our own cultural base. I make no secret of the fact that this is the model I feel most comfortable with, personally and professionally, as either trainer or student.

I think the 'starting with me' approach is best served if we take the time to reflect on our own experience. This is the story of how I met my friend and colleague Golnar Bayat, and whenever I am hosting one of her workshops I introduce Golnar with the following story.

Many years ago, when she and I were student counsellors, we shared the same placement setting in a university counselling service, a suite of counselling rooms in a converted hall of residence. On the occasions when we were both waiting for our next client, we would stand in the corridor chatting and comparing training notes, seeing as we were on different diploma courses. I very quickly noticed how pleasantly close Golnar would stand next to me, and the fact that she would periodically reach out and touch my arm as she talked. It did my self-esteem no end of good, especially at a time in my life when my confidence had taken a battering. Some weeks into this enjoyable 'relationship' I signed up to Golnar's 'working with difference' training. In illustrating how hidden cultural differences can manifest themselves in surprising ways, Golnar described to the group how differences in the distance we stand from one another in social interaction vary from culture to culture. Golnar pointed out how her own behaviour was regularly misunderstood by Western European men and that it was something that could easily lead to misunderstanding. My excitement at learning something new was tinged with regret at my misreading of the signal I thought I was receiving.

The lesson I took from this experience is that cultural difference has both an explicit and a hidden dimension. The explicit, obvious dimension includes language, dress, music, rituals, religious practice and so on. This, however, is just the tip of a very large iceberg, with most of the differences being hidden in beliefs, values and behaviours we cannot see. People from many cultures stand much closer to one another when they talk socially than is common in Western Europe and in cultures with Western European origins.

Recognizing difference

We have looked at a real example of cultural difference: that of space deemed appropriate between people as they talk. This is just one of many that are explored in Edward T. Hall's book *Beyond Culture* (1997). The examples that follow are also from Hall's observations.

Upset and misunderstanding can be caused by different concepts of time. In the West we become obsessed with accurate time-keeping and see it as a sign of good manners, assuming that this is a universal norm. The truth is that in many cultures time is a less rigid concept and it is acceptable to agree to meet people over a much more fluid time span. Subtleties in language can cause confusion, with variation in pitch and volume sometimes conveying very different meaning between one culture and another. A tone of encouragement in one culture may be interpreted as sarcasm or aggression in another, even if the two cultures share a common language. Non-verbal behaviour can be equally confusing. Eye contact, considered an aspect of good manners in some cultures, is interpreted as disrespectful in others. Gestures and body movements convey culturally bound meaning and as such are open to misinterpretation, as is the touching while speaking that I so clearly misinterpreted when I met Golnar.

Universal, cultural and unique

The encounter I relate above reminds me of the three strands we must all consider when interpreting the behaviour of another person, particularly if she comes from a culture clearly different from our own. First, we must consider the *universality* of the person's actions. In Chapter 1 we considered the proposition that grief is universal. We concluded that in all cultures there is grief, yet mourning is *culturally* determined. Likewise, eye contact and smiling in friendship is universal, yet in some cultures prolonged eye contact with a stranger or a person judged to be of superior status would be regarded as threatening or rude. We have already seen that personal distance in conversation is culturally influenced. At the same time there are individual differences in the behaviour of each of us, within our cultural norms. To put it simply, some people are just more friendly, trusting and approachable than others. Their *uniqueness* is expressed in their actions.

None of these three strands are more important than the others. We need to keep an eye on all three, and be careful not to assume that our familiar actions are universally accepted as norms.

Dangerous assumptions

It seems to me that the most dangerous assumption we can make is to interpret the culture of others from the perspective of our own. To return to an earlier example, the meaning I construed from a woman standing very close and touching my arm as we chatted was based on my own cultural view. To work with difference ethically, morally and legally is to learn to view the world differently and to be kind to ourselves for our inevitable mistakes along the way.

The kinds of assumptions we make vary greatly and Paul Pederson (1987) has helpfully listed the common ones as they will apply to helping practitioners. The principal ones are summarized below.

One biased assumption is to see certain behaviour as normal, and thus, by implication, there must exist a concept of abnormal behaviour. Our concept of normality is likely to be based on our cultural perspective, with no meaningful reality that will apply to everyone. A common assumption related to this that Western educated practitioners are likely to make is that individuality is a human universal and hence it is normal to support and attend to the needs of the individual. In truth, the greater part of the world's population doesn't think that way at all. The concept of the individual 'self' is not normal. In Hong Kong, health professionals Chun Tse and Samantha Pang report that following a diagnosis of a life-limiting illness, the family of the patient expect to be informed first, so that they can decide if the patient should be told (Tse and Pang 2006, p.174). In other words, the Chinese concept of self is relational. Brenda Koo and colleagues (2006) have noted that although there is a Chinese picture symbol for an individual person, 人, it is seldom used in isolation, as an individual is viewed in relationship to other. For example, 内人 represents 'wife' (the other symbol represents the interior of a house).

Another major East/West difference exists in the Western way of breaking reality down into discrete disciplines – scientific, religious and poetic truth – in ways that would not be recognized in the more holistically thinking East. Strict adherence to Western philosophy can limit our human understanding, as Fritjof Capra's (1992) exploration of scientific ideas from an Eastern perspective vividly demonstrates. Closely related to this is the Western view of reality as being invariably the result of cause followed by effect. Counselling outcomes are predicated on this belief. In Taoism, however, cause and effect are non-linear and are seen as interrelated aspects, the Yin and Yang of the same whole. In fact, some of the more recent aspects of grief research and theory suggest that rather than being bound by linear stage models of grief, it may help the bereaved person to be immersed in their grief and to trust a process where loss and renewal are integrated parts of one process.

Practitioners in the West are very likely to make assumptions about the benefits of empowering the client to become independent. From this angle the helper could easily minimize the value of the wider family network of support. In the organization where I counsel, it is considered best practice to find out the client's support system and to encourage its best use. In spite of this I could easily make the assumption that it will always be helpful if the client discusses intimate thoughts and feelings, forgetting that people from many cultures would see this as wrong. In fact I believe that we should broach the invitation to share intimate thoughts sensitively with all clients, regardless of what we perceive as their cultural background. More than one of my clients has at first felt disloyal to family by talking to me.

Paul Pederson has suggested that counsellors tend to focus on the present and in doing so neglect the past. This may be true of schools of psychotherapy that focus on the here-and-now. In contrast, although bereavement counsellors will invite clients to attend to their feeling, and emotions in the present, it is considered good practice to set this work in the context of the client's past, in particular childhood and past attachments. The evidence base for this stems from the work of John Bowlby (1969, 1975, 1980) and Colin Murray Parkes (2006). There is a case to be made for exploring the effect of family history on the nature of any client's grief. It is equally important to be aware that for some clients, tribal history, religious stories and ancestral accounts may be important in the linking of past with present. For example, family rituals based on traditional beliefs and practices may be an important part of the expression of grief. If your bereaved client has come from another country and is separated from family, this may restrict opportunity for ritual expression. Such denial of shared opportunity can greatly complicate the grieving process. You may be able to ameliorate this complication if you are sensitive and open to the client's cultural needs. Health practitioners need to be aware of the role that modern health practices may have in denying ritual expression. In some cultures, for example, family members will wish to attend to the body and will wish the body to be touched only by family, only by a person of the same gender, or by those with a shared belief. The family may be content for health staff not of the deceased's faith to wear latex gloves as a way of avoiding touching the body directly. People from any culture can be adversely affected by unhelpful assumptions. I vividly remember meeting one very distressed English mother bereaved of a child while she and her husband were living in the Far East. The body of her child was not afforded the care she would have received in the UK, due to the assumptions of nurses, doctors, mortuary staff and crematorium staff. Her distressing experience greatly complicated her grief.

Assumptions that derive from stereotyping

Earlier in this chapter I made the point that the categories of difference typified by anti-discrimination legislation carry the risk of complication before clarification. If we identify a client by her wheelchair use, ethnicity, sexual orientation or religion, we can find ourselves emerging with a stereotypical view of a group that we impose on the client. Such stereotyping is the basis of many a stand-up comedian's routine in which a minority group is singled out. Some comedians have a clear discriminatory intention that can have the effect of reinforcing prejudice against social groups (for example, there still appears to be an open season on older people even among those comedians who portray themselves as progressive) but others would claim that their intention is to gently point out human folly and make us think. Of course comedians have no control over the way in which their supposed good intentions backfire when stereotypes are reinforced rather than challenged. All of us are quite capable of stereotyping without any help, as I demonstrated with my example of the 93-year-old man in a care home. Stereotypes may encompass the group but they miss the person. On the other hand, if we have, as professionals, taught ourselves the likely pressures, prejudices and assumptions that a client from a minority group is likely to experience, this can be helpful. Knowledge of the lifestyle, values and beliefs that typify a group can also be useful to us. For example, when a gay client came to me following the tragic death of her partner, her sexuality was relevant to our work due to the homophobia she experienced from the investigating police officers and that compounded her grief. For other gay and lesbian clients, their sexuality has held no relevance to the work, and is no more recorded in my notes than would be routine mention of a client's heterosexuality.

Our awareness of the issues that are commonly faced by a minority group is important. Before I became a specialist in bereavement counselling I worked as a student counsellor and there I met Jane. Jane was a black student reading business studies. She had a history of examination nerves and she was coming up to her finals, the most important examinations of her life. She was clearly very able and at heart confident in her ability, but she worried that when she turned over the examination paper she would freak out and her mind would go blank. Jane was as puzzled about her fears as I was at first. We began by exploring her childhood. Jane grew up in a small, exclusively white village in an affluent part of England, with her mum, dad and brother. She and her brother went to a village school of all white children, where both of them did particularly well. On a hunch I asked if the teachers had ever been surprised by her ability and Jane reflected that they had, and that perhaps she had grown up with the inference that everyone is surprised if black children are clever. Then we looked at the cohort in which Jane would sit the exam. Jane would be surrounded by white faces. I don't know the true reality of our shared hunch. I do know that Jane relaxed, confident in her ability and revision skills, and that the examination went well.

If in doubt, should we ask?

None of us can possibly know about every aspect of every world culture. I have been in an audience when trainers in multicultural counselling have suggested that it is better to ask than to make false assumptions, which is true. However, please let me urge caution. Each of us is responsible for our own continuous professional development. Clients do not come to their counselling session or consultation to teach the practitioner about their culture. To expect this is in my view a form of exploitation and if we are charging them for our expertise, it would be reasonable for them to bill us for theirs.

Finding out what your client needs

Clinical assessment used to assess if a service is appropriate for a client's needs is covered in detail in Chapter 8. Once the client work starts, then there remains an ongoing assessment process, whatever her cultural background. It is hoped that you realize that a skilled practitioner learns how to get these answers using the core conditions

(Rogers 1961). In no circumstances should this become a checklist of closed questions on a clipboard. Rather, the skilled practitioner elicits responses from open-ended questions, for example, 'Tell me what you remember about the day that your mother died.'

The client's story

Listen to the unfolding story the client tells you about her loss. If the death was preceded by a long illness, invite her to tell you about the life of the deceased before they were ill, about the diagnosis, family reactions to the diagnosis and the reaction of the sick relative to the bad news. Gently and sensitively lead your client through the progress of the illness, asking open-ended questions about any changing family attitudes and beliefs. Explore family members' willingness to talk to one another and the effect this had on your client. If the death was sudden and unexpected, how have family members reacted?

Dominant message

However the death occurred, are you hearing a dominant family message, spoken or implied, that pervades the grief? Typical messages are 'Be strong', 'Pull together', 'Don't upset each other', 'Nothing can ever be the same', 'Intense grief demonstrates our love', 'Let's talk about it' and 'Let's not talk about it'. What sense has the family tried, perhaps unsuccessfully, to make of the loss? Janice Nadeau (2001, 2008) has conducted some important research into the meanings shared by family members following a loss.

Role of the deceased

Explore the role previously played by the deceased, first in relationship to the wider family, for example, matriarch, patriarch or pacifier and second, in relationship to your client, for example, confidante, guide or mentor.

Family history

This will include your client's childhood experiences and the predominant family values.

Family religion

In particular, explore your client's belief in relationship to the family. For example, she may secretly be renouncing some aspects of the family's beliefs and rituals that may be causing conflict. Religious affiliation can often provide a support system; equally it can become a source of conflict.

Moment of death

Was your client present at the death? If 'yes', is she glad she was? If 'no', does she regret that she was not? Was it important in terms of religion, culture or family tradition that she was present? In Chinese culture, for example, it is very important that the first-born son is present at his father's death (Koo *et al.* 2006).

Unfinished business

Invite your client to talk about any guilt or regrets about anything she has done or omitted to do in relationship to the deceased. For example, was anything left unsaid? Are there any actions or decisions that your client regrets or feels guilty about? Are there any family members that she is avoiding talking to and/or anything particularly that needs to be said? Are there ritual expectations you may be unaware of? Are any of these still to be completed? Are there any circumstances that are preventing this from happening?

The remains of the deceased

Was the body available to your client? In some instances the death may have been in a different country and she may not have been reunited with the deceased. I have known clients unable to be present at both the death and the funeral either for financial reasons or as the result of unresolved family feuds.

Did your client view the deceased after the death? Was the body mutilated by trauma or emaciated by disease? Did she have any part in the preparation of the body for the funeral? What effect did viewing and/or preparing the body have on her? This set of questions needs to be handled with great sensitivity. Your client may have been traumatized by the experience and you risk re-traumatizing her.

Be explicit that your client does not have to revisit this experience. If she chooses not to, make a note, as this may be significant as the grief counselling process unfolds.

Did the funeral arrangements happen as the deceased would have wished? Did they happen as tradition and culture demands? For example, Hindus in the West have to make compromises, witnessed by the moving account of Tanith Carey in *The Guardian* newspaper (Carey 2011).

Does your client visit the grave or the place where ashes are scattered? Is there an additional or alternative 'special place' that she goes to memorialize or commune with the deceased?

Notes for trainers

Perhaps the most important point to begin with is that membership of a minority group is not an automatic qualification to teach 'working with difference'. That said, tutors from a minority group may have experienced oppression, discrimination or false assumptions on a regular basis. Perhaps as a result, these tutors are likely to have given this subject significant thought. On the downside there is the chance that a tutor from a minority group may over-emphasize the work from her own position and so make unhelpful assumptions about other cultural and social groups. Within a course team, the course leader should select the working with difference trainer with full awareness of the assumptions she is making in the selection process.

Openness and honesty

This is part of good practice for trainers and practitioners. It is far easier to encourage open, congruent behaviour in our students by modelling such behaviour than it is to try to teach it from a theoretical standpoint while remaining in the role of an aloof, didactic deliverer of knowledge and skills. I exaggerate here to make the point. The so-called 'expert' has got to this point by reflecting on actions that did not always go so well but from which new ways of being were able to grow. I believe we should support our teaching with examples from our personal and professional experience, including some of our human fallibility, along the way. When we are teaching we are learning as well. I also believe that it helps the relationship with our students if in our teaching we try to maintain the core conditions throughout our class contact time.

Awareness of own culture and its effects

None of us can effectively teach this subject unless we have a good awareness of our own culture and appreciate how it affects how we think, feel and behave in relation to others; we all have a cultural background that is fine-tuned by our family history. I will illustrate this with my own experience, and urge you to consider your own cultural context as a trainer. My father and his father were both butlers in Cambridge University colleges. They attended with humility to the needs of some of the cream of 20th-century academia and knew many great people, albeit as their servants. My father believed that the clever and the wealthy were born to rule. He 'knew his place' and had no time for trade unionism, believing one could better oneself through individual effort rather than collective strength. This curious mixture of deference to authority and a belief that anything is possible with hard work is the legacy I have inherited. It underpins the English middle-class, educated and liberal culture to which I would appear to belong – the part of my personal iceberg hidden below the surface.

Deciding on an approach

The way of working emphasized here has a long record of demonstrable effectiveness, when judged by the course evaluations of many cohorts of students who have appreciated tutors working alongside them rather than addressing them from a position of superior knowledge. Of course there are cultural assumptions inherent in this position. We are concerned with Western-educated students here. My brief and limited experience of teaching a cohort of Asian and Eastern European students quickly taught me that they were confused by a collegiate approach, many of them communicating that it left them feeling unsafe. Much preferred was a clear demarcation between teacher and taught, and a need for the former to impart knowledge that should not be questioned. Tutors must take into account the cultures within the student group and should be willing to respond reflexively to students' needs. Students need the chance to explore their assumptions and the assumptions others have made about them by being given the opportunity to share with one another. They need to feel safe if they are to lay bare their feelings, thoughts and actions in the presence of others. A helpful exercise to begin training is to invite each student to recall and describe an event in her life when an unhelpful assumption was made about her. This introduces students to the idea that whatever our cultural roots, we have all experienced unhelpful behaviour from others based on unfounded assumptions made about us.

Resources
Websites for learning about grief customs and rituals across cultures

www.amemorytree.co.nz/customs.php A New Zealand obituary database with a section on customs across cultures and religions represented in the population.

www.egfl.org.uk A website provided for schools in the Borough of Ealing. Go to the website and at the top enter a search for 'funeral rights website', from where you can download a very comprehensive Microsoft Word document.

www.funeralwise.com A United States website with a very comprehensive list of funeral customs.

Further reading

Chan, C.L.W. and Chow, A.Y.M. (Eds) (2006) *Death, Dying and Bereavement: A Hong Kong Chinese Experience.* Hong Kong: Hong Kong University Press.

(Chapter 19 is particularly important, and essential reading for practitioners working with Chinese clients.)

D'Ardenne, P. (1999) *Transcultural Counselling in Action* (Counselling in Action series) 2nd edition. London: Sage.

Davis, D. and Neal. C. (1996) *Pink Therapy: A Guide for Counsellors and Therapists Working with Lesbian, Gay and Bisexual Clients.* Buckingham: Open University Press.

Lago, C. (2005) *Race, Culture and Counselling: The Ongoing Challenge,* 2nd edition. Maidenhead: Open University Press.

Lago, C. (ed.) (2011) *The Handbook of Transcultural Counselling and Psychotherapy.* Maidenhead: Open University Press.

Sue, D.W. and Sue, D. (2012) *Counseling the Culturally Diverse: Theory and Practice,* 6th edition. Hoboken, NJ: John Wiley.

Freelance training

Golnar Bayat BA, MA is a BACP senior accredited counsellor and independent trainer in cross-cultural issues in the UK.

Email: gbayat2@gmail.com

Chapter 8

Clinical Assessment in Bereavement Support

Before any client begins regular one-to-one support with a skilled practitioner, he should be assessed by a qualified and experienced counsellor. The guidance in this chapter is based on the procedure that has evolved over 20 years in the bereavement service where I work. It fits our purpose very well and we continually fine-tune it.

There are two elements to this assessment. The first is to determine if the model of support offered by the service is appropriate to meet this client's needs, and the second is to assess any risk factors that could arise when working with him. Some counselling services make use of clinical outcome measures, so that within the assessment session your client may also complete a clinical baseline measure using a standardized questionnaire. In general, an assessment can be completed in an hour, although I like to allow for the possibility that it may take 75 minutes and possibly even as long as 90 minutes if a questionnaire is to be completed. Occasionally, for reasons I will explain further into this chapter, the assessment cannot be completed in one session.

Where are assessments carried out?

The ideal place for the assessment is the space where future counselling sessions will take place, since this can help reassure the anxious client. It is also much easier to maintain confidentiality in a dedicated space familiar to the counsellor. In some circumstances, for example where a client is infirm or disabled, he may ask for a home visit. Quite often there are other family members in the house and finding a room to talk in complete confidentiality can be an issue. Home visits also carry personal risk.[1] In the past I have visited a farm with a dog on the loose, flimsy gates on stock pens and moving farm machinery. On another occasion I visited a block of apartments after dark, in an area known for its high rate of youth crime. The visitors' car park was poorly lit and I had to walk 100 yards carrying a briefcase.

Making your client feel comfortable

Remember that this may be the first time that your client has told the story of his loss and talked about his feelings with respect to the loss. He has probably dreaded this session since he received the appointment and very likely is frightened about how upset he may get in front of a stranger. At the end of many assessments, when a client has relaxed, he will admit to losing sleep fretting about meeting me for the first time. Although the assessment is about gathering information and agreeing an ethical contract, I would emphasize that the core conditions of counselling and the skills of active listening are never more important than in this initial session. This could be your client's first introduction to this form of support and you will leave a permanent impression. Meet and greet him with a gentle smile and introduce yourself with a handshake. Once in the counselling room, use your skill to help the client relax and feel comfortable. At this point many clients will begin to tell their story spontaneously. If at all possible, however, intervene gently with a very brief 'verbal confidentiality contract'. This means that before you invite your client to begin, you tell him that what he talks about will remain confidential providing that he does not mention harm to himself or other people. As you begin to listen to the client's story, summon all your active listening skills. Have no paper or clipboard between you and your client and give your undivided attention.

Hearing the client's story

An important question to ask is what it was that has brought the client to this assessment, and why now? Often clients cope for a while, until some event triggers a reaction that results in the client seeking help. The situation may be compounded by past and concurrent losses, or by events that have happened since the death.

---

1   Counselling services should have a lone worker policy and procedure that includes risk assessments for home visits.

As you listen to the client's story it is important to notice both the content of the story (1) and the way the story is told (2). The content will inform you of the likelihood that this client's grief will be complex or prolonged. The way the story is told will give you an insight into how the client is managing his grief (2a). It should also give you clues as to the readiness, willingness and ability of the client to form an effective therapeutic alliance (2b), more of which we will explore below.

1: content of the client's story

Chapter 1 gave the risk factors for complicated grief. In summary, reliable indicators are:

- sudden, violent and traumatizing deaths (especially suicide), and especially if the client witnessed the death or its aftermath

- deaths unexpected because of the age of the deceased, especially the death of the client's child

- deaths of people on which the client was very dependent/ co-dependent

- emotionally and geographically isolated clients with low levels of social support

- clients with a history of depression and/or neuroticism

- clients unemployed or underemployed, perhaps with attendant financial worries

- concurrent or closely consecutive losses and/or stressful life events

- clients for whom the relationship with the deceased had been difficult; this may include instances where the progress of the deceased's illness had resulted in personality changes (for example, as a result of brain injury or tumours).

As a general rule, the more of these indicators you note in your assessment, the greater the complexity of the client's grief. It follows from this that a client for whom many of these situations apply is likely to need an extended period of counselling with a skilled practitioner. As your client tells his story, use clarifying questions to get as much detail as you need in order to assess which of these risk factors are relevant. Remember, however, that you are not just compiling a mental checklist; you are helping a distressed and potentially vulnerable person share painful emotions that may not have been shared before. It is better to get a *sense* of his needs than a definitive record.

Trauma and grief

Some deaths involve trauma. This may seem obvious after a violent, sudden death, but other deaths, including expected deaths, perhaps following over a long period in which the loved-one's appearance has been significantly altered by the disease, can be traumatic, too. The client should be asked if they are experiencing any unwanted images or memories. In some cases a client may be so traumatized that he needs specialist support. It is unethical for any practitioner to work beyond his competence. If you are in doubt you should obtain written informed consent from your client to speak to a named professional about his care. Ultimately this may mean referring the client on to another service.

2a: How is the client coping with grief?

In hearing my client's story, I am trying to find out what coping strategies he has and what support structures he has in place, such as family, friends and social groups. I also want to find out about the client's cultural and spiritual belief system, including where he believes the deceased is now. Clients often get some solace in believing that one day they will be reunited with the person they have lost.

The way your client tells his story can give you an indication of his grieving style. If the client is unemotional and tells the story in clipped sentences with so little detail that regular prompts from you are needed before you can make sense of the story, this suggests that he is devoting considerable energy to maintaining control.

Case study: Kevin

The referral letter from Kevin's physician indicated that Kevin's wife Julie had died in her sleep from a previously undiagnosed condition. At the beginning of the assessment I invited Kevin to tell me the story of Julie's death. Kevin looked at me with a hint of aggression. 'Didn't my doctor give you the details?' he asked.

'He did,' I replied, 'but it helps if you can tell the story in your own words.' Kevin looked at me with some annoyance.

'I took her a cup of tea, tried to wake her and she was dead. What else is there to say?'

This account, based on several real and very similar examples from the assessment sessions of both male and female clients, is an extreme example of a *controlled* response to loss as described by Linda Machin (2009) and as discussed in Chapter 5. It is rare for clients as controlled as in this example to present for counselling unless they are there at somebody else's insistence or persuasion. If it is important for a person to cohtrol his grief to this extreme, counselling would not generally be the person's preferred option. At the opposite end of a continuum is the *overwhelmed* response.

Case study: Marjorie

The referral letter for Marjorie told me that her husband David died from a heart attack. Marjorie related that David was playing squash with his best friend when he collapsed. He was taken to hospital where he was pronounced dead. Marjorie told me in great detail how she suspected that David was not well, although he kept denying anything was wrong. She said she had caught him two or three times holding his chest and said that he had been overdoing it at work. She talked of her anger at him leaving her like this and of her guilt at not insisting he went to the doctor when he first got chest pains. Marjorie sobbed throughout the assessment and kept apologizing. She told me that she cried every day for a large part of the day and thought of David constantly. She told me that she felt life without David would always be pointless and in response to a direct question, indicated a belief that she would feel this way for the rest of her life.

While a short, unemotional account proffered at assessment is a reliable indicator of controlled grief, a client's detailed account is not in itself an indicator of overwhelmed grief. In addition to the detailed story, the assessor looks for overwhelming emotions, a sense of pointlessness and a belief that the future is and always will be bleak. With her colleagues Marilyn Relf and Nikki Archer, Linda Machin has produced a detailed guide for assessing coping styles (Relf, Machin and Archer 2010), based on the RRL model described in Chapter 5. This publication includes user-friendly questionnaires to determine a client's coping response.

Some clients are both overwhelmed and controlled (see Chapter 5). They assume a pessimistic outlook following the loss, but carry the belief that it is best if they bottle up their emotions rather than share feelings with others. Quite often, gentle questioning will reveal a belief that they need to remain strong, and that tears are a sign of weakness.

2b: Is this client ready, willing and able to use counselling effectively?

This idea was covered, with a case study, at the beginning of Chapter 5 but I would like to revisit it in the context of assessment. We meet a person who is referred for counselling in order to decide if what we offer will meet his needs. A counselling model of support is not a universal panacea for the grieving process. When I assessed Mary I asked her what she wanted from our service. She told me that she had lost confidence since her husband had died, and she found it difficult to leave the house on her own. Her daughter had lost patience and they had fallen out, leaving Mary geographically and emotionally isolated. Mary said that she needed somebody to go to her house for a cup of tea and a chat, somebody who could encourage her out of the house and perhaps go shopping with her. It goes without saying that what Mary was asking for did not fit a counselling model of support. Our service could not meet Mary's needs and in the course of the assessment I concluded that Mary could not in any case use a person-centred model of counselling effectively. To offer counselling to Mary knowing that in all probability it would be ineffective would have been unethical, but there was little doubt that she needed practical support. I was able to refer her to another charity that offered a befriending service. Mary got what she asked for and what she needed. The types of bereavement support that do not fit a counselling model include help with finances, help with transport and access to social groups. It is important that counselling assessors have knowledge of what other services, statutory and voluntary, are available in the locality. Models of counselling such as cognitive behavioural therapy (CBT) may help clients unsuited to more person-centred approaches.

Although I did not feel that Mary was sufficiently self-reflective and autonomous to be *able* to use counselling she was *ready* and *willing* to change how she was living and grieving. This could not be said of any of my clients on whom fictitious client Kevin (see earlier) was based. None of them were ready to make use of counselling at this point in their grief. In his inspiring book *Essential Research Findings in Counselling and Psychotherapy: The Facts are Friendly* (2008), Professor Mick Cooper cites James Prochaska's transtheoretical model (for example, in Prochaska, Redding and Evers 2008), which describes the stages of change a person must go through before he is ready to change behaviour, such as giving up smoking. Cooper (2008, pp.74–75) concludes that therapeutic interventions should be tailored to the stage of readiness for change that the client has reached. In assessing readiness for bereavement counselling I suggest that we should also take into account the findings of Henk Schut and colleagues (Schut *et al.* 2001). In reviewing the existing research into bereavement counselling efficacy, these authors concluded that routine referral to a bereavement counselling service was unlikely to be effective, and that self-referral, especially from people experiencing complicated grief, was more likely to be effective. My own conclusion, both from weighing up the evidence and from many years of clinical experience, is that a client's readiness to commit fully to a counselling model of bereavement support is a strong predictor of a positive outcome. This does not mean that clients should only be offered support when they are fully ready, since skilled and sensitive support not only meets the client at his current state of change, but can also guide and support him through all the remaining stages.[2]

The stages of preparation for grief counselling are, I would suggest, concerned with accepting the reality of the death, becoming prepared for the pain of grieving and facing the uncertainty of moving forward without the lost loved-one. Sometimes clients will refer themselves for assessment, not because they are aware that they need it but because their family has commented on their changed behaviour following the bereavement.

If it is clear to the assessor that the client is ready to make use of counselling, it is very likely that he will also be willing to enter into a therapeutic relationship. However, there are exceptions to this.

---

2   Prochaska's 'stages of change' are precontemplation, contemplation, preparation, action, maintenance and termination.

Sometimes the person in front of me is desperately unhappy in his grief and at their wits' end about what to do next. He will say things like, 'Yes I want to try counselling; I've got to do something. I can't go on like this!' and of course our heart goes out to him. We are caring practitioners and we want to help this person. However, before we jump to the rescue, we must be sure of his willingness.

It takes a lot of courage to sit in front of a stranger and share intimate thoughts and feelings, to cry and to release weeks or months of pent-up emotion. At assessment I warn each client that counselling may make him feel worse before it helps him feel better. I warn clients that at the end of some sessions they may feel exhausted, even distraught. Recently I had occasion to telephone a client shortly after the end of the session. She told me she was still in the car park sitting in her car in tears, yet during the session she had remained controlled and detached.

As we assess whether the client is ready and willing to make use of a counselling model of support, we must make a professional judgement about his *ability* to make use of counselling. Of course in practice these judgements are made concurrently, not in sequence, and they are made as part of the active listening process as the client tells his story. In deciding if a client is able to make effective use of counselling, we are making a judgement about her *psychological mindedness*. Research has shown that a client's degree of psychological mindedness is an important predictor that he will benefit from a counselling model of support. A psychologically minded person recognizes that he and others have what Cooper (2008) has called 'internal experiences' (p.74). In other words, he can see himself and others in terms of what drives and motivates people at a psychological level. During an assessment I listen for the client's ability to reflect on his feelings and on her behaviour: in particular how it was and how it is now as a result of his loss. If a client can give a coherent account of both his actions and his emotional processes, can describe the link between the two and can understand aspects of his grieving in psychological terms, then this is the evidence that I need in order to conclude that he is psychologically minded.

Here are two imaginary accounts of a conversation I may have with a client during an assessment, as I attempt to explore his psychological mindedness alongside hearing his story:

Client 1: Since Frank, my husband, died I've hardly been out of the house.

Counsellor: That must make life really difficult, and perhaps quite frightening?

Client 1: Yes.

Counsellor: (After a pause to see if the client adds any more) What do you miss about Frank?

Client 1: Everything.

Counsellor: Anything in particular?

Client 1: (Thinks) No, just everything. (Long silence) And my son Sean hasn't been to work since Frank died.

Counsellor: What do you imagine is Sean's difficulty?

Client 1: I don't know, he won't talk to me.

Client 2: Since Malcolm, my husband died, I've hardly been out of the house.

Counsellor: That must make life really difficult, and perhaps quite frightening?

Client 2: Yes, you're right, it is frightening. Sometimes I worry that I am going crazy. I've lost all my confidence, and when I do go out I feel I should be at home with Frank, silly as that sounds.

Counsellor: I don't think it sounds silly. You were with him a long time; perhaps you are getting used to the idea he isn't at home any more.

Client 2: Mmm... I watch the front gate for him coming home. I listen for his key in the door.

Counsellor: What do you miss about Malcolm?

Client 2: (Pauses to reflect) His sense of humour. I'm a natural worrier, but he could always put things in perspective. He'd laugh at me, tease me, but in a kind, reassuring way. (Long silence)

Client 2: And our son Michael hasn't been to work since Frank died.

Counsellor: What do you imagine is Michael's difficulty?

Client 2: He was always close to his dad, I think he just feels lost, and I'm worried that he is depressed and bottling up his feelings. I've tried to talk to him but he gets upset. I think he is trying to protect me from his tears. I try not to get upset in front of him so I can see where he's coming from.

The reader will have no problem working out which of these two imaginary clients is psychologically minded. Being able to reflect on one's own actions and the actions of others is central to the process of counselling, because this ability makes it possible to choose to do things differently. A person unable to stand back and see what he is doing and why he is doing it does not have this choice. The purpose of the therapeutic relationship is to increase the client's awareness of his psychological process in order to foster change, something that is only possible with the active cooperation of both parties. Some authors have argued convincingly that it is the client's ability to actively self-heal (Bohart and Tallman 1999) that makes the greater difference in counselling outcomes. There is some evidence that a client's self-healing ability is more important than the competence or experience of the practitioner (Cooper 2008, Chapter 5).

Before we leave this section on assessing readiness, willingness and ability, we need to consider one other aspect of the client's ability: psychosocial functioning. Cooper points out the general paradox of counselling for problematic experiences. At one level, the greater the degree of distress, the more effective counselling tends to be (pp.68–69). Schut and colleagues (2001) reach the same conclusions specifically to complicated grief. However, while this is true of presenting problematic issues such as grief, clients with underlying mental health difficulties, including high levels of psychosocial dysfunction, get the least out of therapy. Clients with certain kinds of personality disorder and clients with a dependent personality tend to do particularly badly (Cooper 2008, pp.69–70). In bereavement counselling it is a sad fact of life that those clients who, because of their emotional security, are least likely to need counselling to overcome complications in their grieving, would be most likely to benefit from it when compared with less securely attached clients, since securely attached clients form better relationships with their therapists (p.72). However, all is not lost. A skilled practitioner prepared to give time to a client with poor experiences of attachment, can sometimes build a fruitful and effective therapeutic alliance that can heal the client's grief. When we assess our clients we should be realistic about the extent to which we can help, and we should do our best to provide them with appropriate support competently delivered. Clients can be supported in learning to use counselling effectively and practitioners offering support should be active rather than passive and benign in our endeavour to help clients change. Thomas Attig (1991) has written a helpful and thought-provoking piece about the importance of counselling being an active process.

What do I do if I am unsure about whether a client is ready, willing and able to use bereavement counselling effectively? If I believe that he is not ready to begin facing the reality of the death, I will sometimes invite him for a second assessment and will negotiate a date for this, generally two or three months after the first assessment, to allow time for the natural grieving process. If at the end of the assessment I am still unsure about his willingness and ability to effectively engage in bereavement counselling, I will make an appointment for a second hour of assessment. It sometimes happens that the whole first session is taken up by the client telling the story of his loss, so that it is necessary to invite him back to complete the assessment. If I believe that the client is ready but I am not sure about his willingness or ability or both, I may suggest a small number of sessions with a skilled practitioner to see if he can be helped by what our service offers. Sometimes a client quickly develops a trusting relationship with his Bereavement Supporter and the success exceeds predictions.

There are times when at assessment the client demonstrates a normal grief, a secure attachment style, good psychosocial functioning and well-developed psychological mindedness. In these cases the client may just need gentle reassurance that in spite of the intensity of his grief, what he is experiencing is a normal and healthy process that will proceed quite naturally without counselling intervention. So that clients in this position feel supported and held in their grief, I will contract to telephone them on an agreed date and time to discuss their progress. Very often these clients need no formal intervention but they appreciate knowing that our bereavement service is still there if they need it and that we are available on the end of the telephone. A protocol such as this recognizes Schut and colleagues' (2001) finding, that counselling offered routinely for clients who are grieving normally is of no clinical benefit.

Assessing risk

The second element of assessment involves evaluating risk. There are two strands to this: 1. the client's risk to others, and 2. the client's risk to self.

Client's risk to others

When we assess the risk of a client harming people in our organization, we need to be realistic about the hazard as well as the risk. Risk is concerned with the likelihood that we will be harmed by one of our clients, whereas hazard is the potential for harm. Although the risk of being harmed by one of our clients is extremely low, the hazard is a very serious. Recently in Rochester Prison, Kent, UK, a prisoner held broken glass against the neck of a bereavement counsellor to hold him hostage (Hunt 2013). Bereavement service managers have a duty of care that includes asking referring individuals and organizations of any known risks that could arise from the behaviour of potential clients. It is also good practice for counselling rooms to have panic alarms and for no counsellor to work without colleagues close by and able to respond to an alarm. The risk may be heightened if the client is under the influence of alcohol or drugs. For this reason, at the initial assessment it can be very important to contract with clients that if they present for counselling affected by substance abuse they will be refused support on that occasion.

Client's risk to self

The common risks include substance and alcohol abuse, self-neglect, other forms of dangerous risk-taking and suicide ideation. I will also want to know of any specialist services involved in the client's care whether the client is making use of this. We will consider the risk assessment of each in turn.

By the time I get to this part of the assessment session I have heard the client's story. He will have told me if, based on his experience of the session, he would like bereavement counselling and I will have told him whether this seems appropriate to meet his needs. At this stage the paperwork begins and I also need to work through a checklist and it is important that nothing is missed.

Substance and alcohol misuse

I ask if the client has a history of evidence of alcohol or substance misuse. Sometimes clients find this hard to answer honestly for fear of being judged. Some regard as normal rates of alcohol consumption way beyond what is recommended medically. Clients will sometimes describe their drug use as recreational and not see it as a problem. I try to ask these questions in a way that will not leave the client feeling judged, with the hope that he is able to be honest.

Self-neglect and dangerous risk-taking

I want to know from the client whether he is caring for himself, including eating properly and taking any prescribed medication. I also want to know if he feels he is getting sufficient sleep. I will also ask about any history of self-harm, including cutting and burning. Then I check out in more general terms about dangerous risk-taking. One client admitted to driving dangerously early in his grief, not caring at this point if he lived or died.

Suicide risk assessment

It is common for newly bereaved people to fantasize about falling asleep and not waking up, to feel that they really wouldn't mind if an accident or illness took them. It is fairly common in the depths of grief to take this one stage further and consider ways of ending one's life. When asked, these clients will usually explain why they would never go to these lengths. Often this involves consideration of friends and family. When these clients are asked what stops them carrying out suicide fantasies, they will say things such as, 'I couldn't do it to people I love.' Passing thoughts of suicide, tempered by the effect it would have on others, are a feature of grief. It is quite another thing to plan one's suicide in detail and to gather the means to carry it out. At assessment it is important to ask these questions. It is a myth that asking a client about suicide can put the idea into his head. It is true that previous suicide attempts increase the risk of a suicide attempt. If a client talks in detail about suicide, it is important to move from the general assessment form (see Figure 8.1) to a detailed suicide risk assessment protocol. I am indebted to a colleague in another service, Sharon Cornford (Bereavement Service Coordinator at St Joseph's Hospice, London) for her thoughtful and compassionate work in suicide risk assessment. I would recommend her workshop. Dr Cornford teaches this formula:

> Intention + means + plan + risk factors, minus protective factors = level of risk

Detailed suicide risk assessment

Based on this formula, all services can construct a suicide risk assessment protocol based on the questions that follow the client's expressed belief that he does not want to go on living. If the client says this, he should be asked if he has intentionally considered taking his own life.

If he replies in the affirmative, his plan should be discussed with him and the assessor should determine if he has the means. For example, one client I assessed admitted to stockpiling over-the-counter medication by visiting several chemists to collect what he calculated would be a lethal dose.

A plan and a means should be taken seriously, especially if added to this are known risk factors, such as previous suicide attempts, mental health issues and a lack (real or perceived) of social support. Balancing this may be protective factors, such as a belief system that suicide is sinful, awareness of how it would affect others and trusted support structures that can keep the client safe. In discussion with this client as you complete the assessment together, you must ascertain whether the client can remain safe until his next appointment. Then you must decide if the client's doctor should be informed and, if so, whether this is by an emergency phone call, by a routine call or message within 24 hours, or by notification of a general concern within seven days. All practitioners working in this field should be aware of the systems, policies and procedures in place to keep potentially suicidal clients safe, and should be aware of the contact details of local supportive agencies and services.

Making a safety plan with this client

The plan should include:

- What will help to keep the client safe?

- Who currently knows how he is feeling? Who else could he tell?

- Who could he telephone to ask for help in a crisis moment (this may include friends and professionals such as the Samaritans)?

- Does his GP know how he is feeling?

- What would it take to want to live?

Completing the assessment

All that remains is to explain the nature of confidentiality to the client, including the ethical and statutory limitations. In the UK this includes obtaining a signature from the client under the terms of the Data Protection Act 1998, giving the counselling service permission to keep records on a computer system. In our service our ethical limit to confidentiality concerns the client's suicide risk. As discussed above, our client must agree that we contact the appropriate doctor or medical centre if we judge it to be necessary. Legal limits to confidentiality will vary between nations and states, but there will be similarities, based on the general principle that confidentiality will be breached if there is a credible risk that the client, or somebody known to the client, will harm others. In the UK there are statutory limits to confidentiality covered by the protection of children and vulnerable adults, by anti-terrorist legislation and by serious crime involving drug trafficking. Clear guidelines are issued by the BACP on Information Sheet G2 (Bond and Mitchels 2010), free to members. Figure 8.1, a sample assessment form, includes space for a checklist of tasks completed during the assessment.

Providing the client with feedback

At the end of the assessment it is important to share with the client the conclusions you have reached and what actions you suggest. It is also valuable to share how you see the client to be coping, what strategies he has at his disposal and how he can best move forward.

Whatever you choose to say at the end of the assessment should be recorded on the assessment form.

CONFIDENTIAL

Anytown Bereavement Support Service

Assessment form

Client Name: Date of birth: Case code:

Preferred name: Telephone no: Is it okay to leave a message? Yes No

Assessment date:

Doctor and surgery details:

Name(s) of other professionals involved in the client's welfare:

Information check list   I have explained to the client:

What our service offers

How we evaluate the service

Confidentiality and limits to confidentiality

Signature obtained to keep computer records

Consent form signed to liaise with other named professional

I have explained the Service policy on cancellations and missed appointments

1. What has brought the client now? (recent/past losses, nature of the death, story of the loss)

2. How is the client coping? (Strategies, support, inner resourcefulness, religious, cultural and spiritual beliefs?)

3. Risk assessment

3a Has the client considered ending their life? Is there any history of suicidal behaviour?

No risk   Low   Medium   High risk (please circle one)

*If client at risk, complete detailed suicide risk assessment

3b Does the client have a history of self-harm, alcohol or substance misuse? Please specify:

3c Is the client involved in dangerous risk-taking or self-neglect? Please specify:

Figure 8.1 Sample assessment form

4. In your professional opinion, in what way is this Service appropriate to meet the client's needs? If our service is not appropriate, what needs is this client telling you they have?

5. Is there any trauma associated with the client's grief? (unwanted images and/or memories)

6a Other significant details such as eating and sleeping problems, client's isolation or other important factors not mentioned elsewhere on this form?

6b Relevant medication, e.g.antidepressants

7. Verbal feedback given to the client:

Outcome: Yes   No   Not appropriate   Pending client's decision
*Please circle one
Client's availability:

Male or female support requested?
What does the client tell you (s)he wants to get from support?

Any other action required? e.g referral to another professional or agency
                     second assessment needed
                     telephone call to client arranged on (date and time):

Signature of assessor:
Time and date:

Figure 8.1 cont.

What does the client want from support?

You will notice this question on the specimen form (see Figure 8.1). Record what the client tells you as accurately as you can. Asking this question helps the client to take control, and gives him a shared ownership in the decision-making.

Concluding thoughts

As I read this chapter, with all its complexity, I find myself amazed that my colleagues and I are able to gather so much information and complete ethical contracts with the client in the space of an hour. Yet because of our experience as counsellors we are able to do this on a daily basis, and do it in such a way that we leave clients more relaxed and more reassured than at the start of the process. Many clients find that they gain enough from this process to feel that their grief is following a normal pattern and that they do not need further support.

Notes for trainers

I cannot emphasize enough how important it is for those doing initial assessments to be both experienced and properly trained. Some people referred to bereavement counselling are at risk of self-harm, including suicide, and it is unethical for a service or a training course not to take this into account when allocating clients, either to trainees on placement, or to inexperienced practitioners. A mistake could quite literally be a matter of life or death. I have witnessed first-hand students on a counselling course given free rein to find a placement and then being allowed to assess clients with minimal training and then go on to work with them – very possibly beyond the competence that their minimal experience would suggest. It is unethical for any counsellor to work beyond his competence, and it is a mark of professionalism to refer on clients that one feels unqualified to work with. Trainers should make it very clear to students that a grasp of this chapter is not in itself sufficient to go out and begin assessments, and that considerable counselling experience should be part of the training needed to assess clients. It should also be made clear to students on placement that it is good practice for an experienced and appropriately qualified practitioner to have assessed the student's clients before counselling begins. Any standard short of this puts both client and trainee at risk.

Chapter 9

Personal and Professional Development

So you want to work with loss and grief?

Of all the counselling I have done, grief work is the most rewarding, in large part because of the positive changes that bereaved individuals can achieve when they commit to this therapeutic relationship. At least 99 per cent of the time I see my clients getting colour back into their lives. So often I am in awe of their courage and resilience. I am filled with admiration at how hard some of them work in the therapeutic space, and I see what they share with me as a huge privilege.

Bereavement counselling is never easy. It is demanding by its very nature. Each client should expect your total engagement, however emotionally laden and distressing the narrative she brings to you. Then just minutes later you may be engaged with another client, with equal attention and the same active use of the core conditions. You also have the task of caring for yourself so as to be fully available for each new client. This is far from easy unless you know what makes you tick, and what draws you to the work. Remember that all person-centred counselling involves congruence, which is to be authentic with clients rather than in some kind of professional role. I believe that nowhere is this more important than in grief work.

Competent practitioners in bereavement support possess both knowledge of the subject and skills of active listening. They also have a thorough understanding of their own drives and limitations and have learnt to integrate the personal and professional self. Most importantly they accept that they will never stop learning: about bereavement and loss, about other people and about themselves. What follows is the content of the personal and professional development workshops my colleagues and I have used to train Bereavement Supporters for more than a decade. Our workshops are constantly being updated and refined: The competent trainer accepts that she or he will never stop learning either.

The remarkable human brain

We take most of our cognitive and affective processes for granted, and if you stop to think about this, why would it be any other way? The human brain is the most powerful and sophisticated structure in the known universe. It comes with one primary function: to keep our body safe, enabling us to thrive and play a part in producing and maintaining the next generation (Immordino-Yang and Damasio 2007). The last thing we need in a crisis is a brain that takes time and energy to operate; we just want it to do its job and get us out of trouble. Our brain has an additional important function, which is to network with other human brains in our vicinity (Cozolino 2006). This enables us to make shared decisions and to socialize with others, something we do best if we can imagine the internal processes of those around us. We call this imaginative skill 'empathy'. Zoologists who have observed chimpanzees hunting in a family group report the remarkable ability each of the family has in anticipating the movements, both of their quarry and the other chimpanzees. The group hunts as one, something I suspect our human primate ancestors could do, too. Empathy plays an important part in the survival of our species and we become competent in understanding the mental processes of others when we understand our own. In spite of our ability to think, feel and respond quickly by acting outside of full awareness, each of us has the capacity to experience our own thoughts and actions. The journey towards becoming a helping practitioner requires us to equip ourselves with expertise in our own cognitive and affect processes. One way forward is to study our own learning cycle.

Kolb's learning cycle

Cyclical models of experiential learning owe a debt to David Kolb's learning cycle (Kolb 1984). Kolb was inspired by the work of John Dewey, Kurt Lewin and Jean Piaget and his learning cycle has permeated higher education and vocational training to the present day. I first met the concept of experiential learning, or 'learning by doing', when I

SUPPORTING PEOPLE THROUGH LOSS AND GRIEF

was training to be a teacher more than 40 years ago. Educationalists of the time made liberal use of a popular Confucian aphorism that reads, 'I hear I forget, I see I remember, I do and I understand.' As we shall explore in this chapter, although *most* people learn *most* tasks best by practical activities, *some* people learn *some* tasks best by other means. Effective learning, as Kolb demonstrated, involves more than just completing a task; it involves observing one's own actions and reflecting on them. Figure 9.1 is a simplified version of Kolb's learning cycle, which I have included to illustrate the source of the three-stage TEB cycle (Bohart and Tallman 1999, p.202).

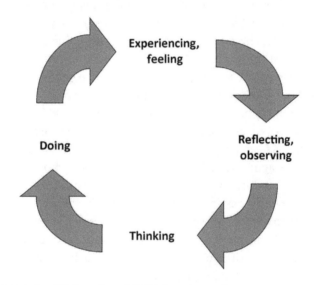

Figure 9.1 A simplified version of Kolb's learning cycle

Thinking, experiencing, behaving: the TEB cycle

In the teaching pack, *Bereavement Counselling: A 60 Hour Introductory Training Course* (Faulkner and Wallbank 1998) the authors built their training around a feelings, thoughts and actions (FTA) model. As a trainer I used this successfully for several years before discovering the therapeutic approach of Arthur Bohart and Karen Tallman (1999). It made sense to me to integrate the principles of Kolb's learning cycle, Faulkner and Wallbank's approach and Bohart and Tallman's description of therapeutic learning into a model of teaching and learning for trainee Bereavement Supporters. I owe much to Faulkner and Wallbank's teaching pack and the principle of the FTA and TEB models is essentially the same. The TEB cycle, be it either with bereaved clients attempting to relearn their world or with trainee counsellors, consists of three interrelated ways of learning new knowledge and skills. It works like this: I try approaching a task in a way I have not tried before; I reflect on how it went; and I learn from the experience (see Figure 9.2). Alternatively, I may start by thinking about a recent experience, reflect on it and decide that, learning from the experience, I will approach it differently next time. From the point of view of helping our clients, different therapies focus on different parts of the cycle. Psychoanalysts are primarily interested in helping clients towards reflecting on and understanding the self and secondarily on experiencing. Humanistic counsellors are primarily interested in experiencing and secondarily in thinking. Cognitive therapists are primarily interested in thinking and behaving. Behavioural therapists focus on behaving and experiencing (Bohart and Tallman 1999, p.202).

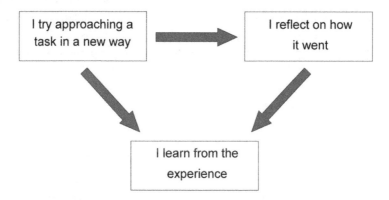

Figure 9.2 The TEB Cycle

Experiencing

This involves becoming aware of the world around us and our place in it. In doing so, we interact directly with our internal and external environment. We notice our bodily sensations including our emotions. This is also the most basic form of 'knowing' and sometimes exists without needing to be conceptualized in language. We 'know' when something is good (just as we know when something is bad, frightening, evil and so on) without needing to explain it. In the course of our busy lives, pure experiencing can be put on the back burner. We may need to make time to fully experience our world. A useful aspect of training counsellors is to begin each taught session with a round. Each course member is invited to say her name and then to say just how she is feeling in the here-and-now. It is surprising how difficult it can be to contact our immediate feelings when we are surrounded by internal and external distractions, but this is very good practice for the demands that this work makes on us.

Thinking

We can use thinking to observe our here-and-now experience as in the exercise mentioned above. Awareness of what is happening in the moment also allows us to reorganize our actions. For example, if I notice that I feel tired or distracted in a task, it may help to take a short break, to do something else for a time and return refreshed. There may be times when I reflect that I mishandled an experience, and in my head I can rewind and play the scene again ('What I *should* have said is…'). By the same token I can visualize alternative scenarios ('What if?' situations) and can 'thrash out' imagined situations in a dialectical exchange with myself. Thinking creatively about experiences expands my choices.

Behaving

Thinking creatively about our experiences in the moment allows us to be more choiceful in our behaviour rather than the alternative, which can be summed up as 'flying on autopilot'. With enhanced awareness comes the possibility of experiment and practice. Once we summon the courage to risk doing things differently, we can evaluate our choice and reflect on the outcomes. With practice and by deliberately developing the habit, we can constantly be modifying and fine-tuning our behaviour.

Case study: Susanne and Mavis

Following the death of her father, Susanne finds it difficult to explain her grief and her ambivalent feelings about Dad to her mother Mavis. Susanne explores her frustration with her counsellor, and in doing so, reflects that Mum is grieving a husband of many years. Susanne discusses this further and reflects that some of her mother's self-centredness is understandable in the circumstances. With further reflection and discussion, Susanne concludes that in spite of making this allowance, she does not feel that her mother has listened to her needs and begins to feel angry. She decides with her counsellor what she is going to say to her mother and summons all her courage. She and Mavis have a constructive conversation. Mavis says she is sorry for not having time for her daughter, and promises to listen to her grief so that they can share feelings.

Notice that Mavis also went through the TEB cycle when she experienced an upset daughter being very honest. We all go through this cycle many times every day, often without even noticing it.

Case study: Susanne and Mavis 2

During her counselling with you, Susanne expresses anger towards her mother, whom it seems is so preoccupied with her own grief that Susanne feels that her own grief for a much loved dad has been discounted. You recognize the value of empathy and of remaining non-judgemental with your client, but you reflect that to do so in this instance may reinforce Susanne in the mistaken belief that her mother is genuinely discounting her grief. You decide that instead of taking a passively empathic position, you will challenge your client. Very gently you invite Susanne to consider what it must be like to lose a husband after 30 years of marriage. Susanne is thoughtful about this. You experience a sense that your intervention was appropriate. Susanne says that while she acknowledges that she has not been entirely fair, Mavis does have a tendency towards self-centredness, and that she will discuss this with her mother. You reflect that this is the time to reinforce and validate your client's choice and you communicate this to her by helping her practise what she can say in a way that will be well received.

Since the likely reason you are reading this chapter is because you intend to become the helping practitioner, it is important that you consider what part of the TEB cycle you feel safest with: *thinking* (*absorbing facts, reasoning*), *experiencing* (*feeling, reflecting*) or *behaving* (*action, doing*). Would you agree with me that your answer is likely to be significant in how you would approach learning to do this work?

The role of a bodily felt shift in the TEB cycle

Sometimes we know what we should do, but nothing seems to change. Bohart and Tallman discussed the importance of a 'bodily felt shift'

(1999, p.220). Your client may say, 'I know what to do, but it's easier said than done.' A cognitive understanding is not enough. Only when your client *feels* what she needs to do does she change her behaviour. We as practitioners have our many blind spots, too. There may be many things about ourselves that we want to change, and as many reasons for remaining the same, particularly if the desire to change is more intellectual than emotional. However, as Henry Ford is attributed as saying: 'If you always do what you've always done, you'll always get what you've always got.' One reason that many trainee counsellors choose to go into therapy as part of their personal and professional development is because the experience allows them to 'know', at both a cognitive and an affective level, how they would like to behave differently in the world. Of course, with the best will in the world, we have no possibility of changing any aspect of our behaviour that is outside of our awareness. If you decide to develop personally and professionally, it may help to learn more about yourself. There are a number of ways of doing this. What follows is an account of the ways my colleagues and I help our students in this journey.

Learning more about ourselves
1: keeping a reflective journal

A very personal way of monitoring your own TEB cycle is by keeping a reflective journal. Nobody can tell you exactly how to do this, since by definition it is personal. There are, however, some guidelines I can offer you. First, you have to have *ownership* of the journal, which is about understanding what you want to get out of it. Tutors on counselling courses are particularly fond of students' journal keeping, with the result that some students keep a journal mainly to satisfy the requirements of the assessed course work. I believe a journal should never be assessed or graded as an assignment. I would even go so far as to say that a tutor should not expect to see your journal. If you feel it will be seen, even judged, by others, you cannot write what you like and you may end up censoring your own content, which entirely defeats its purpose as a tool for personal growth and development. To take ownership of your journal you need to be clear about what you want to get out of it. My own therapist talked regularly about my 'growing points' and it took a very long time to fully understand what she meant. If you look at a growing plant you will see that there are various points on the stem from where the plant can put out new growth, usually at the junction of stem and existing leaves. We, too, have growing points but ours are in our brains. These are the cognitive and emotional places where an awareness of new ways of thinking and behaving start to emerge. As discussed earlier, we experience these growing points as the felt bodily shift described by Bohart and Tallman and often these are very emotional moments. Our clients sometime report these as the moment of realizing 'I can't go on like this', and readiness to change is established (see Chapters 5 and 8).

If you choose to keep a journal and you take ownership of the content, life does not have to reach a crisis point before you make the decision to do things differently. I can attest to the value of finding a quiet, safe space, switching off 'autopilot', and then stopping and resting with a favourite pen and a notebook you have chosen for its design, its quality and luxury, even its smell. Once relaxed into a state of awareness we are ready for the quality of *experiencing* described in the TEB cycle earlier in this chapter. We may contact experiences earlier in the day or the day before, replay them, explore the feelings they have left us with and make decisions about how to behave in the future. Kept wisely and with complete ownership, a journal can be your place to record your unique process of growth and development in whatever way you choose to do it. Some aspects of this journal may be about our personal development, and other aspects may be about our professional development.

Learning more about ourselves
2: daring to receive feedback from others

One of the best ways to learn about ourselves is by asking for feedback from others. The Johari Window (see Figure 9.3), named after its creators Jo Luft and Harry Ingham, is an effective and structured way to achieve this. In an entertaining description of this idea (Luft 1961), Joseph Luft begins his explanation of the model with the story of a happy centipede who is getting along just fine, just as we all do so long as life is not presenting us with a challenge. As you can see, the model resembles a window with four panes of glass. You are invited to write into each quadrant as much as you know about yourself. Quadrant 1 refers to your behaviour and your motivation that is known to yourself and to others. Quadrant 2 is the part of you that others can see but to which you are blind. Obviously you cannot complete this unless and until you ask others to tell you. Quadrant 3 contains the things that you know about yourself but that, for your own reasons, you choose to keep hidden from others. It may take a lot of courage to write these things down if you think somebody else is going to see them. Quadrant 4 are unknown behaviours and motives, about which Luft says, 'We can assume their existence because eventually some of these things become known.' By finding out what is in quadrant 4 you may discover how these things affect your relationships with others.

If we are trusting enough to be deliberately open with others – to share stories, experiences, feelings, fantasies, desires and so on – then quadrant 1 begins to move into quadrant 3 as less things about ourselves are hidden from others. If we trust enough to ask for feedback and others offer it, we encroach on our blind area as we learn from others what they can see in us. The open area of quadrant 1 continues to grow as quadrants 2 and 3 shrink. The process can become reciprocal; as we learn more about ourselves we learn about others. *My* hidden area and *your* hidden area both get smaller as a result. Both of us will be helped in this if we are prepared to be more mindful and less numb in our relationships with others. Joseph Luft ends his story back with the centipede: 'A centipede may be perfectly happy without awareness, but after all, he restricts himself to crawling under rocks.'

	Known to self	Not known to self
Known to others	1. Area of free activity	2. Blind area
Not known to others	3. Avoided or hidden activity	4. Area of unknown activity

Figure 9.3 The Johari Window (Luft 1961, p.6)

Learning more about ourselves
3: drawing your lifeline

In Chapter 1 I described my childhood experience of the death of a mouse that I had befriended. In the same chapter I outlined the importance of the developmental and circumstantial losses that shape our lives, and how small losses prepare the way for greater ones. As we learnt from Chapter 3, the nature of our childhood gives us our attachment style and our sense of how we are valued by others. Each event in our life and each interaction with another person informs who we are and determines who we become. From the sum of our experiences we construct a continually changing narrative of our life, for better or worse. Take a large sheet of paper and on it draw a simple representation of a path or a road to represent your life. Mark significant events, perhaps with words and pictures. Do you notice losses along the way? Do you notice events that did not seem significant at the time? Maybe you can represent these events as forks in the road. Mark where you are now and continue the path into your future where there may be anticipated events. A refinement of this exercise, which I have based on an original exercise by Faulkner and Wallbank (1998), is to chart your life stages by listing memorable events under the following headings:

- preschool years

- 5 to 7 years

- 8 to 11 years

- 12 to 16 years

- young adult

- adult pre-parenthood

- parenthood

- parent of adult children

- grandparenthood.

Your earliest memories may be patchy, so you may need to draw on photographs and on the accounts of family members. One important part of completing this exercise is to consider the extent to which it helps your empathy with others if you are at the same life stage as your client, or have experienced your own version of her current life stage. If you have no direct experience of this, may it help if, as part of your personal and professional development, you have taken time to construct your understanding of life stages by spending time in conversation with others who are older than you? Research suggests that the age of the therapist has little or no effect on counselling outcome, but there is some evidence that where the therapist is more than ten years younger than the client, outcomes are not as good as when the counsellor and client are of similar age (Cooper 2008, p.87). There is also some evidence that counsellor/client age matching matters most to clients under 30 (p.87). Perhaps we can mitigate these effects if we take the time to develop an empathy based on recollecting our past experiences from our life journey.

Learning more about ourselves 4: personal attitudes and beliefs about death and loss

How do you feel when you watch television documentaries about death and dying? Do you carry an organ donor card? Have you made a will? Does your family know how you would like your funeral to be? What would you say was your personal attitude to ageing and death? These are just a few of the questions to ask yourself if you are considering specializing in this field. The Reverend Peter Speck is Honorary Senior Lecturer at the Cicely Saunders Institute at King's College, London. He is a researcher and former hospital chaplain and has for many years specialized in palliative care. In the teaching pack *Bereavement Counselling: A 60 Hour Introductory Training Course* (Faulkner and Wallbank 1998), Peter Speck is quoted as describing four different attitudes to death. The four attitudes are *death defying, death desiring, death denying* and *death accepting*. Death defying people are those who fight and rage against the possibility of death, epitomized by the poem of Dylan Thomas entitled 'Do Not Go Gentle Into That Good Night' (Thomas 1952). This contrasts with the poem 'Ode to a Nightingale' by John Keats (Keats 1985, first published 1819), which Speck describes as a death-desiring attitude. In the poem Keats almost seems to court death. When Peter Speck talks of a death-denying attitude, he is not talking of the denial stage of grief but of the modern attitude towards ageing and death. In the West we live in a culture of prolonged youth, in which Botox treatments and invasive cosmetic surgery are for many normal practice in order to keep ageing and death at bay. Contrast this with a death-accepting attitude. The approach taken by Dame Cicely Saunders, founder of the modern hospice movement, does perhaps encapsulate death acceptance. Her famous quote, 'You matter to the last moment of your life, and we will do all we can, not only to help you die peacefully, but to live until you die,' continues to appear in the mission statements of hospices worldwide eight years after her death and it is my guess that it will do so in perpetuity. In the UK, The Natural Death Centre also represents an attitude towards death acceptance. This organization publishes *The Natural Death Handbook* (Callender 2012), and provides independent funeral advice and information on all types of funeral choices, especially advice and support on family-organized, environmentally friendly funerals. The handbook also maintains a list of UK natural burial grounds.

It may help you to discuss your attitude to death and dying with others you trust, including the questions at the start of this section. If you become professionally involved in this work you will very likely find that your attitude changes over time. I was once very frightened of death. I recall an exercise in my counselling training when we were asked to write down our worst fear, and I wrote, 'dying alone'. Now with the familiarity of the job that I do, I would describe myself as 'death accepting'. You can perhaps discuss your attitudes and fears with friends, family members and colleagues in order to begin to build up a realistic picture of your own attitude to death.

There are some matters you will need to consider before embarking on client work. Perhaps the most important issue is to be clear about your views on suicide. Do you believe people ever have the right to take their own lives? Does your view differ between mental and physical illness, or between young and elderly people? What are your views on assisted suicide and euthanasia? This is not about sharing these views with clients, although they may ask you and you will have to decide how to answer. It is, however, likely that you will, by your approach and responses, unconsciously and unintentionally communicate your attitude. Clients very often ask therapists about their religious views and in particular their position on life after death. Again there are no hard-and-fast rules, but ask yourself how helpful it would be to tell an atheist client about Heaven, or a deeply religious client, that 'once you're dead, you're dead'. We are there to be alongside clients, to work with what they bring to us and to support them in their beliefs. Some clients temporarily lose their faith, but with careful, non-judgemental support, may find it important to discover it again on their own terms.

Are you perhaps drawn to this work because of your own involvement following the illness and death of one of your close family? One of the questions my colleagues and I ask when we are selecting students who wish to train as Bereavement Supporters concerns any recent bereavements, with the supplementary question, 'How have you dealt with this loss?' We regard it as important that our students are not using access to bereavement training for the purposes of their own therapy, and it is important to ask yourself how you feel about your own experiences of loss in relation to working with the grief of others. Clients may ask you about your own experiences. I do not feel that there are any hard-and-fast rules about self-disclosure in this field. However, it is important that if you do tell a client about your own losses you must be sure that this is done for your client's sake, not as part of your own healing process. If in any doubt, discuss this in your clinical supervision.

One final point to make in this section covers the use of euphemisms to describe death and dying. We notice that when we are training many students begin our courses using phrases such as 'passed over' or 'passed on'. It is our position as trainers to use the words 'dead' and 'died', and to explicitly point this usage out to students. With clients we would obviously not correct what they say, but we do not use such euphemisms in our own therapeutic responses.

Learning more about ourselves
5: addressing personal prejudices – attitudes to minority groups, sexuality, age, disability

If we are honest with ourselves, most of us nurse prejudices of some kind. This is not to suggest that we deliberately set out to oppress any particular minority group; it is unlikely that we would be in this kind of work if that was our intention. However, *Chambers's 20th Century Dictionary* (1983 edition) defines prejudice as 'a judgment or opinion formed beforehand or without due examination', something I would suggest we all do from time to time. As I recorded in Chapter 7, I find that I am most likely to be confronted with my own prejudices when I meet somebody who challenges my stereotyping. Personal journal keeping is a good place to record those times when the person you have gone to meet for the first time surprises you because, for whatever reason, they did not match the expectation you had of them.

Making effective use of supervision

One place to pull all of these strands of our personal development together is within the supervisory relationship. Trainee bereavement support practitioners often struggle initially to understand the nature and purpose of clinical supervision. One reason for this is that we will have first met the word 'supervision' in a managerial context, so that we expect clinical supervision of our counselling to be similar to how our manager or employer supervises our work. It is helpful to think of counselling supervision as working with another practitioner skilled in facilitating a new understanding of the work we are doing with our client. Good clinical supervision gives us the opportunity to step back from the relationship with each client and view the therapeutic process from above, hence, *super* (above) *vision*. It is good practice for your supervisor to have no managerial responsibility for you and to be independent of the organization you are working in. For example, in the service where I work, the paid counsellors are free to choose an independent counsellor. Volunteer practitioners in our service may choose to have their own individual supervision, and the service facilitates group supervision, again with independent supervisors who are not service employees but who charge a professional fee for the work.

There are pros and cons for individual as opposed to group supervision. Individual supervision, usually an hour or 90 minutes, gives you the time to discuss several of your clients, whereas in a group of three or four you will have to share time with your peers. The advantage of group supervision is that not only do you have access to the expertise of your supervisor, but you are also able to take a fresh view of your client work through the perspectives of your peers.

A good supervisory relationship is based on mutual trust and honesty. When I begin to work with a new supervisee I make it very clear that my first responsibility is to keep her clients safe and that I will do this by keeping the supervisee safe, and by ensuring that the work she is doing is skilled, ethical and within her level of competence. I can only do this if my supervisee is open about her physical and emotional health and honest about the relationship with the client we are discussing. Trainees may be tempted to play down some of their feelings towards clients for fear of being judged. It is in the nature of the work to have powerful feelings towards clients, including frustration, anger, dislike, admiration, love and attraction. To pretend otherwise when difficult or embarrassing feelings are around benefits nobody. It may also be tempting to hide from our supervisor how stressed we are feeling. If we are so mentally and physically exhausted that our client work is affected then we are working unethically. Supervision is one of the places where we can monitor our wellbeing and look after ourselves. It may help to consider that there are three distinct aspects to the supervisory role. The primary aspect of clinical supervision is the exploration of the client work in order to keep the process skilfully and ethically on track. A second aspect is the training or educational role. The supervisor is likely to be a more experienced practitioner than the supervisee, especially in the first few years of the supervisee's practice. As part of your professional development you can learn from your supervisor. Very often the boundary between the training role and the supervision role becomes blurred, and the supervisor has a responsibility to be sure that the emphasis remains on the clients. The educational aspect of supervision does in any case diminish as the practitioner becomes more competent. The third aspect of supervison is a therapeutic role. From time to time the supervisee may be presented with life issues, for example a circumstantial or developmental loss, which potentially affect her ability to work with clients. The supervisor always has a therapeutic responsibility towards her supervisees and the boundary between therapy and supervision is likely to be blurred at times. Both supervisor and supervisee have a responsibility to keep the therapeutic aspect of supervision within limits, and there may come a point where the supervisee is advised to seek therapy, since this part of the supervisory relationship is assuming too big a part in the work.

For the reader who has never experienced clinical supervision, I will conclude this section with a vignette of a typical supervision session.

The supervisee, who has come well prepared, introduces, or perhaps reintroduces, her client. First names may be used but generally not surnames so as to maintain confidentiality. She may indicate how much of our time she wants to spend on this client and I may time-keep for her. She outlines the work she is doing and then presents the issue she wants to discuss, often in the form of a dilemma, or a choice of ways forward. I ask questions to clarify my understanding of the client and to help my supervisee gain fresh perspectives into the therapeutic process. I may invite my supervisee to explore her feelings towards the client. Usually the supervisee will gain fresh insights into the work, perhaps by looking at the relationship from a new angle, by seeing the client's behaviour in a new light or by getting a surprising insight into her own experience of the client. Sometimes the two of us will get stuck, in parallel with the process the supervisee is experiencing with the client. In such cases I will support my supervisee in staying with the stuck process with the client, since the process may be temporarily stuck for a reason.[1] Usually, however, the supervisee experiences the felt bodily shift described earlier in this chapter, and at this point will reach a decision about how to proceed with the client. I invite my supervisee to sum up her intended interventions next time she meets the client and voice my support for her way forward. We then move on to the next client. This is the basis of a cyclic model of supervision and I was fortunate enough to have been tutored by Val Wosket, co-author with Steve Page, of *Supervising the Counsellor: A Cyclical Model* (Page and Wosket 2001).

Learning styles

Each of the styles described in this section is based on the concept of a polarity with extremes and the possibility to function anywhere along a spectrum. The tendency to favour one polarity over the other is supposed to have a significant effect on how we learn. Allan Paivio (1971) focuses upon a person's tendency to choose one form of processing information, either verbally or visually. Verbalizers prefer words and visualizers learn more effectively through images and diagrams. Geir Kaufmann (1979) investigated two cognitive styles of problem solving, naming the types 'assimilators' and 'explorers'. He concluded that assimilators use tried-and-tested methodical problem solving activities while explorers try novel and creative approaches. Gordon Pask and B.C.E. Scott (1972) described the wholist/serialist continuum. Serialists, or 'step-by-step learners', are methodical and

---

1   Modelling a parallel stuck process in the supervisory relationship is a form of acceptance and trust that eventually there will be a helpful outcome in the client work. Remember that it is the client who does the work and we that facilitate the process; we are not responsible if they remain stuck. We are responsible *to* our clients, ethically and professionally, but we are not responsible *for* them and for how they choose to behave in the therapeutic process (although we may point out their choices to them and challenge their decisions).

analytical. Information is broken down into easily digested, bite-sized chunks that are then built up to reach an understanding of the whole picture. By comparison, holists, or 'global learners', like to see the big picture from the outset. They look for links between disparate pieces of information that are presented to them. Extreme serialists take careful and copious notes in lectures. Extreme holists may take few or no notes but listen to the lecturer and try to make sense of the general idea presented. Effective holists do a lot of focused reading after the lecture in order to increase their 'big picture' understanding.

In the light of this brief exploration of learning styles, reflect on how you learn. Do you learn most effectively from words or by images and diagrams? Do you understand a lecture step-by-step with reams of accumulated notes, or do you sit back to absorb the big picture? Perhaps you are versatile enough to learn either way. Do you approach problems creatively or rely on tried-and-tested, methodical solutions?

A constructivist way of making sense and creating personal meaning in our world

In the middle of the 20th century, the great education pioneer Jean Piaget used a biological approach to observe how children learn. His discoveries changed the nature of classroom learning, moving teachers away from a rigid, didactic, rote learning approach towards a greater emphasis on experiential learning. From these beginnings, constructivist psychology was developed. In 1963, American psychotherapist George Kelly published his version of constructivism as a therapeutic tool, with his book *A Theory of Personality: The Psychology of Personal Constructs* (Kelly 1963). The bereavement practitioner and teacher who has made most effective use of this is Robert Neimeyer, whose inspiring work is very largely based on a constructivist paradigm (see, for example, Neimeyer 2009c; Neimeyer et al. 2006; Neimeyer et al. 2002). I believe that constructivism describes the way that human beings intuitively make sense of the world, and that it is how, when presented with new phenomena, we manage the experience, be it in the learning environment or as the result of attempting to adapt to the catastrophic changes that bereavement presents us with.

Constructivism posits that all our learning builds on previous learning, enabling us to make sense of and construct meaning in our personal world. As we learnt in Chapter 3, our earliest behaviour is instinctive. Through our instinctive behaviours we cling, suck, smile and cry. We quickly learn that such instinctive behaviour keeps us fed, warm and safe. Through imitation and observation we begin the journey of lifelong learning about our world. We acquire our own unique understanding of our environment and the objects in it. Each new experience builds on the last. In our first few years everything is exciting and new – think about how baby humans and other animals watch the world so intently. As we get older we accumulate many similar experiences so that we hardly notice differences between them. For example, think about times when somebody you know has changed their hair or shaved off a moustache and some of the family didn't notice the change until it was pointed out.

Constructivist learning theory uses the terms *assimilation* and *accommodation*. New but similar experiences are *assimilated*. However, if some new experience comes along, such as being presented with a manual transmission gearbox car to drive when you have only been used to an automatic car, new learning must be *accommodated* before the car begins to move. Accommodation is more challenging than assimilation and too many new experiences in a short space of time can lead to psychological stress. Even this is very personal, as some people enjoy change and challenge more than others. Once we understand the nature of constructivist theory we can become more effective both as teachers and as learners. You probably find that abstract concepts are easiest to understand when the teacher reinforces the concept with concrete examples. Often we will read a novel concept in a text book and find the words going straight over our head, until the author cites an everyday example that we can relate to and then we can understand the concept more easily. This is because in general the student learns by matching the explanation of the teacher with examples of her previous experience. Ideas always build on existing ideas and past understanding. What the teacher has tried to teach is only an approximate match to what the learner has learnt and in a class of 20 students there will be 20 different learning outcomes. For example, in teaching students about how grandchildren make sense of a grandparent's death the good teacher will give an anonymous case study example. As the teacher talks, each student in the class who has lost a grandparent during their childhood will be constructing her own understanding of childhood bereavement. It is very possible that at least one student would want to talk about her experience with an appropriate example, which in turn helps others develop their theoretical understanding.

The following exercise is designed to help you to reflect on your own process of assimilation and accommodation. Think of a familiar skill or piece of knowledge that you have used in the past few hours and jot it down (it could be something as obvious as making a cup of tea or walking the dog). Ask yourself these three questions: where did you learn to do that? How did you learn to do that? How long have you been able to do that? Now think of something a little more complex that you have had to learn in the recent past (for example, perhaps involving a new phone, new software, an unfamiliar cookery technique or work-related task). Jot it down. Now ask yourself: what challenges did this new activity present? How did you master this activity? Was this mastery an enjoyable challenge, a stressful chore or somewhere in-between?

Confidentiality

What does confidentiality mean to you? Perhaps it means that your friends can trust you with their secrets, knowing that what they tell you will go no further. What would you do, however, if what they told you could be a risk to their life or to somebody else's? Are there circumstances in your social life when on balance it may be best to break confidentiality? Would you be prepared to face the consequences of your decision?

When we work within a profession bounded by confidentiality, many of these personal decisions are taken out of our hands. Not only will we have the guidelines of our professional body, we will also be bound by the policies and procedures of our organizational setting. There will be clear guidelines, both for the maintenance of confidentiality and for the rare circumstances in which confidentiality is breached in the wider public interest (this was discussed in Chapter 8). It is likely that you will be expected to sign a contract stating what is required of you in the knowledge that there will be sanctions should you be responsible for a confidence being broken. There are many more ways of breaking confidentiality than through a careless, unguarded spoken word. Breaches can occur from unlocked filing cabinets, messages left on an answer machine, dropped scraps of paper bearing an address or phone number, lost and unencrypted memory sticks and confidential notes left on desks in view of unauthorized people. The list of possibilities is practically endless and it is for this reason that all professionals have a responsibility to be alert to unintentional lapses. In time, the maintenance of your clients' confidentiality becomes a regular aspect of good practice.

Organizing your practice so that you see each client in a quiet, safe space will help you to maintain confidentiality. Ideally, nobody needs to know your client's name outside of your department. In the service where I work, receptionists have a daily list indicating the times that counsellors are expecting clients, but the clients' names are confidential. Such practice may not be so easy to maintain if we work from outreach premises, such as medical centres. The room in which you see clients should be designed so that what is said cannot be overheard.

Each organization will have its own policy and procedure on record-keeping so that what follows is just a brief overview of good practice. Notes should be factual, accurate and up to date. This excludes recording opinions and impressions. You should also consider principles of fairness and justice in your notes. For example, if one week out of many your client displays atypically aggressive behaviour, would it be reasonable to record this? If you would be uncomfortable at anything your clients saw you had written, there is probably a flaw in your note-taking. The BACP publish information sheet P12: *Making Notes and Records of Counselling and Psychotherapy Sessions* by Liz Coldridge (2010). It discusses the purpose of notes and records and distinguishes the different kinds of notes; for example, research notes are governed by separate protocols. In this context it is important to mention what traditionally have been called 'process notes'. These are the notes that counsellors often take to supervision. Counsellors in training often keep copious process notes. If a process note can in any way identify the client, by name, code or personal content, then this is not a process note, but part of the client's record, subject to law. Process notes that do not identify the client may be kept, but should be destroyed as soon as they are no longer needed (Bond and Mitchels 2008, pp.68–71). Organizations often have strict rules about seeking the client's informed consent to keep process notes and it is the responsibility of the counsellor to work within these arrangements.

Working to a counselling model of support

Counselling is a term that has many definitions, but most professionals would agree that counselling requires a private and confidential setting with clearly agreed boundaries, and that it involves working with people over either a long or short period of time to explore a difficulty the client is having, so as to effect a change that reduces distress and leads to enhanced wellbeing. Some would add that counselling always requires the client's explicit informed consent, that it is about enabling and empowering the client, and that it involves neither giving advice nor directing a client to a particular course of action. This book is based on such a counselling model of support. The organization where I practise and teach is called a bereavement support service rather than a counselling service. This is because although the core team practitioners are BACP Accredited counsellors, not all of our supporters are qualified counsellors. We all work to a counselling model and adhere to the BACP *Ethical Framework for Good Practice in Counselling and Psychotherapy* (Bond *et al.* 2013). I believe that it is important for all practitioners claiming to offer a counselling model of bereavement support to work within a counselling code of practice. Bereaved people are vulnerable. They should expect to be supported to the highest possible standard and should be able to seek redress if they are treated unethically.

Mid-course blues and how to avoid them

Some way into any training, particularly training that requires personal introspection, there often comes a point when some students begin to feel completely de-skilled. At best, each troubled student seeks a tutorial to address the issue; at worst, one or more students quietly drop out of the course. This is a great shame because actually the students' skills are increasing, but unfortunately not as fast as their feelings of not knowing enough. In management speak, the students' consciousness of what they do not know is increasing faster than the competency required by the course. The origins of this concept have become lost in the mists of time, and one internet source attributes it to a number of possible origins (Chapman 2013). The earliest recorded version of it seems to have originated at Gordon Training International (GTI), a human relations training organization founded in 1962 by Dr Thomas Gordon based in California. More than 30 years ago a GTI employee, Noel Burch, formulated a four-stage model of learning a new skill. The stages he identified he called: stage 1: unconsciously unskilled; stage 2: consciously unskilled; stage 3: consciously skilled; and stage 4: unconsciously skilled. In formulations of later models the word 'skilled' has been replaced by the word 'competence' (Adams 2013).

When we begin to work in a new discipline, for example, beginning some new training, we can be blissfully unaware of how little we know. Basing how we are on the 'ignorance is bliss' principle, we feel comfortable not knowing all there is to know. This state is our *unconscious incompetence*, and we are likely to feel unjustifiably confident in our ability. Gradually, as our training progresses, we become aware of how much we don't know and how much we have to learn. This can feel quite daunting and those with low self-esteem can feel threatened. This is a time when inadequately supported students may quit a course. Confident people can find this time an exciting challenge. This stage, be it unnerving or exciting, is our state of *conscious incompetence*.

If all goes well we begin to notice that we are getting more competent, especially if tutors and peers give us positive feedback for our increasing skill and knowledge level. Tutors have a special role in making students aware of their development. This affirmation helps the student build on her own success. We then arrive at a place of *conscious competence*.

As we become more and more proficient, we begin to take for granted what we can do, to the point where we perform tasks automatically. As an example, the skill involved in using a computer mouse and keyboard do not have to be thought about once we are truly competent; we perform the actions without thinking. We have reached the final stage – the one we call *unconscious competence*. Experienced counsellors and psychotherapists use the core conditions without the sense of deliberation that a novice would have.

There is another way of viewing the model, in terms of a continuum rather than as four discrete stages. A graph (Figure 9.4) illustrates this idea, with degree of consciousness being mapped on one axis and level of competence being mapped on the other. Ideally, the first three stages of consciousness and competence would increase evenly and in direct relationship to each other, so that the result would be a straight line, as is depicted in Figure 9.4. For example, a trainee counsellor begins with both little knowledge of the counselling skills necessary to be effective and limited competence in using these skills.

It would be comforting if both knowledge and ability increased at an equal rate. In the event, this rarely, if ever, happens. Trainees quickly become aware of how much there is to learn and how little they know. In other words, they exist for a time in a potentially demoralizing state of conscious incompetence. Some are tempted to give up at this point. Skilled and sensitive tutors keep an eye out for this seemingly inevitable stage in each student's development and are on hand to normalize and reassure. My experience is that students on counselling diploma courses typically reach a stage of being consciously unskilled towards the end of the first year of training. I know I did; it is recorded in my journal and I vividly remember the unsettling feeling it engendered.

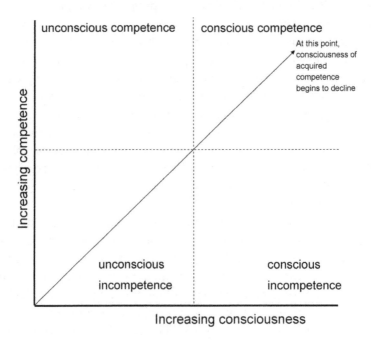

Figure 9.4 The consciousness/competence model

Beginning to work with clients: be reassured

Let us assume that you have managed to get an adequate grasp of the theory and the skills needed to work with bereaved people and you understand the rules of confidentiality. You have your supervision arrangements in place and you are ready to meet your first client. So let us begin with what I believe is the golden rule: because you have chosen to work in a client-centred way, then, overall, the single most important factor in determining a successful outcome, is down to your client's *active involvement in her own process of change* (Bohart and Tallman 1999). Person-centred bereavement counselling works from a belief in the client as 'active self-healer', that is, 'Clients can and do heal themselves' (Bohart and Tallman 1999, p.20). The client is the source of energy that drives the change, information, techniques and procedures offered by the helping practitioner to facilitate clients to focus on their own self-healing. Clients make their own creative discoveries utilizing what the practitioner offers, and most change takes place between sessions as clients integrate the therapy experiences into their lives. Our role as counsellors and helping practitioners is, according to Bohart and Tallman, to provide a well-boundaried place, the opportunity for creative, exploratory dialogue and the resources to help clients construct working solutions. We also have a role to teach and train our clients in specific skills when needed. 'Whether the therapist should be active or non-directive is not an issue. Far more important are the *attitudes* that the therapist holds towards the client and the kind of *climate* that the therapist creates' (Bohart and Tallman 1999, p.20, my italics).

When the client is too psychologically fragile to engage actively in their healing

It would be naïve to believe that all bereaved people come to us with the psychological resilience to immediately begin the process of self-healing. In his book *Interpreting Residential Life*, Atherton (1989) outlines a helpful metaphor to address this difficult and important issue. He describes two modes of living: 'shell' and 'skeleton' (pp.152–175). Although originally a model to describe the behaviour of institutionalized residents in care settings, Atherton has acknowledged its usefulness as a metaphor for therapy. A skeleton is vulnerable to injury while a shell gives protection. On the other hand, a skeleton more easily allows growth and flexibility while a shell is more restrictive. The psychological metaphor of a skeleton offers an internal structure that requires emotional competence while a shell is externally imposed, keeping us safe but likely to limit the possibilities of change. So which alternative do we offer deeply grieving clients? The treatment for a broken limb is the application of a plaster shell until the limb heals and is able to function as part of the skeleton. Likewise, for a time the therapeutic space may offer temporary protection, although the aim of a client-centred practitioner is to return the client to an active, participatory role in the grief process. Clients may begin their counselling in a shell, but we are working towards helping them become a flexible and active skeleton. I find it helpful to begin the work by inviting my client to talk, where possible, about her positive memories of the deceased, including biographical details of good times spent together.

As the work progresses

We can feel reassured that the most important single determinant of a successful outcome is the client's active involvement. It may also help to know the most important quality of the helping practitioner is the nature of the relationship with the client. It is more important than either your expertise or your experience. Former students tell me that they have found, to their surprise and delight, that, as clients talk, it is clear that they are intuitively drawing on the models of grief I have described in Chapter 5. If a client talks about how difficult it is coming to terms with change, she is describing assumptive world theory and you have the opportunity to intervene appropriately. Your client may be searching for meaning, attempting to make sense of the loss or be looking for ways of getting some balance back in her life. You may, over time, be able to help her grow around an undiminishing grief and be alongside her as she discovers resourceful ways to continue a bond with the person who has died. Listen, and your client will guide you in how to be of help. Importantly, she is doing the work herself. Equally important is *the fact that she is not doing it alone.* Try to relax in the therapeutic relationship and your client will relax, too. Trust your client, trust yourself and trust the process. Make good use of your supervisor and draw on the expertise and experience of colleagues. Follow this guide and the work will reward you more than you once ever thought possible.

Notes for trainers

My colleagues and I begin our eight-day training course by explaining the TEB cycle with a PowerPoint presentation. Students are given copies of a grid (see Appendix 9.1) to complete at the end of each session, as an aid towards their journal keeping. We also introduce the consciousness/competence grid (see Figure 9.4) on the first day, as part of introducing our tutorial and pastoral care role. We also remind students about this model periodically so that they don't become daunted.

Through reading, reflection and class discussion, students are encouraged to relate the TEB cycle to Bohart and Tallman's principle of the Active Self-healer. The essence of this principle is reinforced if students' attention is drawn to Mick Cooper's 2008 book. We introduce our PowerPoint discussion on learning styles on the first day and invite class discussion.

The Johari Window, the lifeline and life-stage activities, the attitudes to death and loss and attitudes to minority groups are all exercises we incorporate into our training days. Through group and pairs work and class discussion, this allows us to break up the didactic content to allow for our students' individual differences in attention span and learning style. The lifeline exercise can be a simple drawing exercise, or if you feel that time permits it, a creative exercise involving paints and collage materials. We present the life-stage activity as a grid on A4 paper for students to complete, discuss in pairs, and then feed back to the whole group. The Attitudes to Death and Loss activity can be presented as a grid, as a structured class discussion or as a continuum activity (see Appendix 9.2 for the latter). For our Working with Difference session (see Chapter 7) we involve a specialist speaker and follow this with a class discussion.

Your students may or may not have had previous experience of a counselling model of supervision; many of our students have not, although they may have experience of line-management supervision in their occupation. We find it helpful to introduce our students to a live supervision session, with tutors taking the roles of supervisor and supervisee. In our view the supervisee should present a real (but anonymous) client in this session, rather than use role-play.

Relating What I Have Learnt to the TEB Cycle

(After an Idea by Faulkner and Wallbank 1998)

You may want to complete this sheet for separate activities

Journal sheet

Date:

Knowledge covered today	Skills covered today

Thinking

During the session I found myself thinking...

Now I am thinking...

Experiencing

During the session I experienced...

Now I am feeling...

Behaving

This session has had the potential to change my behaviour in the following ways:
(This may include thinking and feeling differently from before).

The Continuum Exercise

This activity requires a large teaching space. On opposite walls, tack two signs. One should read 'Strongly agree' and the opposite one should read 'Strongly disagree'.

Invite your students to stand in a group mid-way between the two signs. Then read from a list of statements designed to elicit each student's opinion, belief or philosophical position.

For example, you may read out:

'We each have a right to decide when we will die.'

Or:

'I will always strive to prevent a client's suicide.'

Invite each student to stand between the two signs in a place that reflects the strength of his or her feeling. Invite each student to explain his or her position.

Suggested Module Programme

Day 1

1. **Introductions and contracting:**
   Students' individual expectations
   Ground rules, expectations

2. **Models of learning:**
   Kolb's Learning Cycle
   TEB cycle

3. **Johari's Window**

4. **Keeping a reflective journal**

5. **Confidentiality:**
   Personal constructs and professional models

6. **Stages of life experience:**
   Life changes
   Personal narrative exercise

7. **Study skills**
   Internet skills
   Library skills
   Independent study to build up a resource

8. **Listening skills, theory and practice:**
   Listening skills – active listening
   Giving and receiving feedback appropriately

Day 2

1. Attachment and loss:
Presentation of attachment theory
Personal loss exercise
Personal attitudes and beliefs about loss – sexuality, age, disability
Personal attitudes to death and dying

2. The helping relationship:
Working within boundaries
Carl Rodgers and the humanistic philosophy of self-actualization
The core conditions

3. Skills theory and practice:
Introducing triads
Giving feedback in your triad
Active listening
Barriers to effective listening

Day 3

1. Preparing to do the assignments:
Working definitions of 'bereavement', 'grief', 'grieving', 'mourning'
Grief in a historical context
Factors affecting grief
The concept of complicated grief
Attachment styles developed: the work of Hazan and Shaver, and the work of Colin Murray Parkes (2006)

2. Skills theory and practice:
Using the core conditions:
Paraphrasing, reflecting, clarifying and summarizing

Day 4

1. The complexity of grief:
Active self-healing: the client's role
The role of the helping practitioner

2. Models of grief:
Assumptive world theory
Finding meaning, making sense
Grief and growth: Lois Tonkin's Circles Model

3. **Skills theory and practice:**
   Second level skills: focusing
   Deeper level empathy

Day 5

1. **Models of grief:**
   The Dual Process Model
   Instrumental and intuitive grief
   Linda Machin's RRL model
   Continuing bonds theory

2. **Skills theory and practice:**
   Challenge and confrontation

Day 6

1. **Working with difference**

2. **Skills theory and practice:**
   The concept of transference

Day 7

1. **A systems approach to family grief:**
   Family sculpture

2. **Skills theory and practice:**
   Supervision: its function, and how to make best use of it
   Revising and consolidating listening skills

Day 8

1. **Skills assessment**

2. **Rituals and endings**

3. **Ending with one another**

4. **Tutorials**

References

Abraham, K. (1949) *Selected Papers of Karl Abraham* (edited by T. Douglas Bryan and Alix Strachey). London: Hogarth Press and the Institute of Psycho-Analysis. (Original work published 1924.)

Adams, L. (2013) *Learning a New Skill is Easier Said Than Done.* Available at www.gordontraining. com/free-workplace-articles/learning-a-new-skill-is-easier-said-than-done, accessed on 16 July 2013.

Ainsworth, M.D.S., Blehar, M.C., Waters, E. and Wall, S. (1978) *Patterns of Attachment: A Psychological Study of the Strange Situation.* Hillsdale, NJ: Erlbaum.

American Psychiatric Association (2013) *Diagnostic and Statistical Manual of Mental Disorders,* 5th edn *(DSM-5).* Arlington, VA: American Psychiatric Publishing, Inc.

Anderson, C. (1949) 'Aspects of pathological grief and mourning.' *International Journal of Psycho-Analysis 30,* 48–55.

Archer, J. (1999) *The Nature of Grief: The Evolution and Psychology of Reactions to Loss.* Hove: Brunner-Routledge. (Reprinted 2004).

Archer, J. (2001) 'Grief from an Evolutionary Perspective.' In M.S. Stroebe, R.O. Hansson, W. Stroebe and H. Schut (eds) *Handbook of Bereavement Research: Consequences, Coping and Care.* Washington, DC: American Psychological Association.

Archer, J. (2008) 'Theories of Grief: Past, Present and Future Perspectives.' In M.S. Stroebe, R.O. Hansson, H. Schut and W. Stroebe (eds) *Handbook of Bereavement: Research and Practice.* Washington, DC: American Psychological Association.

Atherton, J.S. (1989) *Interpreting Residential Life.* London: Routledge.

Attig, T. (1991) 'The importance of conceiving of grief as an active process.' *Death Studies 15,* 4, 385–393.

Attig, T. (2001) 'Relearning the World: Making and Finding Meanings.' In R.A. Neimeyer (ed.) *Meaning Reconstruction and the Experience of Loss.* Washington, DC: American Psychological Association.

Averill, J.R. (1968) 'Grief: its nature and significance.' *Psychological Bulletin 70,* 6, 721–748.

Begley, S. (2013) *Psychiatrists Unveil their Long-awaited Diagnostic 'Bible'.* Reuters edition US 17 May 2013. Available at www.reuters.com/article/2013/05/17/us-science-psychiatry-dsm-idUSBRE94G04420130517, accessed on 16 July 2013.

Boelen, P.A. (2008a) *Complicated Grief: Possibilities and Limitations in Bereavement Care.* Paper presented at the Anglo-Dutch Day, Grief research and bereavement care: How can the twain meet?, St Christopher's Hospice, London.

Boelen, P.A. (2008b) 'Cognitive behaviour therapy for complicated grief.' *Bereavement Care 27,* 2, 27–31.

Bohart, A.C. and Tallman, K. (1999) *How Clients Make Therapy Work: The Process of Active Self-healing.* Washington, DC: American Psychological Association.

Bond, T., Griffin, G., Casemore, R., Jamieson, A., Lendrum, S. and Potter, V. (2013) *Ethical Framework for Good Practice in Counselling and Psychotherapy.* Available at www.bacp.co.uk/ethical_framework, accessed on 16 July 2013.

Bond, T. and Mitchels, B. (2008) *Confidentiality and Record Keeping in Counselling and Psychotherapy.* London: Sage.

Bond, T. and Mitchels, B. (2010) *G2 Information Sheet: Breaches in Confidentiality*. Lutterworth: British Association for Counselling and Psychotherapy.

Boorse, C. (1976) 'What a theory of mental health should be.' *Journal for the Theory of Social Behaviour* 6, 1, 61–84.

Boorse, C. (1977) 'Health as a theoretical concept.' *Philosophy of Science 44*, 7, 542–573.

Bowen, M. (1976) 'Family Reaction to Death.' In P.J. Guerin (ed.) *Family Therapy: Theory and Practice*. New York, NY: Gardner Press.

Bowlby, J. (1944) 'Forty-four juvenile thieves: their characters and home-life.' *International Journal of Psychoanalysis 25*, 19–52.

Bowlby, J. (1951) *Maternal Care and Mental Health*. Geneva: World Health Organization.

Bowlby, J. (1958) 'The nature of the child's tie to his mother.' *International Journal of Psycho-Analysis 39*, 350–373.

Bowlby, J. (1960). 'Grief and mourning in infancy and early childhood.' *Psychoanalytic study of the child 15,9*, 52.

Bowlby, J. (1961) 'Processes of mourning.' *The International Journal of Psycho-analysis 42*, 317–340.

Bowlby, J. (1969) *Attachment and Loss: Volume 1 Attachment*. London: Pimlico.

Bowlby, J. (1975) *Attachment and Loss: Volume 2 Separation Anger and Anxiety*. London: Pimlico.

Bowlby, J. (1980) *Attachment and Loss: Volume 3 Loss: Sadness and Depression*. London: Pimlico.

Bowlby, J., Fry, M. and Ainsworth, M. (1953) *Child Care and the Growth of Love*. London: Penguin.

Bowlby, R. and King, P. (2004) *Fifty Years of Attachment Theory*. London: Karnac Books.

Bowlby, J. and Parkes, C.M. (1970) 'Separation and Loss within the Family.' In E.J. Anthony and C. Koupernik (eds) *The Child and his Family*. New York, NY: Wiley.

Bowlby, J. and Robertson, J. (1953) A two-year-old goes to hospital. *Proceedings of the Royal Society of Medicine 46*, 6, 425.

Bowlby, R. and King, P. (2004) *Fifty Years of Attachment Theory*. London: Karnac Books.

Bowlby-West, L. (1983) 'The impact of death on the family system.' *Journal of Family Therapy 5*, 3, 279–294.

Bretherton, I. (1992) 'The origins of attachment theory: John Bowlby and Mary Ainsworth.' *Developmental Psychology 28*, 5, 759.

Burke, L.A. and Neimeyer, R.A. (2013) 'Prospective Risk Factors for Complicated Grief: A Review of the Empirical Literature.' In M.S. Stroebe, H. Schut and J. Van den Bout (eds) *Complicated Grief: Scientific Foundations for Health Care Professionals*. Hove: Routledge.

Callender, R. (2012) *The Natural Death Handbook*, 5th edition. London: Strange Attractor.

Capra, F. (1992) *The Tao of Physics: An Exploration of the Parallels between Modern Physics and Eastern Mysticism*, 3rd edition. London: Flamingo.

Carey, T. (2011) My father's Hindu funeral. *The Guardian*, 26 March 2011. Available at http://www.theguardian.com/lifeandstyle/2011/mar/26/father-hindu-funeral-cremation-tanith-carey, accessed 4 November 2013..

Carr, D., Nesse, R.M. and Wortman, C.B. (2006) *Spousal Bereavement in Late Life*. New York, NY: Springer Publishing Company Inc.

Chan, C.L.W. and Mak, J.M.H. (2000) 'Benefits and Drawbacks of Chinese Rituals Surrounding Care for the Dying.' In R. Fielding and C.L.W. Chan (eds) *Psychosocial Oncology and Palliative Care in Hong Kong: The First Decade*. Hong Kong: Hong Kong University Press.

Chapman, A. (2013) *Businessballs Free Online Learning*. Available at http://www.businessballs.com/consciouscompetencelearningmodel.htm, accessed 4 November 2013.

Childs-Gowell, E. (1993) *Good Grief Rituals: Tools for Healing*. Barrytown, NY: Station Hill Press.

Clukey, L. (2007) '"Just be there": hospice caregivers' anticipatory mourning experience.' *Journal of Hospice and Palliative Nursing 9*, 3, 151–158.

Coldridge, L. (2010) *Information sheet P12: Making Notes and Records of Counselling and Psychotherapy Sessions*. Lutlerworth: BACP.

Cooper, M. (2008) *Essential Research Findings in Counselling and Psychotherapy: The Facts are Friendly*. London: Sage.

Cooper, R. (2013) 'Complicated Grief: Philosophical Perspectives.' In M.S. Stroebe, H. Schut and J. van den Bout (eds) *Complicated Grief: Scientific Foundations for Health Care Professionals*. Hove: Routledge.

Counts, D.A.and Counts, D.R. (1991) 'Loss and Anger: Death and the Expression of Grief in Kaliai.' In D.A. Counts and R. David (eds) *Coping with the Final Tragedy: Cultural Variation in Dying and Grieving*. Amityville, NY: Baywood Publishing Co.

Cozolino, L.J. (2006) *The Neuroscience of Human Relationships*. New York: Norton and Company.

Darwin, C. (1859) *On the Origin of Species by Means of Natural Selection, or the Preservation of Favoured Races in the Struggle for Life*. London: John Murray.

Darwin, C. (1872) *The Expression of the Emotions in Man and Animals*. London: John Murray.

Darwin, C. (1881) *The Descent of Man, and Selection in Relation to Sex*. London: John Murray.

Davis, C.G. (2001) 'The Tormented and the Transformed: Understanding Responses to Loss and Trauma.' In R.A. Neimeyer (ed.) *Meaning Reconstruction and the Experience of Loss*. Washington, DC: American Psychological Association Books.

Davis, C.G., Wortman, C.B., Lehman, D.R. and Silver, R.C. (2000) 'Searching for meaning in loss: are clinical assumptions correct?' *Death Studies 24*, 497–540.

Doka, K. (ed.) (2002) *Disenfranchised Grief*. Champaign, IL: Research Press.

Engel, G.L. (1961) 'Is grief a disease? A challenge for medical research.' *Psychosomatic Medicine 23*, 18–22.

Faulkner, A. and Wallbank, S. (eds) (1998) *Bereavement Counselling: A 60 hour Introductory Training Course*. London: Cruse Bereavement Care and Help the Hospices.

Folkman, S. and Lazarus, R.S. (1980) 'An analysis of coping in a middle-aged community sample.' *Journal of Health and Social Behavior 21*, 3, 219–239.

Freud, S. (1957) *Mourning and Melancholia*, J. Strachey edn, Vol. 14. London: Hogarth.

Gabrieli, V. (1955) 'A new Digby letter-book: in praise of Venetia.' *The National Library of Wales Journal 9*, 2, 113–148.

Gabrieli, V. (1956) 'A new Digby letter-book: in praise of Venetia.' *The National Library of Wales Journal 9*, 4, 440–462.

Gabrieli, V. (1957) 'A new Digby letter-book: in praise of Venetia.' *The National Library of Wales Journal 10*, 1, 81–106.

George, C., Kaplan, N. and Main, M. (1985) The Berkeley adult attachment interview. Unpublished protocol, Department of Psychology, University of California, Berkeley.

Gerson, R., and McGoldrick, M. (1985) *Genograms in family assessment*. New York: W.W. Norton and Co.

Gilbert, K.R. (1996) '"We've had the same loss, why don't we have the same grief?" Loss and differential grief in families.' *Death Studies 20*, 3, 269–283.

Graves, D. (2009) *Talking with Bereaved People: An Approach for Structured and Sensitive Communication*. London: Jessica Kingsley.

Grosskurth, P. (1986). *Melanie Klein. Her World and Her Work*. London: Karnac.

Gündel, H., O'Connor, M.F., Littrell, L., Fort, C. and Lane, R.D. (2003) 'Functional neuroanatomy of grief: an fMRI study.' *American Journal of Psychiatry 160*, 11, 1946–1953.

Hall, E.T. (1997) *Beyond Culture*. New York: Anchor Books.

Harlow, H.F. (1961) 'The Development of Affectional Patterns in Infant Monkeys.' In B.M. Foss (ed.) *Determinants of Infant Behaviour*. London: Methuen.

Hazan, C. and Shaver, P. (1987) 'Romantic love conceptualized as an attachment process.' *Journal of Personality and Social Psychology 52*, 3, 511–524.

Horowitz, M.J. (1986) 'Stress-response syndromes: a review of posttraumatic and adjustment disorders.' *Psychiatric Services 37*, 3, 241–249.

Horowitz, M.J., Siegel, B., Holen, A., Bonanno, G.A., Milbrath, C. and Stinson, C.H. (1997) 'Diagnostic criteria for complicated grief disorder.' *American Journal of Psychiatry 154*, 904–910.

Horowitz, M.J., Wilner, N. and Alvarez, W. (1979) 'Impact of Event Scale: a measure of subjective stress.' *Psychosomatic Medicine 41*, 3, 209–218.

Hunt, K. (2013) Prisoner Tony Suckling holds counsellor against will at Rochester Prison. *Kent Online*. Available at www.kentonline.co.uk/kentonline/home/2013/april/3/counsellor_held_in_prison.aspx, accessed on 16 July 2013.

Immordino-Yang, M.H. and Damasio, A. (2007) 'We feel, therefore we learn: the relevance of affective and social neuroscience to education. *Mind, Brain and Education 1*, 1, 3–10.

Jacobs, M. (1988) *Psychodynamic Counselling in Action*. London: Sage.

Janoff-Bulman, R. (1992) *Shattered Assumptions: Towards a New Psychology of Trauma*. New York, NY: The Free Press.

Jordan, J.R. (1990) *Loss and Family Development: Clinical Implications*. Paper presented at the 98th annual meeting of the American Psychological Association, Boston, MA.

Jordan, J.R., Kraus, D.R. and Ware, E.S. (1993) 'Observations on loss and family development.' *Family Process 32*, 4, 425–440.

Jupp, P.C. and Gittings, C. (1999) *Death in England.* Manchester: Manchester University Press.

Kai, J., Spencer, J. and Woodward, N. (2001) 'Wrestling with ethnic diversity: toward empowering health educators.' *Medical Education 35,* 3, 262–271.

Kaufmann, G. (1979) 'The explorer and the assimilator: a cognitive style distinction and its potential implications for innovative problem solving.' *Scandinavian Journal of Educational Research 23,* 3, 101–108.

Keats, J. (1985) 'Ode to a Nightingale.' In H. Vendler (ed.) *The Odes of John Keats.* Cambridge, MA: Harvard University Press.

Keesee, N.J., Currier, J.M. and Neimeyer, R.A. (2008) 'Predictors of grief following the death of one's child: the contribution of finding meaning.' *Journal of Clinical Psychology 64,* 10, 1145–1163.

Kelly, G.A. (1963) *A Theory of Personality: The Psychology of Personal Constructs.* New York, NY: Norton and Company Inc.

Kissane, D.W. and Bloch, S. (2002) *Family Focused Grief Therapy: A Model of Family-centred Care during Palliative Care and Bereavement.* Buckingham: Open University Press.

Klass, D., Silverman, P.R. and Nichman, S.L. (1996) *Continuing Bonds: New Understanding of Grief.* Philadelphia, PA: Taylor and Francis.

Klein, M. (1948) *Contributions to Psycho-analysis 1921–1945.* London: Hogarth Press.

Klein, M. (1975) *Love, Guilt and Reparation and Other Works 1921–1945.* New York, NY: The Free Press.

Kolb, D.A. (1984) *Experiential Learning: Experience as the Source of Learning and Development.* Upper Saddle River, NJ: Prentice-Hall.

Koo, B.W.S., Tin, A.F., Koo, E.W.K. and Lee, S.-m. (2006) 'When East Meets West: Implications for Bereavement Counselling.' In C.C.W. Chan and C.A.Y.M. Chow (eds) *Death, Dying and Bereavement: A Hong Kong Chinese Experience.* Hong Kong: Hong Kong University Press.

Kübler-Ross, E. (1969) *On Death and Dying.* Toronto: MacMillan.

Kuhn, T.S. (1962) *The Structure of Scientific Revolutions,* 2nd edn, Vol. II Number 2. Chicago, IL: University of Chicago Press.

Latham, A.E. and Prigerson, H.G. (2004) 'Suicidality and bereavement: complicated grief as psychiatric disorder presenting greatest risk for suicidality.' *Suicide and Life-threatening Behavior 34,* 4, 350–362.

Lazarus, R.S. and Folkman, S. (1984) *Stress, Appraisal, and Coping.* New York, NY: Springer Publishing Company.

Lazarus, R.S. and Folkman, S. (1987) 'Transactional theory and research on emotions and coping.' *European Journal of Personality 1,* 3, 141–169.

Lee, C.W. and Cuijpers, P. (2013) 'A meta-analysis of the contribution of eye movements in processing emotional memories.' *Journal of Behavior Therapy and Experimental Psychiatry 44,* 2, 232–239.

Lee, L. (1959, 2002) *Cider with Rosie.* London: Vintage Books, Random House.

Lewis, C.S. (1961) *A Grief Observed.* London: Faber and Faber.

Lindemann, E. (1944) 'Symptomatology and management of acute grief.' *American Journal of Psychiatry 102,* 2, 141–148; reprinted in 1994 in the *American Journal of Psychiatry 151* (Sesquicentennnial Supplement).

Lindsay, M. (2013) Joyce Robertson Obituary: Writer and researcher who studied the effect on children of separation from their parents, particularly in hospitals. *The Guardian,* 19 May 2013.

Luft, J. (1961) 'The Johari Window: a graphic model of awareness in interpersonal relations.' *Human Relations Training News 5,* 1, 6–7.

McGilly, K. (2013) Personal communication.

Machin, L. (2009) *Working with Loss and Grief: A New Model for Practitioners.* London: Sage.

Machin, L. (2014) *Working with Loss and Grief: A Theoretical and Practical Approach,* 2nd edition. London: Sage.

Main, M. and Solomon, J. (1986) 'Discovery of an Insecure-disorganized/disoriented Attachment Pattern.' In T.B. Brazelton and M.W. Yogman (eds) *Affective Development in Infancy.* Westport, CT: Ablex Publishing.

Martin, T.L. and Doka, K.J. (2000) *Men Don't Cry ... Women Do: Transcending Gender Stereotypes of Grief.* Phildelphia, PA: Taylor and Francis.

Mill, J.S. (1856) 'Of Ethology, or the Science of the Formation of Character.' *A System of Logic: Book VI On the Logic of the Moral Sciences,* 4th edition. London: John Parker and Son.

Nadeau, J.W. (2001) 'Family Construction of Meaning.' In R.A. Neimeyer (ed.) *Meaning Reconstruction and the Experience of Loss.* Washington, DC: American Psychological Association Books.

Nadeau, J.W. (2008) 'Meaning-making in Bereaved Families: Assessment, Intervention, and Future Research.' In M.S. Stroebe, R.O. Hansson, H. Schut and W. Stroebe (eds) *Handbook of Bereavement Research and Practice*. Washington, DC: American Psychological Association.

Neimeyer, R. A. (2006) 'Widowhood, grief and the quest for meaning: A narrative perspective on resilience.' In D. Carr, R. M. Nesse and C. B. Wortman (Eds). *Spousal bereavement in later life* (pp.227–252). New York: Springer.

Neimeyer, R.A. (2009a) 'Constructions of Death and Loss: A Personal and Professional Evolution.' In R.J. Butler (ed.) *Reflections in Personal Construct Theory*. Chichester: John Wiley and Sons.

Neimeyer, R.A. (2009b) *Conference Workshop*. Paper presented at the Researching Meaning-Making: Narratives of Grief and Loss Conference, St Ann's College, Oxford, 14 July.

Neimeyer, R.A. (2009c) *Constructivist Psychotherapy*. Hove: Routledge.

Neimeyer, R.A., Baldwin, S.A. and Gillies, J. (2006) 'Continuing bonds and reconstructing meaning: mitigating complications in bereavement.' *Death Studies 30*, 8, 715–738.

Neimeyer, R.A., Botella, L., Herrero, O., Pacheco, M., Figueras, S. and Werner-Wildner, L. A. (2002) 'The Meaning of Your Absence: Traumatic Loss and Narrative Reconstruction.' In J. Kauffmann (ed.) *Loss of the Assumptive World: A Theory of Traumatic Loss*. Hove: Brunner-Routledge.

Nesse, R.M. (2006) 'An Evolutionary Framework for Understanding Grief.' In D. Carr, R. M. Nesse and C. Wortman (eds) *Spousal Bereavement in Late Life*. New York, NY: Springer.

Noll, R. (1983) 'Shamanism and schizophrenia: a state-specific approach to the "schizophrenia metaphor" of shamanic states.' *American Ethnologist 10*, 3, 443–459.

O'Connor, M.F. (2013) 'Physiological Mechanisms and the Neurobiology of Complicated Grief.' In M.S. Stroebe, H. Schut and J. Van den Bout (eds) *Complicated Grief: Scientific Foundations for Health Care Professionals*. Hove: Routledge.

O'Connor, M.F., Wellisch, D.K., Stanton, A.L., Eisenberger, N.I., Irwin, M.R. and Lieberman, M.D. (2008) 'Craving love? Enduring grief activates brain's reward center.' *Neuroimage 42*, 2, 969–972.

Page, S. and Wosket, V. (2001) *Supervising the Counsellor: A Cyclical Model*. Hove: Routledge.

Paivio, A. (1971) *Imagery and Verbal Process*. New York, NY: Reinhart and Winston.

Parkes, C.M. (1965) 'Bereavement and mental illness.' *British Journal of Medical Psychology 38*, 1, 13–26.

Parkes, C.M. (1970) 'The first year of bereavement: a longitudinal study of the reaction of London widows to the death of their husbands.' *Psychiatry: Journal for the Study of Interpersonal Processes 33*, 4, 444–467.

Parkes, C.M. (1981) 'Evaluation of a bereavement service.' *Journal of Preventive Psychiatry, 1*, 2, 179–188.

Parkes, C.M. (2002) 'Grief: lessons from the past, visions for the future.' *Death Studies 26*, 5, 367–385.

Parkes, C.M. (2006) *Love and Loss: The Roots of Grief and its Complications*. Hove: Routledge.

Parkes, C.M. (2013a) 'Elisabeth Kübler-Ross, On Death and Dying: a reappraisal.' *Mortality 18*, 1, 94–97.

Parkes, C.M. (2013b) Personal communication.

Parkes, C.M. and Brown, R.J. (1972) 'Health after bereavement: a controlled study of young Boston widows and widowers.' *Psychosomatic Medicine 34*, 5, 449–461.

Parkes, C.M and Prigerson, H.G. (2010) *Bereavement: Studies of Grief in Adult Life*, 4th revised edition. London: Penguin.

Parkes, C.M. and Weiss, R.S. (1983) *Recovery from Bereavement*. New York: Basic Books

Pask, G. and Scott, B. (1972) 'Learning strategies and individual competence.' *International Journal of Man-Machine Studies 4*, 3, 217–253.

Payne, S. (2001) 'The role of volunteers in hospice bereavement support in New Zealand.' *Palliative Medicine 15*, 2, 107–115.

Payne, S. (2002) 'Dilemmas in the use of volunteers to provide hospice bereavement support: evidence from New Zealand.' *Mortality 7*, 2, 139–154.

Pedersen, P. (1987) 'Ten frequent assumptions of cultural bias in counseling.' *Journal of Multicultural Counseling and Development 15*, 1, 16–24.

Piaget, J. (1929) *The Child's Conception of the World*. London: Kegan Paul.

Piaget, J. (1952) *The origins of intelligence in children*. New York: International Universities Press.

Piaget, J. (1954) *The construction of reality in the child*. New York: Basic Books.

Powell, J. (1999) *Why Am I Afraid to Tell You Who I Am?* London: Fount Paperbacks.

Prigerson, H.G. (1995) 'Inventory of complicated grief: a scale to measure maladaptive symptoms of loss.' *Psychiatry Research 59*, 1–2, 65–79.

Prigerson, H.G., Bierhals, A.J., Kasl, S.V., Reynolds III, C.F. *et al.* (1996) 'Complicated grief as a disorder distinct from bereavement-related depression and anxiety: a replication study.' *American Journal of Psychiatry 153*, 11, 1484–1486.

Prigerson, H.G., Bierhals, A.J., Kasl, S.V., Reynolds III, C.F. *et al.* (1997) 'Traumatic grief as a risk factor for mental and physical morbidity.' *American Journal of Psychiatry 154*, 5, 616–623.

Prigerson, H.G., Frank, E., Kasl, S.V., Reynolds III, C.F. *et al.* (1995) 'Complicated grief and bereavement-related depression as distinct disorders: preliminary empirical validation in elderly bereaved spouses.' *American Journal of Psychiatry 152*, 1, 22–30.

Prigerson, H.G., Horowitz, M.J., Jacobs, S.C., Parkes, C.M., Aslan, M., Goodkin, K. *et al.* (2009) 'Prolonged grief disorder: psychometric validation of criteria proposed for DSM-V and ICD-113.' *PLoS Medicine 6*, 8, e1000121.

Prigerson, H.G., Vanderwerker, L.C. and Maciejewski, P.K. (2008) 'A Case for Inclusion of Prolonged Grief Disorder in DSM-V.' In M.S. Stroebe, R.O. Hansson, H. Schut and W. Stroebe (eds) *Handbook of Bereavement Research and Practice: Advances in Theory and Intervention.* Washington, DC: American Psychological Association.

Prochaska, J.O., Redding, C.A. and Evers, K.E. (2008) 'The Transtheoretical Model and Stages of Change.' In K. Glanz, B.K. Rimer and K. Viswanath (eds) *Health Behavior and Health Education: Theory, Research, and Practice*, 4th edition. San Francisco, CA: Jossey-Bass.

Rando, T.A. (2002) 'The 'Curse' of Too Good a Childhood.' In J. Kauffmann (ed.) *Loss of the Assumptive World: A Theory of Traumatic Loss.* Hove: Brunner-Routledge.

Rando, T.A. (2013) 'On Achieving Clarity Regarding Complicated Grief: Lessons from Clinical Practice.' In M.S. Stroebe, H. Schut and J. van den Bout (eds) *Complicated Grief: Scientific Foundations for Health Care Professionals.* Hove: Routledge.

Raphael, B., Jacobs, J. and Looi, J. (2013) 'Complicated Grief in the Context of Other Psychiatric Disorders: PTSD.' In M.S. Stroebe, H. Schut and J. Van den Bout (eds) *Complicated Grief: Scientific Foundations for Health Care Professionals.* Hove: Routledge.

Relf, M., Machin, L. and Archer, N. (2010) *Guidance for Bereavement Needs Assessment in Palliative Care*, 2nd edition. London: Help the Hospices London.

Robertson, J. and Bowlby, J. (1952) 'Responses of young children to separation from their mothers.' *Courrier du Centre International de l'Enfance 2*, 131–142.

Rogers, C.R. (1939) *The Clinical Treatment of the Problem.* Boston, MA: Houghton Mifflin.

Rogers, C.R. (1942) *Counselling and Psychotherapy.* Boston, MA: Houghton Mifflin.

Rogers, C.R. (1951) Client-centered Therapy: Its Current Practice, Implications and Theory. Boston, MA: Houghton Mifflin.

Rogers, C.R (1959) 'A Theory of Therapy, Personality, and Interpersonal Relationships: As Developed in the Client-cenered Framework.' In S. Koch (ed.) *Psychology: A Study of a Science, Vol III. Formulations of the Person and the Social Context.* New York, NY: McGraw-Hill.

Rogers, C.R. (1961) *On Becoming a Person: A Therapist's View of Psychotherapy* (1967 edn). London: Constable.

Rogers, C.R. (1963) 'Actualizing Tendency in Relation to "Motives" and to Consciousness.' In M.R. Jones (ed.) *Nebraska Symposium on Motivation.* Oxford: University of Nebraska.

Rogers, C.R. (1975) 'Empathic: an unappreciated way of being.' *The Counseling Psychologist 5*, 2, 2–10.

Rogers, C.R. (1980) *A Way of Being.* Boston, MA: Houghton Mifflin.

Rogers, C.R. (1986) 'Rogers, Kohut and Erikson.' *Person-centered Review 1*, 2, 125–140.

Rolland, J.S. (1988) 'Family systems and chronic illness: a typological model.' *Journal of Psychotherapy and the Family 3*, 3, 143–168.

Rolland, J.S. (1994) *Families, Illness, and Disability: An Integrative Treatment Model.* New York, NY: Basic Books.

Rolland, J.S. (2005) 'Cancer and the family: an integrative model.' *Cancer 104*, (S11), 2584–2595.

Schmideberg, M. (1937) *After the Analysis—Some Phantasies of Patients.* Presentation to the British Psychoanalytic Society, (Published in 1938 in *The British Psychoanalytic Quarterly*).

Schur, M. (1972) *Freud: Living and Dying.* New York, NY: International Universities Press.

Schut, H., Stroebe, M.S., van den Bout, J. and Terheggen, M. (2001) 'The Efficacy of Bereavement Interventions: Determining who Benefits.' In M.S. Stroebe, R.O. Hansson, W.E. Stroebe and H.E. Schut (eds) *Handbook of Bereavement Research: Consequences, Coping and Care.* Washington, DC: American Psychological Association.

Schwartz, J. (1999) *Cassandra's Daughter: A History of Psychoanalysis in Europe and America.* London: Allen Lane The Penguin Press.

Seay, B., Hansen, E. and Harlow, H.F. (1962) 'Mother-infant separation in monkeys.' *Journal of Child Psychology and Psychiatry 3*, 3–4, 123–132.

Senn, M.J.E. (1977) Interview with John Bowlby. *American Child Guidance Clinic and Child Psychiatry Movement Interview Collection 1975–78.*

Shand, A.F. (1914) *The Foundations of Character.* London: Macmillan.

Shapiro, E.R. (1994) *Grief as a Family Process: A Developmental Approach to Clinical Practice.* New York, NY: The Guilford Press.

Shapiro, E.R. (1996) 'Grief in Freud's life: reconceptualizing bereavement in psychoanalytic theory.' *Psychoanalytic Psychology 13*, 547–566.

Shapiro, F. (1989) 'Efficacy of the eye movement desensitization procedure in the treatment of traumatic memories.' *Journal of Traumatic Stress 2*, 2, 199–223.

Shear, K.M., Boelen, P.A. and Neimeyer, R.A. (2011) 'Treating complicated grief: converging approaches.' In R.A. Neimeyer, D.L. Harris and H.R. Winokuer (eds) *Grief and Bereavement in Contemporary Society: Bridging Research and Practice.* New York, NY: Routledge.

Shear, M.K. and Frank, E. (2006) 'Treatment of Complicated Grief: Integrating Cognitive-Behavioral Methods with Other Treatment Approaches.' In V.M. Folette and J.I. Ruzeh (eds) *Cognitive-behavioral Therapies for Trauma*, 2nd edition. New York, NY: Guilford Press.

Shear, M.K., Frank, E., Houck, P.R. and Reynolds, C.F. (2005) 'Treatment of complicated grief: a randomized controlled trial.' *Journal – American Medical Association 293*, 21, 2601–2608.

Shear, M.K., Gorscak, B. and Simon, N. (2006) 'Treatment of Complicated Grief Following Violent Death.' In E.K. Rynearson (ed.) *Violent Death: Resilience and Intervention Beyond the Crisis.* New York, NY: Routledge.

Shear, M.K. and Mulhare, E. (2008) 'Complicated grief.' *Psychiatric Annals 38*, 10, 662.

Shear, M.K., Simon, N., Wall, M., Zisook, S., Neimeyer, R., Duan, N. (2011) 'Complicated grief and related bereavement issues for DSM-5.' *Depression and Anxiety 28*, 2, 103–117.

Solecki, R.S. (1977) 'The implications of the Shanidar Cave Neanderthal Flower Burial.' *Annals of the New York Academy of Sciences 293*, 1, 114–124.

Stiles, W.B. (1999) 'Signs and voices in psychotherapy.' *Psychotherapy Research 9*, 1, 1–21.

Stroebe, M.S. (2011) *The Dual Process Model: Latest Thinking.* Paper presented at the Colin Murray Parkes Open Meetings. 16 February 2011, St Christopher's Hospice, London.

Stroebe, M.S., Hansson, R.O., Schut, H. and Stroebe, W. (eds) (2008) *Handbook of Bereavement Research and Practice: Advances in Theory and Intervention.* Washington, DC: American Psychological Association.

Stroebe, M.S., Hansson, R.O., Schut, H. and Stroebe, W. (2008b) 'Bereavement Research: Contemporary Perspectives.' In M.S. Stroebe, R.O. Hansson, H. Schut and W. Stroebe (eds) *Handbook of Bereavement Research and Practice.* Washington, DC: American Psychological Association.

Stroebe, M.S., Hansson, R.O., Stroebe, W.E. and Schut, H.E. (2001) *Handbook of Bereavement Research: Consequences, Coping, and Care.* Washington, DC: American Psychological Association.

Stroebe, M.S. and Schut, H. (1999) 'The Dual Process Model of coping with bereavement: rationale and desciption.' *Death Studies 23*, 197–224.

Stroebe, M.S. and Schut, H. (2000) 'Meaning Making in the Dual Process Model of Coping with Bereavement.' In R.A. Neimeyer (ed.) *Meaning Reconstruction and the Experience of Loss.* Washington, DC: American Psychological Association.

Stroebe, M.S., Schut, H. and Stroebe, W. (2007) 'Health outcomes of bereavement.' *Lancet 370*, 9603, 1960–1973.

Stroebe, M.S., Schut, H. and van den Bout, J. (eds) (2013) *Complicated Grief: Scientific Foundations for Health Care Professionals.* Hove: Routledge.

Stroebe, M.S., Stroebe, W. and Hansson, R.O. (1993) *Handbook of Bereavement: Theory, Research and Intervention.* Cambridge: Cambridge University Press.

Stroebe, W. and Stroebe, M.S. (1987) *Bereavement and Health.* Cambridge: Cambridge University Press.

Stroebe, M.S., Stroebe, W., Schut, H., Zech, E. and van der Bout, J. (2002) 'Does disclosure of emotions facilitate recovery from bereavement? Evidence from two prosepctive studies.' *Journal of Consulting and Clinical Psychology 70*, 1, 169–178.

Stukely, W. (1936) *Memoirs of Sir Isaac Newton's Life.* London: Taylor and Francis.

Thomas, D. (1952) 'Do Not Go Gentle into that Good Night.' In *The Poems of Dylan Thomas*, revised 2003 edition. New York, NY: New Directions.

Tonkin, L. (2007) *Certificate in Grief Support: Extending Your Skills in Working With Grieving Adults.* Christchurch, New Zealand: Port Hills Press.

Tonkin, L. (2013) Personal communication.

Tse, C.Y. and Pang, S.M.C. (2006) 'Euthanasia and Forgoing Life-sustaining Treatment in the Chinese Context.' In C. Lai Wan Chan and A. Yin Man Chow (eds) *Death, Dying and Bereavement: A Hong Kong Chinese Experience.* Hong Kong: Hong Kong University Press.

van den Bout, J. and Kleber, R. (2013) 'Lessons from PTSD for Complicated Grief as a New DSM Mental Disorder.' In M.S. Stroebe, H. Schut and J. van den Bout (eds) *Complicated Grief: Scientific Foundations for Health Care Professionals.* Hove: Routledge.

Wakefield, J.C. (1992) 'The concept of mental disorder.' *American Psychologist 47*, 3, 373–388.

Wakefield, J.C. (2007) 'The concept of mental disorder: diagnostic implications of the harmful dysfunction analysis.' *World Psychiatry 6*, 3, 149.

Wakefield, J.C. (2013) 'Is Complicated/Prolonged Grief a Disorder?: Why the Proposal to Add a Category of Complicated Grief Disorder to the DSM-5 is Conceptually and Empirically Unsound.' In M.S. Stroebe, H. Schut and J. van den Bout (eds) *Complicated Grief: Scientific Foundations for Health Care Professionals.* Hove: Routledge.

Walter, T. (1996) 'A new model of grief: bereavement and biography.' *Mortality 1*, 1, 7–25.

Wikan, U. (1990) *Managing Turbulent Hearts: A Balinese Formula for Living.* London and Chicago, IL: University of Chicago Press.

Worden, J.W. (2009) *Grief Counselling and Grief Therapy*, 4th edition. New York, NY: Springer.

Wortman, C.B. and Silver, R.C. (1989) 'The myths of coping with loss.' *Journal of Counselling and Clinical Psychology 57*, 3, 349–357.

Further Reading

Attig, T. (2011) *How We Grieve: Relearning the World*, revised edition. Oxford: Oxford University Press.
Bohart, A.C. and Tallman, K. (1999) *How Clients Make Therapy Work: The Process of Active Self-healing*. Washington, DC: American Psychological Association.
Bowlby, J. (1969) *Attachment and Loss: Volume 1 Attachment*. London: Pimlico.
Bowlby, J. (1975) *Attachment and Loss: Volume 2 Separation Anger and Anxiety*. London: Pimlico.
Bowlby, J. (1980) *Attachment and Loss: Volume 3 Loss, Sadness and Depression*. London: Pimlico.
Childs-Gowell, E. (1993) *Good Grief Rituals: Tools for Healing*. Barrytown, NY: Station Hill Press.
Dickenson, D. L., Johnson, M. and Samson Katz, J. (eds) (2000) *Death, Dying and Bereavement*, 2nd edition. London: Sage in collaboration with Open University Press.
Graves, D. (2009) *Talking With Bereaved People: An Approach for Structured and Sensitive Communication*. London: Jessica Kingsley.
Janoff-Bulman, R. (1992) *Shattered Assumptions: Towards a New Psychology of Trauma*. New York, NY: The Free Press.
Jupp, P.C. and Gittings, C. (1999) *Death in England*. Manchester: Manchester University Press.
Kauffmann, J.E. (2002) *Loss of the Assumptive World: A Theory of Traumatic Loss*. Hove: Brunner-Routledge.
Kissane, D.W. and Bloch, S. (2002) *Family Focused Grief Therapy: A Model of Family-centred Care during Palliative Care and Bereavement*. Buckingham: Open University Press.
Klass, D., Silverman, P.R. and Nickman, S.L. (1996) *Continuing Bonds: New Understandings of Grief*. Philadelphia, PA: Taylor and Francis.
Lewis, C.S. (2013) *A Grief Observed*. London: Faber and Faber.
Machin, L. (2014) *Working with Loss and Grief: A Theoretical and Practical Approach*, 2nd edition. London: Sage.
Martin, T.L. and Doka, K.J. (2000) *Men Don't Cry... Women Do: Transcending Gender Stereotypes of Grief*. Philadelphia, PA: Taylor and Francis.
Mearns, D., Thorne, B. and McLeod, J. (2013) *Person Centred Counselling in Action*, 4th edition. London: Sage.
Neimeyer, R.A. (2001) *Meaning Reconstruction and the Experience of Loss*. Washington, DC: American Psychological Association.
Neimeyer, R.A. (ed.) (2012) *Techniques of Grief Therapy*. Hove: Routledge.
Parkes, C.M. (2009) *Love and Loss: The Roots of Grief and its Complications*. Hove: Routledge.
Parkes, C.M. and Prigerson, H.G. (2010) *Bereavement: Studies of Grief in Adult Life*, 4th edition. London: Penguin.
Parkes, C.M., Relf, M. and Couldrick, A. (1996) *Counselling in Terminal Care and Bereavement*. Leicester: British Psychological Society.
Raphael, B. (1990) *The Anatomy of Bereavement: Handbook for the Caring Professions*. Hove: Routledge.
Stroebe, M.S., Schut, H. and van den Bout, J. (eds) (2013) *Complicated Grief: Scientific Foundations for Health Care Professionals*. Hove: Routledge.
Wallbank, S. (2010) *The Empty Bed: Bereavement and the Loss of Love*. London: Darton, Longman and Todd.
Worden, J.W. (2009) *Grief Counselling and Grief Therapy*, 4th edition. New York, NY: Springer.

Subject Index

Author Index